INSATIABLE

Celebrating
30 Years of Publishing
in India

Praise for the book

'Shobhaa Dé has been fearless, frank, direct, straightforward, explicit, unambiguous and unvarnished, both as a person and a celebrated journalist and writer! *Insatiable*—her voracious and unquenchable thirst for more could not have been better described than [in] the title of her book. May the accolades for her endeavour never end!'

—Amitabh Bachchan

'I grew up reading Shobhaa Dé's columns in newspapers. She exposed me to a new way of seeing the world. Then, years later, I met her. First as a fan. Then as her friend. And I still read her, enjoying the way she explains the world to me: rooted, grounded, yet adventurous and fun.'

—Devdutt Pattanaik

'Shobhaa Dé is a phenomenon. She is not just insatiable, she's completely unstoppable, and as this chatty, witty, perky book shows, she remains one of the most vivacious writers at work in India today.'

—William Dalrymple

INSATIABLE

My Hunger for Life

SHOBHAA DÉ

HarperCollins *Publishers* India

First published in India by HarperCollins *Publishers* 2023
4th Floor, Tower A, Building No. 10, Phase II, DLF Cyber City,
Gurugram, Haryana – 122002
www.harpercollins.co.in

2 4 6 8 10 9 7 5 3 1

P-ISBN: 978-93-5629-600-8
E-ISBN: 978-93-5629-601-5

The views and opinions expressed in this book are the author's own
and the facts are as reported by her, and the publishers
are not in any way liable for the same.

Shobhaa Dé asserts the moral right
to be identified as the author of this work.

Typeset in 11.5/16 Adobe Garamond at
Manipal Technologies Limited, Manipal

Printed and bound at
Thomson Press (India) Ltd

MIX
Paper
FSC FSC® C010615

This book is produced from independently certified FSC® paper
to ensure responsible forest management.

To
*the select few I love deeply (you know who you are!) and the ones who
love me back even after knowing sab kuch!
It's a question of taste, na?*

She's got a ticket to ride
But she don't care

'Ticket to Ride', The Beatles

CONTENTS

INTRODUCTION

'Anything worth doing, transcends borders. Should I do nothing at all...?'

—Geetanjali Shree, *Tomb of Sand*

PERHAPS THE 'CONVERSATION' WITH MYSELF BEGAN IN JAIPUR IN 2022. At the fifteenth edition of the iconic Jaipur Literature Festival (JLF), I found myself looking for Anuradha in the lit-fest crowds, rushing from one session to the next. Anuradha, the little girl who got lost in the melee decades ago but continues to show up in my dreams to remind me that she's still very much alive. I just have to look much harder. I have been searching for Anuradha for more than seventy years. No luck so far. Does she even exist? *Did* she ever exist? Have I invented Anuradha? And who is Anuradha, you may ask.

I was born under the Anuradha nakshatra and my parents named me after it—as per the tradition in Saraswat Brahmin homes. And then, Tatya, my father's despotic brother, decided the name was too long.

'How will her full name sound later in life? Anuradha Rajadhyaksha? Change it to something shorter. Call her Shobha, and pray she brings some "shobha" to your family. Now that you have a third daughter and fourth child let us at least name her correctly,' he had said.

My parents promptly obeyed. Nobody challenged Tatya. Least of all a brother who was twenty-two years younger—my father, Govind Hari.

Maybe Tatya killed Anuradha there and then without knowing it. When the story was narrated to me, I was around five years old. I burst into tears. I cried and cried. I hated my very pleb-sounding name—Shobha! I begged my parents to start calling me Anuradha. But it was too late. Shobha stuck! I preferred Anuradha; it was classy and classical. I felt Anuradha. I still feel Anuradha. I want to be Anuradha. Only Anuradha.

After my session at the festival, as I was escorted to the book-signing tent, the voice spoke to me again. But softly. I was reminded about a commitment I had made as I inched closer and closer to a landmark birthday in January 2023. A book was expected. It had to be written. I had no idea what to write. Zero. I was sure about what I didn't want to write: '75 Life Lessons'. At heart, I remain a vagabond, a loafer, a gypsy, a voyeur. I have no 'wisdom' to impart. No gyaan. I feel within what I have always felt—I remain an easily excitable, capricious, unruly, rebellious, uncontrollably impetuous, joyously immature schoolgirl constantly in search of 'newness', adventure, discoveries. But, frankly, one thing was clear and shouting for attention: I one hundred per cent wanted to mark my seventy-fifth with a book. Call it ego, vanity, a childish, attention-seeking need to declare, 'Hey! It's my special birthday! I may have finally grown up!'

In Japan, when a person turns sixty, they don a big red hat to celebrate a second childhood. I was closing in on my third! A red hat alone seemed inadequate. A red cape? Why not?

So here's my book! Indulge me and I promise not to be three things—profound, pedantic and pretentious. Qualities I abhor! Instead, how about being authentic? Chatty and chatpata? Conversational and conspiratorial, as I jump from memories of food and friendships, family and fabulousness? Textures and colours and snacky tidbits from my life. This is my personal food court, folks, and you are all invited! The masala mix is my very own recipe with a bit of mirch, khatta–meetha elements and dollops of spice to tease the palate. Tongue pe lagaam rakho? Never! I take food far more seriously than I take people. Food speaks to me in a language of unfiltered, uncensored love. Food fidelity counts! It remains the most passionate and enduring affair in my life, with negligible collateral damage. My heart, mind and stomach are in a committed relationship with all things edible ...

Being a compulsive people-watcher, I love to spy on the unsuspecting enjoying their meals. How, when, where and what someone eats tells you as much as the person's janam kundali. It reveals habits, upbringing, attitudes, sensitivities, preferences, fetishes, cravings, hang-ups, obsessions ... You are warned! I am watching!

—⚭—

'Friendships must be built on a solid foundation of alcohol, sarcasm, inappropriateness and shenanigans ...'

—Anonymous

What if I had written this book while sipping wine, not chaas? Would it have been different or same-same? Right now, I'm sipping chilled chaas, not chilled Dog Point (my all-time favourite Sauvignon Blanc, accidentally discovered by Avantikka and me in Dubai, after escaping from a dry Sharjah Lit Fest), and staring crossly at a rapidly wilting chrysanthemum—a beauty I had bought for two hundred rupees from my neighbourhood florist, who gives me a discount (I'm really cheap and love discounts) because he used to be Mr Dé's stockist for orchids and anthuriums years ago. It's a good feeling to retain sentimental relationships that have nothing to do with 'matlab'. The chrysanthemum had seductively beckoned me when I was at his shop surveying dozens of liliums cooling off in blue plastic buckets. I was debating whether to buy unopened lilium buds or go for button daisies that resembled pretty nipples when the chrysanthemums caught my eye and I grabbed one. My subsequent disappointment was because the flower was sulking and not doing what it's supposed to do, according to Japanese legend—keep unfolding its beautiful petals, layer by layer.

After getting it home, I had done my best by placing it in a cut-glass bud vase. More importantly, I had added last evening's leftover white wine, and some sugar to keep up the bloom's spirit, given the beastly heat. But there it is now ... baleful and pouty, despite the place of honour given to it on my dining table, right next to my most favourite possession—a plastic desk calendar I cannot live without.

My entire life is tabulated on the leaves of such calenders. It even bears records of menstrual cycles—mine, when I was still menstruating—and now my daughters'. If I've not created an entry, then sorry, it doesn't exist, whatever it is. One quick look at the leaves before going to bed tells me how my life is going to pan out over the next few months. Blank leaves suggesting a certain waywardness and caprice—I could be anywhere, go anywhere, do as I please.

The plastic desk calendar is my security blanket. It's my walking stick, my crutch. Without it, I'm disoriented and irritable. 'Why don't you use the Notes app in your phone, Mother?' the children ask, perplexed by my dependence on the ugly, brown, box-like thing which accompanies me on all my travels, including weekend getaways. How will they understand what I feel about my calendar? They aren't used to the idea of physical calendars or diaries. And I am addicted to both.

I only trust what I write down myself. If the writing ain't mine, please ignore whatever you read. My devotion to the calendar borders on the manic. Withdrawal happens if I open my suitcase in some exotic destination and discover I've left the calendar behind. My vacay is ruined right there and then! If people text about something I have to attend/ complete/start/reject, instant panic sets in. I feel flustered and start to stammer, apologizing profusely for not being able to commit one way or the other till my return, when I'll reunite with the blessed calendar! 'That's pretty pathetic, Mother,' my children comment, rolling their eyes. I am adept at ignoring the eye rolls. Roll away, I say!

The plastic desk calendar works just fine for me as it has done for years. I happily acknowledge the dependency. It's my drug, this plastic calendar. Come September, and I get withdrawal symptoms. I have to place the order for next year's calendar with the local stationery dukaan. My eyes light up expectantly when it arrives. Wow! What does next year look like? Busy? Great! What's so amazing about voice notes and memos stored in the iPhone? It's just a device! It can be misplaced or stolen. Then what? Who'll steal my ugly desk calendar, huh? And, excuse me, it's not just an object. It is my lifeline.

No calendar: No focus. No structure. No schedule. No discipline. No life. One big blank.

I start flipping through the hectic schedule scribbled on the leaves. The year is already looking overcrowded with multiple commitments. I'm starting to feel 'extra', like Priyanka Chopra or Kim Kardashian. Wow! How am I going to manage my time in 2022 without messing up? Of course, I prioritize! But I need serious pruning if I am to keep pace with all that I have to honour.

Flipping through this little calendar, I'm suddenly struck by inspiration. Of course ... the structure of my book is right in front of me. And so the book starts writing itself, month by month, following the same rhythm noted in the calendar. The narrative comes to life in my mind as snippets and reflections of a year in my life. Connecting all of it is food—delicious, glorious khaana, definitely some peena, and all the emotions that go into stirring the memory pot, the flavours and aromas shared with family and friends as we speed through 2022, gaining experiences and definitely gaining kilos while consoling ourselves. This is a personal ode to food, family and friendship—my way of expressing gratitude to all the ingredients that have added so much zest to my seventy-five years.

They say the tongue never lies; watch your words, darling! And pass me the menu.

JANUARY

'Birthdays are good for you. Statistics show that the people who have the most live the longest.'

—Larry Lorenzoni

IT'S FIVE DAYS BEFORE MY BIRTHDAY. I HAVE SURVIVED THE THIRD wave of COVID-19. Arbitrarily and arrogantly, I have officially declared the pandemic over inside my head. No more of this nonsense. We have suffered enough. Let the party begin. It's a brand new year. The lockdown restrictions must go; most already have. The few friends I've invited to my party on the 7th in Pune are worriedly asking if I'm planning to go ahead with the celebration. I am! I am! Definitely! Why are they even asking? We are good to go, right?

Wrong!

'If you don't have friends who are miserable and sniffling in bed with the bloody COVID-19 virus right now, you don't have friends. Everyone I know has had it at least once,' exclaims a gorgeous neighbour, dressed in couture as she steps out to attend a glamorous soirée, imported sanitizer in one hand, designer mask over her nose and mouth. It's a throwaway comment. But chilling.

Thanks a lot! Dear lady, you just ruined my birthday plans for me! But I am not a COVID coward.

Prasad calls from Bengaluru. 'Shobes, the fourth wave … are you sure you want to do this? I mean … our tickets are booked and all that. But a party at this time?'

Fashion guru Prasad Bidapa, his wife Judith and their kids, Adam and Aviva, are more than family to us. We have been close friends for over forty years and to think our friendship started with a handwritten letter from Prasad, delivered by a postman to my office address when I was the editor of a glossy publication. Prasad is the most fun, creative and loving person I know—he's the younger brother I never had. That voice! Those legs! The Coorg swag. The discerning eye for all things beautiful—fashion, architecture, textiles, art. A born aesthete—when in doubt about a dodgy outfit, a potential fashion faux pas, I call Prassssss.

Judith is a dog- and horse-whisperer—there's little she doesn't know or get about animals. Strong, practical, capable—Judith is the go-to gal in any and every emergency—physical and emotional. My best food memory of her is from Paris—when the rest of us were in search of the best crêpes, croissants and macarons, Judith was craving for ghar ki kadak chai with pav (no baguettes, merci beaucoup!) while desperately searching for a riding crop from a specific equestrian store. Our children meld and merge when they meet.

Prasad brings me back to earth with that question about going ahead with the party. What am I even thinking? The menacing microbe is still around; I can hear it singing, 'Every breath you take, and every move you make … I'll be watching you …' My favourite track by The Police. The party is beginning to look grotesque—like a scene from a Fellini film. Damn! Just as we are ready to cheerily kiss the bloody pandemic goodbye and reclaim our old lives, our old selves, another lethal wave is sweeping victims away. Newspaper reports with scary statistics are being hastily shared with me by nervous invitees. And I am feigning nonchalance because I want to block out the inevitable—the virus has gone nowhere. Perhaps it never will. COVID-19 has killed our spirit without our realizing just how powerful the body blow has been. We have changed forever. I need to drink undiluted, unadulterated joie de vivre straight out of a bottle. Unless someone can inject it directly into my veins.

Recklessly, I declare to Prasad and the others who have called, 'Fourth, fifth or tenth wave—life has to go on. We can't stop living. Or having fun. Come onnnnn … what's with you?'

My party plans are very much in place: crates of my favourite champagne (Veuve Clicquot) have been transported to my apartment in Pune, along with artisanal gins from Goa and specific malts for the silly snobs who insist they drink just from those particular distilleries even if they can't tell the difference. And now this! Fourth wave, my foot!

'Rubbish!' I tell Prasad. 'I don't go by alarmist stories. You watch too much television! Himmat hai toh come on over.'

Brave words. But the reality is always different—isn't it? Strict COVID-19 protocols have been imposed, yet again, across Maharashtra. Then there is the irritating question about the host's 'responsibility'. Yes, I can still go ahead and have the fairy lights up on the balcony and a few daring friends will show up. We will clink glasses, after lowering our masks and drink champagne with ambulance sirens providing the background score. The caterer, dearest Ashish Chandani, will send the preordered gourmet treats in sealed boxes with disposable plates and cutlery. We'll try and beat the 10 p.m. curfew and pretend we are having a grand time. *Scheisse*!

There is really no point in being defiant. Baba, my late father, would have called it 'immaturity' and misplaced bravado. My children (Censor Board) provide the much-needed reality check: 'What if someone tests positive after attending your dinner, Mother? This is not just about you and a cancelled birthday party. It's plain irresponsible!' Definitely didn't need that. So, it's 'bye-bye, Pune'…

And hello, Mumbai!

'Shobhaa, listen … I have the perfect plan: let's meet at Wodehouse Gymkhana—I'm a member. We can safely host up to fifteen people on the lawns as per the rules—the food's amazing and the bartender makes a great hot toddy. We will scrupulously follow all COVID-19 protocols and behave ourselves … Let's do this!'

This cheery suggestion has come from Manjeet, a darling girlfriend I have known since her days as a journo in *Bombay* magazine (established in 1979). Former India bureau chief of *Business Week*, and now a well-respected director of Gateway House—an important foreign policy think tank—with degrees in law, English, history, and a master's in international relations from Columbia, Manjeet Kripalani (nicknamed 'Honey Bunny' by me) is what we call a soliddddd friend. Solid … and liquid as well! We like our vino. She is like a delicious platter of all things irresistible—tangdi kebab for sure. Bright, attractive, cerebral, well-travelled, well-read, hot, successful and such a sport! She does what caring girlfriends sweetly do—seamlessly take over during a crisis! This think tank–wali is a super strategist! Over to you, Honey Bunny!

Earlier the same day, when my children and grandchildren had come over to cut a cake and wish me, I had started to weep, visibly and unselfconsciously. Birthdays (mine and other people's) turn me into instant mush.

Puzzled by my tears, the babies had asked, 'Why is Nani crying? It's her birthday! Please don't cry, Nani …'

Happy tears are the best tears, I wanted to explain. But they are still a bit too young to understand that. The day they do, we will weep together. The daughters popped the champagne, clicked pictures, shot videos while the babies lisped 'Happy Birthday, Nani …' I tore open my gifts, read the birthday cards painstakingly created with crayons and felt pens by the little ones and then it was time to party! 'Big people party' as the little people put it.

Honey Bunny is waiting for us in the Wodehouse Gym lobby. Being a meticulous and impeccable host, she'd come earlier to make sure things were tickety-boo. She needn't have stressed. Things are always tickety-boo around Honey. Of course, she is looking terrific—so New York! The menu has been planned by her with the smart F&B manager of the club, keeping in mind how demanding we all are when it comes to khaana. Then the peena generally takes a back seat.

There are fairy lights in the garden of the charming club (started in 1909 and named after Sir Phillips Wodehouse, who was governor of Bombay from 1872 to 1875), the bartender in the old-fashioned wooden bar room is waiting for our drink orders … This was one thirsty lot! The chairs and tables have been arranged keeping COVID-19 restrictions in mind. We are the only ones on the lawn, with a skeletal staff getting trays of drinks and platters of food to us, while we try hard not to think of death on a birthday. I feel like a schoolgirl playing truant as I wait for my wonderful friends to show up and give me a birthday hug (masks firmly in place, of course). Soon, we have lagaoed countless margaritas and started to imagine we are partying on the full moon hanging over our heads.

Much later, I realize how ravenously hungry we were on that cool January night. Hungry for company, eye contact, touch, laughter, conversation … and food we could enjoy together.

Isolation has awakened so many dead emotions and senses during the wretched COVID-19 times. *Everything* appears exaggerated in this 'new' post-COVID-19 universe. Most of all, our own altered selves. Changed forever. Food had assumed a crazy, new importance during the pandemic. We'd become food-obsessed! What do I order next? From which home delivery kitchen? What should we cook next? Which food show to follow? To bake or not to bake? Our greed knew no bounds! And then there was greed beyond food. We had become greedy for emotional scraps thrown our way. Tactile greed—there was nobody to hold! Aural greed—I missed the blaring horns of city life at its busiest. Even olfactory greed—toxic diesel fumes on highways we once travelled on without a care in the world. And then—the sight of strangers! Yes—strangers. Not just the people we were stuck with at home during the punishing lockdown. We grabbed at anything that reminded us how fortunate we were to be alive. Alive! Pulsatingly alive … my own heartbeat had become my music of choice.

My friends—Raisa, Olga, Bhawana, Rashmi and Priya—turn up looking smashing, and I feel instantly chuffed. All five of them have been family to me for decades. These are women with exceptional qualities and talents. Just as I have changed over time, so have they. We look different. Some appear a little drawn and saddened. Some retain the original ebullience. The main change is age. Our lives have come with enough challenges—medical, emotional, professional. But here we are exchanging hugs and feeling great just being together!

While the spinach ricotta triangles are much appreciated, all of us pounce on the piping hot (pun!) wasabi prawns, crispy Bombil, egg fried mutton chops and asparagus rolls. Imagine ... there is still room enough in our tum-tums for Mangalorean sukkha chicken with lachha paranthas, Balinese curry, lasagne and fried noodles. This is the asli fun of 'club grub'—one can order erratic, technically incompatible dishes and relish them all! Oh, I forget the gooey chocolate cake and the baked Philadelphia cheesecake that made the dinner insanely indecent! We danced and sang uninhibitedly, aware our time on the lawns was limited. Later that night, after my head cleared somewhat, hazy images and memories surfaced in uneven patterns as I looked back and reviewed ... Well ... everything! My life, loves, hopes, disappointments, fears ...

How many of you lost friendships and witnessed cracks in close, personal relationships during the past eight years? Think about it. I fell out with a few old and trusted friends because each time we spoke, there were heated arguments and pointless debates. All of them to do with politics. I was flabbergasted and hurt by the vehemence of the 'discussions'. The political became personal. And a great deal of avoidable negativity finally ruined what we once shared—call it love, although I prefer respect. It is the polarizing phenomenon that interests me more than politics. Families have been divided and marriages broken, because of one despotic individual. I talk of rifts, having experienced them in a rather brutal form. And it makes me wonder: what does ideology have to do with love, friendship, commitment, marriage? Actually, a lot more than we care to acknowledge and dare to admit.

I had heard that solid, successful marriages in America are based on a shared political ideology—a Republican never marries a Democrat. For the first time in India, we are looking at marriages falling apart when one partner is an avid fan of a political cult figure and the other is not. It's not difficult to figure it out—a totally different value system with diametrically opposite beliefs in what is fundamentally right or wrong. It's as basic as that. A little like dedicated carnivores doomed to spend their life with equally dedicated vegetarians—both militant about meal choices, and unwilling to co-exist. Food, sex and politics have a lot in common. It's about what's considered palatable/acceptable by both partners. If politics is chosen over you, don't feel guilty if you decide to decouple or go in for 'conscious uncoupling' like Gwyneth Paltrow and Chris Martin.

But tonight, there is no such conundrum. On the moonlit lawns of the Wodehouse Gymkhana on the night of my seventy-fourth birthday, my friends' invigorating presence is all I need. It serves as a tonic, an elixir, an instant pick-me-up! The overall mood across India may be despondent. Nobody is in the frame of mind to say 'cheers!' to or about anything. The shaky economy, heightened hate politics, enforced divisiveness and the wretched COVID-19 virus have generated unprecedented doom and gloom. But, despite the despondency, my beloved family and friends are here for me on my special day. And we are determined to make an occasion of it, knowing our cut-off time at the club is 10 p.m. as per government directives. Drink up! Nibble away! Bars and restaurants have shut again, after a brief period of staying open. A few of my dearest friends are still in mourning, grieving for family members they've lost to the virus; yet, despite their personal loss, here they are on this lawn, enjoying an extra glass of bubbly, eating an extra kebab, chatting animatedly to my bachchas and husband—all of us putting our best 'party' selves forward. These are gold-standard acts of love and thoughtfulness that I shall cherish for life. FFF (family, friendships and food) will never be the same again. In fact, all three just received a massive upgrade!

Before the burly durwan throws us all out, I drain my last sip of a killer margarita and we jump into our cars. We must beat the curfew before an overzealous hawaldar books us for unruly, drunken conduct.

—m—

'Your 40s are good. Your 50s are great. Your 60s are fab.
And 70 is f*@king awesome!'

—Helen Mirren

Last night was spooky. I was kept awake by noisy fruit bats attacking the fruit on the gigantic jamun tree right outside my bedroom window. It's a weird tree, this one. It attracts all kinds of creatures. This time it was monstrously large bats with a wingspan of three feet, quarrelling over the fleshy purple fruit that had ripened just two days earlier and begun to drop on the watchman's cabin with a messy and audible splatchhhh.

A few months ago, an aggressive brahminy kite couple had built a roomy nest in the crook of the branches leaning dangerously close to the window grill. They were ferocious and lethal, attacking anybody who dared to stand near the large French window facing their nest. My neighbour's wife, who lives one floor beneath ours, was saved just in time after the male bird swooped right over her head, claws out and screeching menacingly. I had gone eyeball-to-eyeball with this nasty chap—but from behind the safety of a thick glass. He would have come crashing through it, but an overhanging ledge made that short flight impossible. There were dog and cat attacks galore, and even the tiny kids in our residential complex were asked to stay indoors till this menace was tackled. It sounds heartless, but I had the nest removed—the kite family was summarily evicted one fine morning, with the help of the irreplaceable Ramlal, the major domo of our building, and assistance from the local fire brigade. Before you ring Maneka Gandhi and get me arrested, please note: I waited patiently for the eggs to hatch and the kite babies to learn how to fly and hunt for prey. After that, sorry—they were unwelcome neighbours!

I have no solution to the fruit bats who keep me awake. I keep thinking of Wuhan and fretting as I wonder if these bats could be cousins of the Wuhan bats visiting Mumbai with a fresh virus. Since I'm wide awake, I imagine all kinds of wild stuff. I also hear sounds that seem to emanate from another dimension. I conclude the room is haunted for sure, and someone from another astral dimension is trying to reach me. I have to instantly distract my racing mind and calm down. It's 3.45 a.m. The water tankers will start rolling up at 4.30 a.m. The young men who wash cars begin their rounds at 5 a.m. The building dogs go for their potty stroll at 6 a.m. and bark hearty greetings to one another while pooping. The anda-bread-wala arrives at around the same time. So does the chaiwala on a cycle, ringing the ting-ting bell, as sleepy watchmen on night duty stir lazily to hand over the ledger to the men on the next shift. Everyone wants piping hot 'cutting chai'. So do I!

I decide not to toss and turn and wait for the morning light. With intent and great determination, I walk up to my cupboard and open it to survey my clothes, which have been neatly rearranged last week by Lakshmi. Hmm. I have far too many clothes! Or do I? I survey the neatly folded pile of saris and the casual jackets on the hangers. Where will I wear any of these? When? I have saris going back forty years. Even if I decide to change saris twice a day, I will still have many waiting to be worn. My daughters are indifferent, even disinterested in my precious collection. Who do I leave these beautiful saris to? Each one has a story. Most have been handpicked from weavers directly by me. I sit down at the edge of the bed and feel teary. Clothes and memories. I still have the haldi-yellow silk sari with a kumkum-red border that I wore on my first date with Mr Dé. And the shapeless pomegranate pink Gajji silk Gurjari kurta with a Kutch embroidery yoke that I wore when we met for the first time. Only I know their stories. Only I value the significance and sentiment. Why am I hanging on to garments nobody else will have the slightest interest in preserving after I'm gone? Damn the fruit bats. It's all their fault!

Suddenly, I'm overcome with feelings of self-loathing and immense guilt. A strange new emotion considering it's triggered off by the sight of my neatly arranged clothes minding their own business on the shelves of the closet. Clothes I have forgotten I possess and haven't worn in years— do I ever really need these heaps and heaps of garments? For someone who has always enjoyed dressing up and stepping out to meet family and friends, what is happening to me suddenly? Renunciation does not suit my personality at all. Some creature comforts are non-negotiable—pretty clothes certainly deserve more respect.

Faint, pale-pink light is beginning to creep in through the blackout blinds. The early birds (over-enthu walking groups) have started on their rounds. Crows and house sparrows start squabbling much before the garbage truck arrives to haul gigantic bags of segregated rubbish. And here I am, staring balefully at clothes that are giving me dirty looks for not acknowledging them in my present avatar. I hear the newborn on the seventh floor wailing piteously—is the mother's breast empty of milk? Gas problem? Diaper change? More annoyance.

I switch on my cell phone, which charges at a respectable distance from my bed—I have to walk up to it in my early morning daze and say a polite 'Good Morning … wakey, wakey…' I check random messages. There are three shaadi invitations and two high-profile 'Save the Date' announcements. I have the choice to attend (or not) any or every one of these glam events. And that's when it strikes me—I've forgotten the contents of my cupboard for the past two-and-a-half years! The pandemic had mandated there was no need to update one's wardrobe—there was nowhere to go! I had happily lived through those unending, silent and tragic months, dressed in what we call 'ghar ka kapda'—comfy, roomy, baggy, shabby cotton caftans. Wearing even a touch of make-up had long ceased to be an option. Clothes I had eagerly bought before the lockdown stared accusingly at me; they were still lying folded up in the original packages I had purchased them in. That's it. I had not made any effort to go through my clothes—old or new. What on earth for? There was no where to go, no one to impress. This had become a shared syndrome world over—a symbol of our collective isolation. And yet, those unopened packages provided an incentive. It was important to believe I would be donning those silken wonders soon.

—⁘—

'Please don't retouch my wrinkles. It took me so long to earn them.'
—Anna Magnani

Going by the social euphoria in the air, it certainly looks like we can consider the pandemic officially over. The rules have been relaxed once again. Yes, we still need to mask up. But we are out of jail … out on bail. The floodgates have been thrown open, people are rediscovering a vibrant and stimulating life outside their homes. The life they had taken so much for granted till it was snatched away. Art galleries are springing up at great new venues, snazzy boutiques have started flashing news about sexy summer collections, multiplexes beckon with mega movies releasing every weekend. New showrooms, gardens, parks, theatres … Mumbai is pulsating after a lull that I'd feared would permanently alter the city's frenzied rhythm. I smile. I reread the invitations—some in the form of slick videos with great music and smart graphics. So … people have not forgotten me after all.

It's time for me to get out of my nightie-mentality and reacquaint myself with the beautiful silks and mulmuls I have always loved to wear. But first, I'd have to reintroduce myself to myself. The pre- and post-pandemic person who had almost forgotten who she'd been not all that long ago. Here was my dilemma: what should get skinnier first—the wardrobe or moi? Keep the clothes and lose weight, Dé. The pandemic is over. Figure out what to do with all the matching-matching masks. Thinking bikini tops. But first, intermittent fasting and warm 'limbu' paani to melt the tyres.

Mumbai's social calendar is calling. It's going to be a bubbly time from now on. But priority demands I catch up on my lost sleep first. No amount of tinted concealer can camouflage eye bags.

My image in the mirror is issuing urgent instructions: call Nasreen. Now! Fix the earliest hair appointment. Hair's a mess. Stop behaving like Judi Dench. She wears her hair and lines with panache. She is Judi Dench! *You* need Nasreen.

Nasreen has been fixing my badly behaved hair at a friendly neighbourhood salon for years. She knows my scalp better than I do. When I say 'fixing my hair', I need to specify: Nasreen colours the greying roots, touches up the crown where the grey shows the most and gives me a basic hair trim thrice a year. Like countless women across the world, I was forced to cut my own hair during the lockdown and did a lousy job of it. Nasreen is someone I missed a great deal during this trying period, and not just because my hair was a total mess, growing wild like defiant weeds in a neglected garden. I missed her quiet, neat presence and our honest conversations. We discuss real stuff as women—the state of our uterus, heaviness in the breasts, sensitive medical issues. The trust levels are high and mutual. I admire her tenacity and discipline, and look forward to meeting her when I visit Butterfly Pond, the salon she works in.

Her boss, the owner, is the petite, attractive Sylvia Chen, who makes the most delicious pork stew with dried shitake mushrooms for her mother-in-law. Sylvia is originally from Kolkata, like so many talented hair stylists of Chinese descent who moved to Mumbai years ago, when life was made difficult for their parents and grandparents during the Chinese conflict in 1967. By a marvellous coincidence, I discovered that Henry, her handsome father-in-law, and I were college mates in St Xavier's College, before he went on to become a successful dentist. I loved running into him each time he visited the salon for a hair wash and the salon girls would whisper, 'Uncle has come … Uncle has come …', hastily pretending to be far busier than they actually were.

The salon changed its location a few years ago. It is still in Colaba, but I preferred the earlier place, even though Sylvia has kept the vibe the same, with plastic butterfly streamers, fairy lights and a playlist put together by her husband who is a model and has an eclectic taste in music, going from retro to club to lounge to house (though never rap). I go to Butterfly Pond as much for the music as for the company of their clientele. Most of us are regulars and have watched one another age. Since men also patronize this unisex salon, we have trained ourselves to cover our knees and watch the neckline while getting a shampoo followed by a blow dry. Some of these salon friendships go back ten years—but numbers are never exchanged and there's no contact outside the salon. We sip green tea, joke and giggle and diss Bollywood stars, while the salon girls scamper around, sweeping cut tresses from the floor, replacing towels, fetching hair sprays from the rack, mixing hair colour in plastic bowls, getting mani-pedi kits ready, offering feet and shoulder massages while we wait for the hair colour to kick in and transform us from crones to glam grannies in under two hours.

There are a few reassuring constants, like Nasreen. And Vishal Lohar, the visually challenged gentleman who gives the best foot massage ever, and knows his way around the space, rarely bumping into anyone or anything. My fascination though is reserved for the tall, statuesque 'Bhabhiji'. Who is Bhabhiji? Well, she's someone's bhabhi and that's all I know. She was employed to do the work of replacing brushes and rollers, keeping the salon neat and tidy. At the time, she wore salwar–kameez or sari, sindoor in the parting of her hair, and her gaze was permanently lowered. The dramatic transformation to the woman she is today happened gradually. Bhabhiji has worked her way up the ladder and now handles manicures, pedicures, shampoos with confidence and charm. Her appearance and body lingo have altered too. She wears fitted jeans and trendy tees, has had her kinky hair straightened, and could easily be a ramp model, with her great posture and height. I asked about her antecedents and was told she's from the Banjara tribe of casual labourers who work at construction sites in Colaba. Their women wear a distinctive ghagra–choli ensemble, with large mirrors and colourful embroidery embellishing the backless choli. The Banjaras rarely stay in one place for long and camp in any available open space near the sites they work in. Once the project ends, they move on. So how come Bhabhiji escaped that trajectory? It had to be love! It was! A local guy fell in love with her and a shaadi followed. Today, Bhabhiji is earning good money at the salon, has put down her roots and made Mumbai her home. I love her story!

All these hard-working women are my friends. This much I can state with confidence. They are kind, warm and loving, when they could just be efficient and professional. On my last birthday, I walked in for a quick shampoo and blow dry at 5 p.m. The salon was unusually busy and I could see all the girls were a little harrowed, with walk-in customers dropping in for last-minute manicures and touch-ups. Nasreen tackled my hair quickly and I got ready to leave. When I reached the cash counter, I found a birthday celebration was being hastily put together. Someone was arranging a red velvet cake on the counter, someone else was lighting candles; balloons had appeared out of nowhere. And there I was asking stupidly, 'Is this for me?'

Nasreen and I hugged as she grinned and asked, 'Then, who else?'

I have never been this moved. What a lovely gesture! So genuine and generous! We cut the cake together, sang and danced and laughed and cried. Thank you, Butterfly Pond, for creating this beautiful memory.

It's more than just their affection that draws me to this salon. Butterfly Pond nurtures so many young women (and a few men) from across India—the girls from the North-east, in particular. Then there is Nasreen and her sister Farzeen. Sylvia and her family. There are Muslims, Christians, Hindus, Buddhists, tribals working together in quiet, comfortable harmony. It's a microcosm of India in all its diversity—a place where all festivals are celebrated with equal enthusiasm, home-cooked food shared generously across faiths, and each client treated like a family member. Someone's doing something right in that beautiful space. Very right.

—◊—

'Old age is an excellent time for outrage. My goal is to say or do at least one outrageous thing every week.'

—Maggie Kuhn

Friday night and lockdown restrictions have been fully lifted. Now we are in the grip of post-pandemic hysteria. The pandemic is *so* yesterday. Pushed into the past. Never mind that the 'past' is not even a month old. Mumbai has rebooted. Its hectic night life (and day life, and twilight life and pre-dawn life) are back with a vengeance. The party never stops in this mad megapolis. It's like COVID-19 never happened. Not to us. Not to the world. It's a blur. Nobody refers to the virus in polite company—even those who lost near and dear ones during the pandemic. It's vulgar to bring up something as low level as a microbe when one is gushing over a hideous canvas and sipping a perfectly chilled rosé, as limousines roll up for another art gallery opening.

I am at one such chi-chi art gallery opening. It feels like I'm walking into a past life. This used to be my beat, my turf. I knew most of the 'big names' in the art world. We were on 'dak naam' terms. I should be okay, I tell myself. Reconnecting is going to be easy. I'm meeting this lot after years. I'm dressed suitably arty (there's a 'look' that is mandatory at these hideously self-deluded functions). It can't be grungy, but it can't be OTT as that. Accessories have to be crafted out of bamboo, recycled fabric, paper, beads, wood. Ideally, the hair should be electric green or shocking pink. The expression on the face is important—a snooty sneer works best.

But since I have put my foot in it, I am going to enjoy myself.

It is a gathering of narcissists—the usual gallery-hopping suspects looking for free wine and fancy hors d'oeuvres. Everyone looks, dresses, talks alike. It's a delightfully incestuous, self-indulgent bunch of hangers-on, and determined, but often supremely ignorant 'patrons' who modestly shell out upwards of Rs 40 crores and more for a work they may secretly detest but one which will create mighty waves when it becomes a big talking point in auction circles. Outside this bubble, they are irrelevant and unknown. But once inside the welcoming womb of an art gallery, they reclaim their confidence quickly and gush over whatever is on display, making sure to sound like Ranjit Hoskote. Perhaps, they memorize a few lines from his most recent, terrifyingly knowledgeable reviews. But these peeps aren't Hoskote. They are pretenders. Their wallet is the ticket to gatherings that celebrate all things nouveau-riche and gloriously mediocre. Yup. I'm in a snarky mood. Mainly, I figure, I may have finally grown up and outgrown this circus, these unimaginative, dull acts of social acrobatics.

Despite that, I'm listening to a school friend introduce me to an oily moneybag (a gym rat, going by his skin-tight, fitted shirt), nonchalantly saying, 'She was the naughtiest girl in class (Hello, Anuradha!).' The guy looks startled but impressed. 'Still getting into trouble all the time!' the lady adds helpfully.

His eyes start gleaming. I can guess his fantasy. 'Naughty' is definitely his thing.

Does she even know how juvenile she sounds? Then she switches on her rehearsed recording, 'I, on the other hand, am involved in several projects. You know … refugees and so on … I don't call myself an activist but I do have a strong social conscience and I'm pained to see what's happening in Kashmir.'

Honey, then you should be there, na? Not standing around grotesque sculptures that, when sold to one of the chumps in the room, could feed hundreds of hungry children in Kashmir. So much pain, uffff, so much pain! But the wine is lovely, thank you, even though the cheese platter could have been better.

After a while I start enjoying myself in a twisted kind of way. My smile widens and I happily greet strangers who look like they have no business being strangers. Maybe I had known them once. Maybe I still know them. Or maybe I never knew them. It doesn't matter because nobody here is actually listening. Everyone is chattering—a stream of words floating above the ugly ceramics.

'Charlie finally flogged his Tyeb … 37 crores, I hear.'

'Not 37 … 45 … could be 41 …' Like, who counts after that?

'I adored the Gaitonde ... he's the one to invest in at the next big-ticket auction before he becomes totally unattainable. There are just so many Gaitondes floating around unlike the hundreds of Husains and Aras and Souzas ...'

The man in a chanderi kurta with zari detailing and elaborate minakaam buttons sniggers, 'My driver's name is Gaitonde. I should treat him with more respect and give him a paintbrush.'

I stop 'being in the moment' since the moment itself is gross and unappealing. Perversely, I start playing a familiar game by walking up to a small group of people (dressed in recycled jute) who are gathered in an intimate huddle. A few surreptitiously eye each other's bespoke accessories, playing with their hair, making sure those solitaires catch the overhead spotlights and flash brilliantly enough to blind the unwary, making bigger and bigger donkeys of themselves. They stare. I stare. I say something that is shockingly inane. They stare some more. Mission accomplished.

I leave feeling light and freed. 'Naughty' schoolgirls stay naughty. Ideally, they become naughtier and naughtier as they grow older. Getting into trouble becomes an addiction. The force is with me! Take that, you activist-shaktivists. See you in Srinagar.

—〰—

Being partial to all things weird, I like weird food combos the most. Have you ever tried crumbling digestive biscuits over spicy idlis, after adding green chutney to the mixture? No? Well, you must, because green chutney goes with everything! Even cake.

Let me tell you what I just had at lunch, and you decide.

Freshly prepared dhokla with a thick layer of just-ground pepper and sprigs of kothmir (coriander) embedded into the diamond-shaped pieces. Dhokla is to Gujaratis what pizza is to Italians. It can be enjoyed anytime, anywhere, and Gujjus never leave home without at least two dozen dhoklas and a stack of methi theplas packed in foil, tucked into their bags. Well-made dhokla must be light and correctly fermented to give it that khatta kick. This batch I'm eating was lovingly sent by Minal, our daughter-in-law Radhi's mother. Minal's amazing table is pretty well known in her circles, and I look forward to being invited over at hers a bit too often. But this afternoon, the dhokla arrived via a chauffeur, along with Gujju aamras (a no-frills, chilled fresh mango juice).

The Gujju aamras is a bit too watery and sweet for my taste and why they add ghee and sontha (dried ginger powder) to it, I'll never understand. For once, the Maharashtrians score over the far more affluent Gujaratis in the aamras stakes—our aamras is thicker and pulpier, with no additives. We don't dilute it with milk to add volume. We make sure we are able to extract every micro-ounce of the precious mango juice by soaking the fruit in a large degchi of water, before squeezing the daylights out of it. And yes, we prefer our aamras made from pricey hapus, not the tail-end of the season mango—the langda or pairi varieties. Ha! At least we are one up in something culinary!

All this over-indulgence was topped with a small bite of Swiss chocolate dipped into Italian coffee. That was my lunch.

I also enjoy my Sunday dosas with Chinese chilli chicken, and hakka noodles with thick mutton stew poured over it. Make sure there are enough bean sprouts around to add crunch to each bite. Crushed banana wafers as garnish are a bonus.

Incompatibilities are most attractive. Purity can be deathly dull, tedious and boring. I love hybrid everything! There is so much more richness in people, dogs, cats, food, fashion, dance, movies and music when interesting experiments or accidents create something entirely new and unexpected. Children of mixed marriages are invariably more attractive than the products of safe, controlled procreation. Some of the craziest people I love hanging out with have a mandatory twist in their stories.

I love Pushpa's food for this reason—it is as 'mixed up' as she is! She has still to make up her mind about where she's from—Andhra? She speaks and writes Telugu. Gujarat? She speaks Gujarati and cooks Gujju food. Maharashtra? She speaks Marathi and cooks Maharashtrian cuisine. Just as she cannot make up her mind which state of India she belongs to, whatever she produces on the table reflects her identity crisis—if it is indeed a crisis for anyone other than her. I see it as a delightful streak—her so-called Gujju kadhi with whole bhindi, often has a Southie style tadka to it. Thank god, Pushpa doesn't Sindhify the kadhi by adding besan. When she makes Maharashtrian puran poli, it is not powdery, flaky and feather-light but heavy with filling, thick and flavoured with nutmeg and not cardamom. Why? Just!

Mr Dé considers Pushpa the house-help, not a cook. That title is reserved for Anil. In most traditional Gujarati homes, it is the maharaj (cook) who reigns like the emperor of the rasoda. Even the ladies of the house know their place—and it is not inside the rasoda, unless the maharaj allows it. Bongs employ bawarchis, and don't treat cooks like demigods or maharajs. Pushpa is technically not our maharaj. The Dé parivaar prefers Bong cooks. In any case, Mr Dé prefers Bong everything, and other family members with their non-Bong food preferences don't really count. He is of the belief that Maharashtrians can only make vada pav and dahi misaal—he dislikes both. But let me assure you, subtle, sophisticated Maharashtrian cuisine does exist. It is multi-textured and varies from family to family. It's easier for me to keep mum than to convince Mr Dé—and not just about food, mind it! A man who knows his mind, knows his mind. A woman who knows he knows what he knows, shuts up and puts up. Why? It saves time and energy. Keeping mum is not a compromise. It is a tactic.

But back to Pushpa. It is she who decides what I should eat at lunch. We have a pact. Today, it was Minal's dhokla, Pushpa's theplas (with ajwain and methi), Raju's chicken curry (our neighbour's cook who steps in when Anil is on leave) and a frothy lassi with a large pinch of roasted cumin and coriander. Pushpa calls the meal 'light' and wonders why I have skipped Minal's aamras. There's also a slice of cinnamon cake on standby—just in case I'm still hungry. The cake has been baked by Mahek, Anandita's batchmate from her catering-college days, who runs a successful bakery business in Delhi. It has travelled well and is light as air. I eat a sliver to be able to provide truthful feedback to Mahek who is staying with us for a couple of days.

All these 'incompatible' dishes and tastes work well for me. This is how I grew up—eating idhar udhar se, and relishing most foods, being adventurous and open to cuisines from everywhere. I recently suggested to a Michelin-star chef that he should serve gobi manchurian (a bizarre enough desi invention) with vanilla ice cream, dotted with chilli flakes as dessert. Imagine the explosion of tastes on the tongue! And the crunchiness of the deep fried gobi! Who would have thought pineapple ice-cream with green chillies would work? But it does! Try it!

Food must have a wicked, adventurous, playful element to it. Like the imli laddoos I used to love as a child. Remember them? Ripe tamarind balls made with rough sea salt, red chillies and a bit of sugar? As schoolkids, we'd often steal stored tamarind left on a kitchen shelf to be soaked and pulped for rasam/sambar later, and make imli 'lollypops' out of it, using twigs from neem trees in the garden to hold the gooey lump together. A really hoarse and terribly sore throat was guaranteed the next morning. Yipeee—no school!

Which brings me to my belief that our moods too should always be in hybrid mode—switching and metamorphosing into dramatic, troubling, intriguing, exciting forms for no reason. Like mine, right now. I am listening to a song titled 'The Last Ride' sung by a rebel rap singer from Punjab called Sidhu Moose Wala who was brutally gunned down earlier this week, while looking at pictures of a homemade mango panna cotta on my phone, sent by a Pakistani diplomat friend, a scholar who lives in Lahore, while Lakshmi, our Nepali help, wearing a T-shirt made in China, hovers around pouring Darjeeling tea into porcelain mugs from Tibet, placed on a bamboo lacquered tray I'd bought in Cambodia. It's a lot like the meals I truly enjoy, which erratically combine cultures and flavours. Try eating green Thai curry with jeera pulao. Or a cheese omelette dipped into rasam.

My palate is as adventurous as I am. The only time I get indigestion is when I am forced to eat my words …

FEBRUARY

'Before I got married, I had six theories about bringing up children. Now, I have six children and no theories.'

—John Wilmot, Earl of Rochester

FEBRUARY IS SUCH AN ANNOYINGLY 'IFFY' MONTH. IT SAYS NOTHING, promises nothing. I love January in a childish, narcissistic way. January signals new beginnings. I sing, 'Hey … it's my budday month', to myself and feel energized.

'Stop behaving like an Eveready battery commercial, Mother. Calm down! We can't handle it. You are too extra and charged up.' The Brood frequently reminds me. I start feeling diminished and go phut! Am I really like those baniyan boys of Bollywood who are always onnnnn?

Aaah—meet the Brood. Our secret society of five. We have our own lingo, codes, abbreviations, nicknames, barbs, insults, put-downs, compliments, prejudices, hang-ups, partialities, slang and signals. Frankly, I would've hated being the subject of a Brood chat had I not been a member.

The Brood comprises Aditya (Padu), Avantikka (Avant), Arundhati (Aru85), Anandita (Ana Banana) and me (Motherji). Aditya, after graduating from Boston College, plunged into business. As a fourth-generation entrepreneur, he followed his passion for luxury, leisure and lifestyle by launching India's first membership-only night club. Today he is the force behind another first-of-a-kind venture—a real estate and hospitality project—Avās Wellness at Alibaug. Being the only man in this intensely female zone, Aditya provides male perspective and tells us when we are f-ing up big time in our relationships. As a Virgo, he is impossibly finicky, and all of us fall over backwards to impress him. He shares his breakfast of freshly baked croissants with his live-in buddies Momo and Pacho, two hyper-energetic Shih Tzus. Breakfast is a top priority for our Padu. Even Momo and Pacho know it's the only meal he is going to share with them, since his whereabouts remain mysterious and uncertain at other hours.

Avantikka, mother of three, has been in the media and fashion world for seventeen years. She holds the position of creative director at *Hello! India* magazine, which is every celeb's favourite. She is the Brood's Buddha—calm, wise and incredibly kind. Her husband, Dr Pramod Raju, is a former surgeon (with a doctor of medicine degree from New York University), who shifted out of the surgical ward and jumped into Wall Street. He's a first-generation entrepreneur focusing on finance, climate change and sustainability. His foundation based in Mumbai has built one of the world's largest ecosystems that works with other companies, big and small, each one involved in combating climate change in their own way. Theirs is a crowded life with three young children (Anasuya, Ahiliya, Adhiraj), two dogs (Leo and Kai) and countless friends. They chill when they need to and work tirelessly when required.

Arundhati calls herself a 'jewellery genie' which is such an evocative and apt description for what she does so brilliantly—Aru85 is a private fine-jewellery advisor, who got her master's degree from ESSEC specializing in the marketing of luxury. She has interned with Cartier and, with over a decade of experience in fine and high jewellery sales, attracts niche clients from India and overseas. Aru85 is the Brood's Miss Proper. I am very scared of her judgements and think of her as a Jane Austen heroine—so very correct at all times. With her faultless eye for all things glittering and beautiful, I crave her approval each time I buy a bauble. Arundhati's husband, Sahil Sheth, is the family's 'Mr Secure' (his nickname at school was 'Secure' for obvious reasons—the girls depended on him to see them home safely after a party). He is a third-generation businessowner in the import and supply of automotive suspension parts for European cars. They have two kids, Aryaman and Ayesha, who are better travelled than I am.

My youngest child, Anandita, the Piscean, is the surprise package—she has hidden depths which emerge at the most unexpected moments, catching all of us off-guard. Brave and courageous, dreamy and deep, she is fearlessly herself, while making a success of her natural talents. She may be foolish enough to become a writer like her mother someday. Till then, she curates luxe events and is a freelance contributor at various upscale lifestyle publications. Her professional identity is interesting—she is a luxury lifestyle consultant, offering event planning and PR services. Her life revolves around Bijou, her apricot mini-Poodle—the biggest threat to Gong Li, my very own nine-year-old Peke. Bijou has her own Instagram handle (@bijouthebeauty) and Anandita insists Bijou is seriously 'famous'.

Baap re … Coincidentally, all these bachchas are connected to the L-word (luxury), while their middle-class mother suppresses a laugh! The only luxury I recognize and value is a four-letter word called 'time'; I never have enough of it!

The Brood functions as a collective. It's a tumultuous, fraught equation given how opinionated and outspoken all of us are. We are one another's gurus, therapists, counsellors, sounding boards, anti-depressants and occasionally double up as cans of Red Bull. The things we say! The things we think and shamelessly share! Are we really so lowdown and lethal? Err—next question. The Brood is my strongest support system, my comfiest comfort zone, my personal comedy club, my hot chocolate on a cold night … What can I say? We are in sync, and we are at loggerheads. We fight, sulk, snarl, insult, hurt, make up, exit the group, beg to get back on it, miss the non-stop banter when travelling, get mental in places where there's no Wi-Fi to chat … Speaking for myself, it's the only chat group that gives me withdrawal symptoms on long, international flights. I am hopelessly hooked. There, I said it!

We also spy secretly on one another and look for carefully concealed clues on Instagram. We compete. Nobody is spared this intense scrutiny, so it's a bit hopeless to expect even a modicum of privacy given our blatantly intrusive attitude when it comes to us. We are sickeningly, obsessively into each other's lives. I know of at least two girlfriends in Aditya's life who broke up because they felt excluded from the Brood and turned paranoid about what they imagined was being said about them! All true! Hahaha!

I am not the Dalai Lama. I have no shame admitting I am emotionally needy. Emotionally greedy. I need love, acceptance, understanding, validation from the Brood. 'We have infinite emotional reserves within ourselves …' a friend assures me before leaving for a mastectomy overseas on her own. I don't know how she can be this strong facing surgery alone. I would feel vulnerable and emotional.

The Brood is my censor board—critical and exacting. I am terrified of attracting their scorn—worse, their rejection. When we fight, I feel the full weight of an elephant's foot on my heart. Sure, they don't read all my columns and they may have read half my books, if that, but they scrutinize my social media posts like hawks and come down on me heavily if I cross some arbitrary line. It's not all terrible! I do receive praise occasionally … and live on the memory of that high for months!

The Brood obsesses over food, starting with pictures of breakfast trays (Aditya's is always the best in terms of visuals and the perfectly balanced breakfast cravings). All our outings are planned around where we're going to eat—extensive research goes into planning a food itinerary. Arundhati does not cook, but her table is always beautifully arranged with shuddh Jain specialities, some of which come from her grandmother-in-law, Naliniben Sheth's kitchen, cooked with hand-pounded masalas and served with good-looking garnishing. Avantikka does not cook either but she knows exactly what to order for whom and meals at her home have something for everybody, including smashed green-pea samosas for Mr Dé, and the best kebabs coated in almond flour for all of us. Aditya is an ice-cream snob, and prefers to serve home-cooked delicacies from his own kitchen when he entertains. Raj, his talented Nepali khansama, can outdo the best Japanese chefs when it comes to making the lightest prawn tempura. With her background in hospitality and catering, Anandita loves baking the most. Her financiers are worthy of a Parisian competition, and her sausage pies might impress King Charles III, with his much-mocked 'Sausage fingers'. Anandita makes killer hummus as well, with just the right amount of sundried tomatoes from Lucerne to give the velvety hummus a little extra sexiness.

The Brood talks food. Dreams food. Devours food. Some of us watch the scales. I certainly don't.

—∞—

But this February is different.

Avantikka is spending her birthday in Galle, Sri Lanka, at a posh resort with close friends, and I am feverishly planning a trip to Shimla to catch the snow before it melts. While Avantikka finds bliss on the beaches of Galle, Mr Dé and I are lovingly shown around Shimla by our good friend of many decades, author–publisher and traveller—Ashok Chopra—born and brought up in the 'Queen of Hill Stations'. I loved his last novel, *The Lovers of Rampore*, and the earlier one, *Memories of Fire*. We are meeting for the first time after the pandemic and there is much to catch up on over the evening gup-shups that define our holidays together, with Ashok sipping his drink thoughtfully while Mr Dé indulges in his monologues and I chat with the Brood on my phone, hoping the two men don't notice. We are a compatible trio.

Like us, Ashok goes where good khaana beckons. On this trip, the star is the unbelievably yummy, khatta-meetha, teekha-teekha: smashed samosa chaat. That, and the fluffy, light-as-air kulchas we devour at Ashok's favourite stop on the busy Mall Road—Sharmaji's Chaat Shop, which has been going strong since 1938. Rabdi and jalebis with garam chai—ohoho! Thank you, Bhagwanji. Dil khush hua.

Before that is the discovery of freshly squeezed kinnow juice on the drive up to Shimla from Chandigarh. I have never tasted kinnow juice and had no idea it is our neighbour Pakistan's biggest fruit export. Kinnow is described as a 'high-yield mandarin' and is a hybrid of two citrus varieties. Commercial cultivation began in 1935 and, according to estimates, 95 per cent of the total kinnow produced across the world is grown in Pakistan.

The three of us are standing near our car, waiting expectantly for the kinnow-wala to squeeze the juice and serve it. I take a sip, and nearly fall off the cliff in my excitement. It is delicious—not too sweet, not too watery, not too cold. The pulpy texture of the fruit, that grows in abundance near Shimla, is particularly welcome. Some kinnow fans prefer to drink strained juice, but I love texture. Kinnow is like an orange, or a malta, but distinctly different in its taste. The fruit is harvested when its external colour turns a bright orange, between mid-January to mid-February. Our timing is perfect! All along the circuitous roads there are high poles of kinnow waiting to be crushed in electric juicers connected to car batteries.

Well, our neighbours are winning the kinnow war for sure!

We are back at the Oberoi Cecil in Shimla after twenty-five years. Mr Dé is busy narrating stories about our last visit when we'd been guests of the legendary hotelier, former chairman of the Oberoi Group, Padma Vibhushan 'Biki' Oberoi. Biki is the ultimate hotelier, revered in the hospitality trade, not just in India but across the world. Soft-spoken, suave, sophisticated and as sharp as his kitchen knives—qualities that are getting rarer and rarer in people these days. We have known Biki over time and spent many wonderful evenings in his company. At ninety-three, he continues to charm and impress all those he grants an audience to. But back in 1997, when we accepted his generous invitation to attend the grand reopening of the iconic hotel on the famous Mall Road, he was a sprightly, dapper and very dashing sixty-eight-year-old.

Cut to 2022. The youthful managers hovering around us at the bar are in their thirties … I nudge Mr Dé seeing the glazed look in their eyes as he mentions some old-timers from the Oberoi Group who are our good friends even now. 'Much, much before our time, Sir …' one of them says with a polite smile. Neither my nudge nor the manager's comment deter the determined Mr Dé—he wants to finish his story.

The pianist in the lobby guesses our vintage and promptly starts playing old Raj Kapoor tunes, looking meaningfully in our direction. We clap pointedly, before he switches to K.L. Saigal songs or tunes from the Silent Era. As a compromise, he settles for 'Que Sera Sera' and we focus on the food, which is dreadful. To make up for it, the chefs promise an elaborate Himachali thali the next night. The poor pianist plays on plaintively to an empty bar downstairs.

We part company with the wise and wonderful Ashok Chopra at Chandigarh airport after five packed days of snow overdose but not before he gives me a parting gift—his words. In a measured tone, he says, 'As long as your neeyat is good, don't worry about anything or anyone else—let it go.' The issue I had been fretting over for days (hurtful exchanges over text messages with a close family friend) melted away as if by magic. I hugged him in gratitude. And went off to buy a phulkari dupatta at the airport boutique.

Later, after boarding our flight to Mumbai, as he waited on for his to Delhi, I finally figured that if you like the same books, chances are your value systems will match. Just his use of the word 'neeyat' had added to my emotional vocabulary, setting me free.

'An archaeologist is the best husband any woman can have: the older she gets, the more interested he is in her.'

—Agatha Christie

From packing for Shimla like we were embarking on an Arctic expedition needing multiple layering—thermals, coats, scarves, shawls, gloves, woollen socks, Aussie Uggs—it is now all Kanjeevaram silks and cotton caftans for the pilgrimage to seek darshan of Meenakshi Amma in Madurai on the occasion of our wedding anniversary. Mr Dé's planning is in overdrive as he plots with Siddharth Jain, the most adorable and enthusiastic general manager at The Gateway Hotel Pasumalai, Madurai, with his attentive aide, Vinoth, in charge of looking after guests.

Post the traditional Madurai-style welcome with a zari-embroidered ceremonial umbrella to shield us from the sun, and prancing resident peacocks to greet us, we are led to a gigantic suite—the most impressive one in the heritage property that was once the home of a gora burra sa'ab, a nineteenth-century textile magnate. Sweetheart Siddharth points to the huge bed and says proudly, 'Our Prime Minister Narendra Modi slept on this very bed during his recent visit.'

I gulp. Will I be able to sleep soundly after digesting this? Forget nightmares, I tell myself, focus on the ceremony tomorrow. What ceremony? Well …

Mr Dé has decided to renew our marriage vows in the presence of the Goddess (Meenakshi Amma) who presides over this magnificent sixth-century CE temple complex. I want to impress Meenakshi Amma and seek her blessings. A good night's sleep is essential.

So … here we are, bright and early, dressed a tad ridiculously (no, I wasn't dressed as a Manish Malhotra bride in a bralette and diaphanous lehenga; I was clad in a trad Kanjeevaram sari!) for the ritual, which involves an exchange of heavy garlands and the tying of a mangalsutra, with a senior priest chanting mantras and blessing us—all this with tourists milling around wondering what the hell is going on. Mr Dé decides to make things easier for the gawking crowds. He holds up his hand, spreads his fingers and announces proudly, 'Paanch baar shaadi kiya ...' There is a collective gasp—and a great deal of respect for the octogenarian who is bravely marrying for the fifth time. Mr Dé's abominable language skills have prevented him from explaining that this is the fifth time he is renewing his marriage vows with the same woman—me!

We treat ourselves to a heavy Andhra meal at a tiffin house. But we face a major problem—language! Mr Dé resorts to mime and asks for teetar ('udta chidiya'), by flapping his hands wildly. No teetar. We are offered what the staff calls 'dove' (pigeon). He wants crab and starts crawling and swimming in the air. No crab. Wild boar? I make him stop the dumber-than-dumb charades before he starts grunting and points to what's written on the menu in Tamil. We get a mound of rice with mutton curry. A katori of hot ghee is poured over the dish. We eat and eat and eat. The renewal of wedding vows has made us ravenously bhookka ... for 'saapad', nothing else.

When we stagger back to the hotel, we find that Sweetheart Siddharth had totally got carried away and laid out a wedding banquet. He's also decorated the suite with yards and yards of mallipoo (the divine jasmine of Madurai).

Oh God! Suhaag raat at our age? That too using the same bed on which NaMo had relaxed a few months earlier? Perish the thought!

'You are only young once, but you can stay immature indefinitely.'
—**Ogden Nash**

Even without faking a suhaag raat for Sweetheart Siddharth's benefit, I am bone-tired when we get back to Mumbai. I desperately need Babita's magic fingers kneading my tense back, getting those tight knots out of my neck muscles. I leave a voice note for Babita, my go-to maalishwali for decades. (Her father, a liftman in our building, had recommended his daughter for the task when he'd overheard me talking to a neighbour about reliable maalishwalis in the area.) She arrives promptly at 7 p.m. with her special Ayurvedic massage oil. We are meeting after months.

Babita has just married off her stubborn daughter—the one who wanted to get into the army but fell short of a few marks. She wanted to become a fauji and not a vada pav stall owner's wife in suburban Mumbai. Nor did she want to follow in her mother's footsteps and opt for a career as a maalishwali, kneading the pampered flesh of privileged ladies like myself.

A fiery, feisty Telugu girl, Babita is married to a local Maharashtrian— her second husband who had offered her and her three children a home after her abusive, alcoholic first husband had thrown her out of his. She was very grateful to her 'aadmi' (she never called him by his name) for looking after the four of them. She had just one fervent desire as she slaved ten hours a day, giving what she termed 'Ayurvedic massage' to ladies only ('no massage for mards—too dangerous'): to get her son educated and daughters married off. The problem was, the daughters went ahead and got themselves educated through scholarships. Then came the question of dowry. Babita's sisters had married well and saved enough to cover their girls with sona–chandi when the time came. They frequently taunted Babita, asking her if maalish could get her any gold at all. Well, at least enough for her to get the girls properly married. ('Two hundred guests, Bhabhi, good caterer, cold drinks, vaghera …')

The pandemic had hit her trade badly—and I idly wondered how the massage addicts had survived without Babita's ministrations. I know how much I had missed her for two years. She is not just a maalishwali; we are friends. Her life, her world interests me deeply. Babita is shrewd, practical and wise—there is much I have learned from her. She is a proud woman. If she is compelled to ask for a loan to finance her son's entrance exam fees, she does so with utmost dignity, works doubly hard and repays the loan to the last paisa. Nirav Modi should meet Babita.

This visit is different. Babita has her palms on my back while my face rests on a pillow. I am feeling suffocated. I cannot see her expression, and she can't see mine. She starts off softly. Oh no, I can tell where this is going. Babita's diction while speaking Hindi is unique—she sounds drunk. All the soft 's' sounds get transformed into 'shhh', like she's slurring after several down the hatch.

'Bhabhi ...' Long pause. And then ... here it comes, 'Aapka weight ... aapki body ...'

Exactly the words I had anticipated and dreaded. Say no more, I say, and then go on to giving her a lame explanation about my sedentary life during the pandemic and how I had busted my left knee trying to play football with Anasuya Devi, my then ten-year-old granddaughter. I start blubbering like I am confessing deep dark secrets to a priest at the Vatican.

'I have given up sugar, wheat, milk products, deep fried food ... What more can I give up?' I didn't say 'sex' ...

All true.

Radio silence. She does not make cooing sounds to soothe me. Instead, she carries on ragdo-ing my back vigorously.

Finally, I muster up the courage to ask, 'All over or just ...?'

She pats my thickened thighs, buttocks and lower back. Enough! Khamosh. I become Shatrughan Sinha in an instant. I am about to cry.

As an afterthought, Babita adds solicitously, 'Upoor bhi ...'

She means my breasts. Yayyy! New bras! Bigger cup! I nearly hug her before controlling myself and hastily adding, 'Toh theek hai ...'

Women and their breasts! I tell you, it's one of the oddest relationships in the world.

Two evenings earlier, I'd gone to a high-profile event, where the three of us (nameless gal pals, please) had conducted an animated discussion on breasts—our own and other women's—after three glasses of Malbec. If only someone had recorded the conversation! We were not 'high'—just more unguarded and less uptight, having known one another for decades. Noticing the rather deep neckline of a black jump suit worn by Lady A, we commented on her super-hot appearance.

Lady B teased, 'Showing cleavage, huh?'

Lady A hastily pulled up her neckline and protested, 'Noooooo! I hate showing cleavage! In fact, I prefer mounds to cleavage ...'

Huh? We laughed and went in search of other 'mounds'.

Women and breasts—there is so much that is linked to those bloody mammary glands! Books and deconstructions of this complex relationship can never truly capture what a woman actually feels when she sees the changing shape of her breasts over time—from pre-puberty buds, to blossoming girlhood titties, to post-menopausal pendulums and, finally, shrunken prunes when it is time to cross the border and make it to the great beyond. Breasts, not vagina, which is too hidden and down there to establish any meaningful contact with unless you go looking for it. Breasts are just there—under your chin! Can't miss them. We watch them grow as little girls, with alarm or delight, depending on our upbringing. And then we watch them change over the years. If babies and breastfeeding are involved, the change is pretty dramatic and not always pretty. Regardless, breasts at twenty are breasts at twenty. If you have a healthy communication going with them, you can observe the waxing and waning of the twin orbs with interest.

Women spend a considerable amount of time staring at their bared breasts in the mirror. Most times, the gaze is critical, since I don't know of a single woman who likes her breasts unconditionally. There's always something to fault—the size, the shape, the overall appearance. One breast is often smaller, and nipples are rarely identical. There could be patches of discoloured skin, or hair around the nipples that require plucking. Too droopy? Too heavy? Or non-existent? No matter—there is always a major body 'defect' women are able to detect and agonize over for their entire lives. Mammary glands—well-shaped, proportionate, firm and perky—command a premium in most societies. For women, stressing over boobs—their own and other women's—is a major preoccupation, whether they admit it or not. Most women covet another women's breasts, even if their own are just fine. Slyly checking out other women's breasts is a fairly common trait. Just like men sneak a peek at another guy's penis while peeing in the stall of a urinal. It's normal. It's human. From the size, the shape and the texture of the nipples, to the overall appearance of breasts, women do invest time, energy, effort and even money trying to acquire the perfect pair of tits.

I'm not sure how men feel about their private parts since they are obliged to hold their genitals several times a day while peeing. It's impossible to maintain a healthy distance when physical proximity is this intimate. I guess it's okay for them to affectionately call their thingie 'Buddy'. Women also stare at other women's breasts, but the opportunities to do so are far fewer. Women could also play the 'mine are bigger than yours' game with breasts but who will ever admit whose are better-shaped?

Which is why the running joke ('mounds, not cleavage') has caught on in our small group. I am sitting on the fence. Why choose? Mounds and cleavage together work the best.

Fingers crossed, my children skip this part of the narrative and move on … That is, assuming they will read this book. I always get an evasive/ defensive response when I ask. I no longer embarrass either myself or them by enquiring. Does it hurt me? Umm, yes. Do I sulk? A little. But at least they're honest. Mr Dé? He reads everything I write and memorizes every line. Especially lines about himself.

Babita leaves with a big tip and smile on her otherwise permanently dukhi face. She looks puzzled as she slips into her slippers and says matter-of-factly, 'Umer ke hisaab se, aapki body theekh-thaak hai.'

Saved!

But I have a bigger question: Who massages Babita when she's feeling down and out?

—ɯ—

'The best way to get most husbands to do something is to suggest that perhaps they're too old to do it.'

—Shirley MacLaine

Bongs are born drama queens. The men in particular. They all want to be Uttam Kumar and go into emotional overdrive with melodramatic dialogues like, 'Aami morey jaabo', at the drop of a hat.

Show me one Bong who doesn't throw these three priceless words during moments of strife. 'I will die' is the literal translation which does not remotely convey the drama involved. Most Bongs are born actors, capable of high histrionics. Mamata Didi has publicly demonstrated her impressive acting chops at countless 'performances'.

Non-Bongs react differently when they are at the receiving end of this dialogue. The first reaction is generally of genuine fright—what if the threat is carried through? Will the actor rush to the kitchen, pick up the biggest knife and slit a wrist? Is there a handy bottle of rat poison tucked away in the closet, just in case it is urgently required? It's a line designed to generate guilt, pain, remorse, wretchedness ... however, by the hundredth repetition it generally backfires. Melodrama degenerates into full-blown jatra, and the only sensible way to respond to the threat is to clap. Well-timed applause can defuse the worst crisis. But most people in the audience resort to apology and tears during the dialogue delivery. Moorkhos! Idiots! Drama queens and kings thrive only when the people in the front row fall for their tired lines. Try singing a song instead! And assure the person everyone is going to die someday ... big deal!

Sorry! But I most certainly do not fall into the 'aami morey jaabo' category. No chance! I neither want to 'maro' nor 'maaro' anybody.

Mr Dé and I had had a useless argument about some useless topic that had nothing to do with either of us. Before we reached the 'aami morey jaabo' stage, I deflected the conversation to food. Politics is less appetizing by far and gives me indigestion.

I have a theory about sulking and food—don't laugh. Ask yourself how you deal with meals when you are angry and upset.

Do you 'take it out' on food—which is perfectly innocent and has not harmed you in any way? Do you starve yourself, hoping others will notice, feel bad and rush to your side with samosas? Do you sit at the table and nibble in an obvious way, pushing favourite dishes around? Do you fume at the serving staff and complain loudly about what's on your thali? Do you orchestrate a scene, throw cutlery/plates/napkins around to express rage? Do you push back your chair midway through a meal and leave the table in a huff? Do you stomp off and lock yourself in a room, refusing even water? Do you deliberately walk to the bar and pour yourself a stiff one while the rest eat? Do you stare fixedly at the screen of your phone and pretend you are chatting with someone who understands you far better? Do you play loud music that clearly disturbs others? And this is just the home scenario—scores to be tabulated later.

If an argument takes place in a bar or restaurant, then what? Do you remind yourself you are in a public place and must maintain decorum no matter what? Do you visibly seethe? Speak through gritted teeth? Order another drink and down it rapidly? Raise your voice regardless of company—even with other diners staring? Do you abruptly leave the table and not return?

Fight resolution is an art—our mothers don't teach us a thing! In the old zamana, parents and children and friends handled conflict in a more controlled, civilized way. Yes, there were 'scenes' galore, but somehow they seemed less toxic.

Aie had a short temper. So did Baba. She sulked for days and months; he forgot all about the argument within a few short hours. She preferred to cook and serve his meals, leaving me to wonder what might have happened had she gone on strike and refused to perform her wifely duties at dinner. Remember, those were pre-Swiggy, pre-home-delivery days. I don't think my father ever went to bed hungry and deprived. My mother most certainly did! Too proud to swallow a morsel when her throat was constricted and her voice refused to emerge. Her eyes would be blazing, but her mouth would be shut! Which way works better? The jury is out on this one.

As for me, confession time: I have occasionally disgraced myself. And, yes, in a public space, too. I strongly believe couples need to *have* a conversation—not *make* it! If couples cannot talk to one another without filters, how can they possibly relate on other levels? Compatibility in bed and compatibility in conversation—both are equally needed! My mother used to let her blazing eyes do all the talking without uttering a word, unlike me, who cannot zip it.

I find food always comforts when emotions are in a turmoil.

Never starve yourself when angered. I would rather go to bed angry than hungry. Fight to the finish, or forever hold your peace! Never argue on an empty stomach. An audibly protesting stomach disrupts logical thinking. No key decisions should be made or contracts signed when the stomach is growling. I remember advising a close girlfriend, when she was abruptly fired from a job she loved, to go home, eat a nourishing hot meal and then respond to the nasty CEO. We laugh over the memory today, but she often tells me how she postpones taking a call on something that matters till she's had a bite. And I readily admit how even a mug of garam chai and a packet of Glucon-D bikkies have saved me during tough negotiations and long treks to attend meetings with people I dislike.

Food fortifies. Food is our friend. Food is fundamental. Why antagonize bichara khaana–peena? What has the poor bhindi done to you?

But wait—food is no substitute for emotional well-being either. Revenge eating is as self-destructive as doing six shots of tequila in a rage. Binge drinking or binge eating do not solve the problem. Nor does food deprivation. When food becomes your ally, you learn how to extract reassurance from it. As is commonly believed, cooking can be very therapeutic. Making yourself a great omelette or a delicious, hearty soup, with chunks of seeded, whole-wheat bread, or steaming hot chawal with ghee-soaked toor dal (roasted garlic papad on the side, and maybe aam ka achhar), can make your blues vanish—at least temporarily. Till you can think things through in a calmer frame of mind—and win the bloody battle.

Today, it's possible for a single woman to give herself a short break, go to a friendly neighbourhood café and treat herself to something she enjoys—could be a falooda, cold coffee, fresh limbu soda or a masala dosa with steaming kaapi. The idea is to insist on 'alone' time and think in peace about what went wrong. Not sure if too many guys feel the need to clear the air—for most, the air is perpetually clear, never mind the fog over their happy heads. They simply do not understand why women are 'so wound up' over 'trivial stuff'. Sorry! I can only speak as a woman—if she is hurt and upset, it is *not* because she is pre-menstrual, post-menstrual, menopausal. Don't pass the buck. Don't duck. It is also not because she likes jhagda—nobody likes fighting. It is because she is in pain. And pain doesn't just disappear if you ignore it. Pain needs to be addressed. Or else it can lead to a chronic condition called unhappiness. Don't trivialize a woman's emotions because those 'inconvenient' emotions make you squirm. When men can't control a woman's brain and emotions, they control the purse strings. Women should remember that and never sell out. Exercising control over another human being using the power of money is nothing short of cruelty. One more key point to permanently etch on a woman's brain and heart: never settle for less. For example, sex-on-demand in a marriage should automatically go with financial-security-on-demand. This is not 'transactional'. This is called a 'fair exchange'. Kaiko compromise karna … Kyon?

Respect. It's a seven-letter word. We often lose sight of it, much to our own peril. Give it. Earn it. Not that tough. But then that's like telling a cook the easiest thing to make in the kitchen is dal–chawal. When, in fact, it's the toughest to master.

Phew! I have released more steam keying in these last few paragraphs than the pressure cooker I can hear whistling in the kitchen as Anil gets my dahi chicken going for dinner and Pushpa steams crunchy haricot beans. It's a challenge to convince the kitchen crew that food can be cooked and enjoyed without ladling oil or ghee into it. This afternoon, Pushpa attempted onion soup for the first time. It wasn't bad, but I have to tell her to hold the cloves. Lavang in an onion soup? She laughed when I told

her to steal some chicken or mutton stock from the meals she makes for
Bijou and Gong Li and then add the onions.

'You want to eat doggy-log ka khaana?' she asked in disbelief.

Why not? Especially if it's better than ours.

These doggy-log are fastidious eaters … Gong Li loves mutton samosas
and roast mutton in gravy from Gaylord's, my favourite restaurant at
Churchgate. Bijou likes chicken liver pâté from the club and deep-
fried Bombay duck. And as a tea-time snack, they both crave parmesan
shavings, the cheese meticulously curated by a cheese connoisseur and
importer at the deli in Alibaug.

Doesn't Pushpa know—Dogs R Us?

—m—

MARCH

'The older I get the less I listen to what people say and the more I look at what they do.'

—Andrew Carnegie

THIS YEAR, 2022, THE JAIPUR LITERATURE FESTIVAL IS BEING HELD at a brand-new venue. It's also been moved from cool January to March and the afternoon sun gives us no respite. There is much anticipation, and much hesitation as well. Will the organizers of the event, the Holy Trio (writer and editor Namita Gokhale; prolific historian William Dalrymple; and the festival's turbo-charged managing director, Sanjoy Roy) pull it off after a two-year break? The world is just about emerging out of the pandemic which has scarred humanity in ways that are still to be decoded and tabulated, much less understood.

Being among a tribe of celebrated, accomplished writers is in itself a scary experience. This year, it will be even more so. I have packed my bags with trepidation and a great deal of self-doubt. Will I be 'accepted'? How will my own session on the last day of the festival be received? The sun is high in a cloudless sky. The heat is draining me of all enthusiasm and energy. Will anybody even turn up for my big moment on the stage? Even twenty or thirty interested folks? Even if it is just to take shelter from the sun under the shamiana? Insecurity is a constant. Insecurity about my appearance. Insecurity about my life's work. About every little aspect of me. Insecurity has been a loyal companion. I am used to the feeling, and laughing secretly whenever people refer to my 'confidence'. What confidence, yaar? Dekho!

Two hours before my scheduled JLF session, I rushed halfway across Jaipur to my favourite boutique, tucked in a tiny space inside a sprawling haveli owned by the Tholia family. The extended Tholia family resides in a heritage haveli located on the main commercial street of Jaipur—the famous M.G. Road. It's a fascinating road, lined by established jewellery stores selling the most eye-popping pieces created for royalty through the centuries. Serious stuff. I have known two branches of the Tholias for several years and always make it a point to visit the brothers (Ajai and Jai), their wives and children. Theirs is a gracious way of life that appeals to me.

On this day, I wanted something hip and cool to wear on stage. Everyone I met or spotted on the grounds of the new and improved JLF was carefully attired and colour-coordinated. Ladies in arty saris worn with leather belts and designer juttis. Men in quilted Jaipur jackets worn over pink shirts with camel or elephant motifs. Frighteningly young, hugely talented and supremely arrogant writers lounging on low chairs and cracking 'in' jokes with other terrifyingly bright people. Stalwarts with an entourage—sure of their brilliance and place in the literary universe. Agents, publishers, groupies … And me, agonizing over an appropriate purchase at Nayika (the boutique). This hidden gem specializes in beautifully detailed quilted jackets in silk. Some are block-printed, others embroidered, and a few embellished with gold gota-patti. These classic jackets can be worn in just about every context, depending on what you combine with their easy, unfussy lines. I have Nayika jackets going back more than fifteen years, which always stand out for their simplicity and elegance. And let me not start on their potlis in vivid mithai colours with playful tassels and frills that add to their charm. You can keep your Dior bags, ladies. Give me a Nayika potli any day.

I tried on a few long kurtas with churidars. Nope! Not working! I was wearing a black, strappy Zara dress with a 'gaunti' and a dizzyingly gaudy yellow cape embellished with fluorescent green pompoms thrown over it. Off came the cape. I spotted a black silk chunni with discreet mukaish kaam. I draped it over my bare shoulders. Yup. Working. I figured I didn't need a bra—gone! Jacket and bra were thrown into a gigantic recycled plastic tote.

Boom! It's showtime! The stage is ours. I squint into the glare. It's a full house!

People are standing three deep, some seated cross-legged on the ground. No chairs! Good sign. I am 'In Conversation' with the bright and beauteous author Gurmehar Kaur—who is younger than my youngest child. The session is planned around my work—books, attitude, thinking, choices. It is supposed to be an open-ended exchange, so to speak. I'm beaming as I turn to look at Gurmehar, who is looking at notes on her iPad. I catch Mr Dé's eye. He seems tense; he always is before I open my mouth—privately or publicly. Not another bombshell, Wife! Please use your words with care. We don't want more morchas at our doorstep. He nods his head imperceptibly. I want to be Ramachandra Guha that very instant. Instead, I feel like Gangubai Kathiawadi.

The session starts off on an alarming note which takes me off-guard. 'You are the sexiest writer in India …' says the lovely Gurmehar, sidelong glances and naughty smile in place.

Whatt?! Stop it, girl! She's thrown me completely. Fortunately, what follows is a lively, well-researched discussion on my definition of feminism and much more, including my stated political stands which have generated a great deal of debate and got me into quite a few hairy 'situations' that deserve a separate book. Don't remind me!

She asks me how I prefer to be addressed. By my name, I answer! 'Call me Shobhaa.' Quick glances are exchanged between her and her friend Anish Gawande, the son of a family friend. He'd asked me the same question earlier. 'Should I call you "Aunty"?' I had laughed and replied, 'Call me Mauvshi, Aji, Aatya, Akka … anything but "Aunty" or Shobhaaji …'

Age! And the charming cheekiness of youth. Still, it's a whole lot more welcome than the snarky remark made by a fellow writer at JLF to another writer, 'One day Shobhaa Dé will surprise us all by writing a great novel!'

The same man wants me to endorse his father's book today. And he still has to write his own great novel and surprise ... himself!

—∭—

There are two rituals I always follow in Jaipur—have chilled lassi at the lassiwala on MI Road and go for a chakkar to the overcrowded Haldiwali Gali near Hawa Mahal in the Old City. The asli lassiwala does not proclaim his lassi leadership with banners and posters. People who know, just know! They go straight to his stall, despite its inconvenient location (no parking space for miles). The pretenders are still there, trying to lure away loyal customers from the dour-faced, unsmiling man, briskly making fresh lassi from a huge container with set dahi—he is sure of his positioning.

After all, his shop was started in 1924—take that, you pretenders! He barely makes eye contact as he fills earthenware tumblers (kulhads) with freshly whipped, frothy lassi, not too sweet, not too thick, and at just the right temperature. Mr Dé stares guiltily at me and then boldly has his large lassi with a thick layer of malai. I pretend not to hear the instructions.

You see, I have a guilty secret too. I have quietly ordered piping hot moong dal and onion hing kachoris from the halwai close by and am planning to enjoy them while he slurps his lassi and gets a malai moustache. This is no ordinary lassi, I swear. It is a magic potion. Or so I tell myself, as I walk into Haldiwali Gali in a trance, looking for Guptaji's pedhi. It is tucked away inside an abandoned, crumbling haveli that once belonged to royal jewellers who created magnificent meenakari, jadau jewellery for the maharajas, maharanis and various hierarchies of 'hukums' in the former princely state. Guptaji's forefathers were given a hole in the wall by the new landlords to operate his modest dukaan. His set-up is unimpressive but his eye is infallible. Guptaji says emeralds speak to him. I believe him. That is, when I can figure out what he's saying. His words are muffled; he barely opens his mouth. He can't! It's stuffed with paan!

Emeralds and lassi—strange combo you might think. But not so. Both satisfy yearnings I find hard to explain. I know very little about emeralds, and my knowledge of the Jaipuri lassi is equally dodgy. Neither featured in my childhood. At home, we used to have taak—thin, watery buttermilk, hand-churned by my mother in a large ceramic barni or jar, using a heavy hand-crafted wooden churner. Sometimes she added roasted jeera powder to it, but mostly we gulped it down with a pinch of salt during hot Delhi summers. When we moved to Bombay, Aie continued to make taak just like she used to in Delhi. This was a far cry from the creamy rich Jaipuri lassi I crave.

Emeralds? Ha!

The only jewellery my mother possessed was crafted out of gold—her mangalsutra with black beads (to ward off nazar), four daily-wear bangles, one or two more gold sets, and the traditional diamond 'kudis' my father bought for her on their twenty-fifth wedding anniversary. These ear studs featuring seven diamonds were her pride and joy—a symbol that her husband had made it in life. She also had a brilliantly enamelled peacock sari brooch in silver to hold her pallu over her left shoulder, but I don't recall her wearing it. I was not exposed to fine jewellery till much later in life, but I was attracted to its mystery and beauty. Not in a covetous fashion—I just love the way certain ladies wear their emeralds and pearls, with the ease and nonchalance that comes with being born into wealth. Riches become your confidantes. Today, I have several glittering confidantes. Back then, it was only after I started earning much more than I did as a trainee copywriter (Rs 350 a month) that I started to buy a few pretty baubles for myself.

Emeralds came later in my life, but when they arrived, my oh my, did they floor me! I love looking at them. Holding the smooth, sensuous pebbles in my palm (I prefer tumbles, not the far pricier faceted stones). It's almost as though I'm hypnotized. Like I'm looking into Ava Gardner's eyes—assuming hers were emerald green. Talking of emeralds and my weakness for the green stones, there is a wicked JLF story Sanjoy Roy loves repeating (partly true—only partly!). He says I once turned up late on stage for a session because I was busy buying gleaming emerald strings by the kilo at Johri Bazaar, the crowded jewellery market located in the stunning colonnades painted in shades of terracotta and orange!

I swear, I was just lukkin'.

Every well-dressed lady in Jaipur is automatically addressed as 'hukum'. I still have to make the 'hukum' cut but I so love it when I am thus addressed by gallant Jaipurwalas.

Jaipur seduces on so many levels. Emeralds are yummy, but I can't eat them. Let me tell you what goes best with emeralds—laal maas.

If you have not tasted laal maas, you have missed out on one of life's most delectable experiences. Essentially, it is goat cooked in a creamy red gravy. It is the inclusion of Mathania (a village of the Jodhpur district) chillies that impart that particular 'redness' to the meat preparation, which is not all that complicated to make at home—provided you have a bagful of these chillies. And don't get nervous about the chillies setting your tongue on fire. They are misleadingly fiery to look at, but mild to taste when cooked. The character of the chillies is well camouflaged! Visual deception works in their favour, I'd say. Right now, I'm drooling over the laal mass cooked by the Leela Palace Hotel's chef de cuisine, Pushpinder Singh Saini. He describes himself modestly as a culinary guru. After enjoying his laal maas with crunchy churra parantha and stuffed kulchas in Jaipur, I am ready to bow!

Years ago, I persuaded a senior chef at the magnificent Umaid Bhawan Palace Hotel in Jodhpur to give me these dried chillies, properly sealed in a zip-lock bag. The previous night, he had served the most memorable laal maas I had ever eaten and I wanted to carry a taste of it back for the family.

There is hardly a trip I have been on and not brought back edibles in some form or the other. On that trip, it was the beautiful chillies. But I often bring back biryani and raan, samosas and kachoris, cheeses and chorizo. Pretty much anything that packs easily and that I have relished in particular. I miss my family in an aching, ridiculous sort of way each time I travel. More so when I enjoy a meal and they aren't there to laugh and joke and dabao it with me.

Back in Mumbai, my version of the laal maas with the chef's neatly packed chillies and his secret recipe turned out to be a complete disaster in my kitchen. What appeared at dinnertime was a miserable-looking, orangish bowl of watery soup with a few pieces of maas drowning in the mess. I guess even the friendliest chefs keep that one key secret ingredient to themselves. If they generously passed on all their culinary tricks to every curious customer, we'd all become master chefs. Great cooks never fully share their recipes—they always hold back. Being possessive about your craft is only natural. Food and democracy? Ha! Go wage your own recipe war … I ain't parting with mine!

—⁓—

Laal maas, maach and Bong dhutis are avidly discussed with Nobel Laureate Abhijit Banerjee (I definitely want to be his BFF) when we meet at the chole–bhature counter of the lavish breakfast buffet at the hotel we are staying at during JLF 2022. The foodie–economist (or economist–foodie) is as distressed as I am that there is no Uttar Pradesh (UP) style puri–bhaji that morning. The UP-style aloo tarkari in a thick gravy goes brilliantly with hot puris, and while travelling to the north, I book hotels in the hope of being served this delicious breakfast specialty. The gravy has to be dense, not watery, and the tadka, just right with a hint of hing and plenty of jeera, sometimes with an additional pinch of saunf too. Green peas are optional but add to the simple flavour of the preparation.

We are staring forlornly at the chole before our eyes meet. Abhijit hastily looks away as I boldly introduce myself. He smiles and confesses, 'I wanted to speak to you, but I felt shy!'

I squeal like a schoolgirl and say, 'So did I! I felt shy as well but decided it was a now-or-never moment.'

I tell him how much I had adored his cookbook, *Cooking to Save Your Life*. How I read it in one go and how it had made me drool in admiration for the man who knew his kitchen and palate as much as he understood global economics and the behaviour of fickle currencies. His passion for food, his knowledge of wine, and the pleasure he took in feeding his family and friends was beyond astonishing. He could write a thesis on ways to cut veggies. After reading that book, reviewers suggested Abhijit be given another Nobel for food writing. Happy to recommend this new category to those stuffed shirts on the Nobel committee. Imagine not awarding a man who suggests Bong tomator chutney with tortillas and insists fish jhol with potol (pointed gourd) is a complete meal in itself.

I don't dare tell him I am a total dud at economics and haven't read his other seminal work *What the Economy Needs Now* in the fear that he will lose interest and go back to his table with a dosa, thus ending a potential relationship right there! No! I have to keep him engaged somehow, so I throw in a few Bangla words and tell him that my husband is a great cook—just like him! Abhijit seems pleased but unconvinced by that tall claim and asks me to join him and the lovely Olivier Cheyenne, who's a vegetarian. Olivier worked as an au pair in the Banerjee household before qualifying as an illustrator. I babble on (a nervous habit) as we walk to the table and, inevitably, the conversation turns to food.

First up is the paean to paanch phoron, the combination of four whole—not powdered—aromatic spices and one legume that are to a Bong what bechamel sauce is to French households. It comprises cumin seeds, nigella seeds, wild celery seeds, fenugreek seeds and is used for tempering tadka. We briefly refer to beguni (thin slices of baingan deep fried in a light batter with a sprinkling of nigella and poppy seeds or posto) done just so. I avoid mentioning ghonto, another Bong staple, because it really sounds terribly sexual.

At some point, I mention the dhuti he had worn to the Nobel ceremony and that I admired his bold, sartorial choice at such a stuffy ceremony at which dress code was the staid and boring black tie. Then it was back to food and wondering why the chefs had skipped the bhaji and served oily chole.

Food connects people in the most unexpected places and in the most delightful ways. Now that Abhijit has extended a warm invitation to visit him in Boston where he would cook for us, I am feeling 'accepted'.

In return, Mr Dé promises to cook doi maach for Abhijit when he's in Mumbai. Mr Dé has cooked doi maach for 125 guests and I can confidently declare him a doi maach world champion. Fair exchange. I say I'll be happy to eat whatever the two men produce in the kitchen. We talk more food … major Bongness is happening. There goes our flight, I think. Note to self: Don't start even a casual convo involving khaabar (or khaana) with hungry Bongs around. Forget skipping sex—they'll happily skip their son's graduation as they salivate over Pishi-ma's topshey maach or Mashi-ma's chorchori. We part company reluctantly after exchanging contact details and lingering looks.

On the flight, I think about how our time with the genius was way too short. Mr Dé tells me he noticed Abhijit's strong wrists and muscular arms on an otherwise lean and mean frame. We conclude he must play tennis. Must remember to ask while enjoying our Bong repast. Mercifully, I think, nobody brought up the 'K' word or all of us would have in earnest missed our flights.

Kasundi conversations make all Bongs very emotional. Well, most things make Bongs super emotional. I love mustard in any form—ground into a smooth paste and covering a plump slice of hilsa, or in a tadka. I like sharp English mustard the most, preferring it to the milder French version, but offer me kasundi with just about anything and I'll finish the bottle. The kasundi kick is hard to put into words—it's simpler to put kasundi in your mouth and taste it for yourself to know what makes it so distinct. Yes, it's bitter but also sweet. There are sour notes lurking within and a sharpness that doesn't damage your sinuses like English mustards often do. Kasundi is mellow and gentle and it definitely deserves a major celebration on haute cuisine menus across the world.

When I was newly married, I started hoarding bottles of kasundi after each trip to Kolkata. I saw these trips primarily as Mission Kasundi. My relatives found it bizarre that Mr Dé and I would come armed with bubble wrap, elastic bands and more in order to transport our stash without spillage. Ever seen spilled kasundi? Looks like a toddler's kakka. The caution was needed. So was the extra suitcase for the precious bottles, which along with wheels of nolen gur, made the bag so heavy that porters would groan and protest. When the kasundi supply was down to three bottles on the kitchen shelve, I'd hit the panic button and start rationing it, counting the days left for the next trip to 'maike'.

I generally polish off half a bottle at lunch. Kasundi goes with everything. Try dotting a gooey chocolate cake with Bengali mustard—heaven! I wallop my bottle over 'maach bhaja' (fried fish) or mince cutlets, but I also use generous amounts in creamy, mayo-heavy, egg sandwiches from Bombay Gymkhana. An artisanal beer from Goa washes it down rather well. The last time I treated myself to a kasundi overkill, I'd checked the city's temperature—it was 39 degrees Celsius. It was easy to blame the heat wave … easier by far to eat one more anda sandwich and go take a nap.

—∿—

Much more than the unbeatable taste of kasundi was avidly discussed when Abhijit Banerjee kept his date with Mr Dé and came home, en famille, to an informal dinner. Since I had missed the Nobel Laureate's energetic bhangra, clad in colourful attire, at the incredibly amazing Writers' Ball that closes the JLF celebrations, I was hoping for a little naach-gaana at home. But Mr Dé would have none of it.

'Nonsense!' he said. 'He is coming to our home to eat … not dance!'

I stopped myself from saying, 'He can do both—eat, dance, and drink too.' By then, Mr Dé had thrown himself into the job of locating the best fish for the paturi maach, the best meat (thank you, Ansariji) for the kosha mangsho, and the best prawns for the malai chingri. He would leave the bhaaja moonger dal to Anil, who makes it consistently well.

I was wondering whether the assembled Bongs would go into the predictable lineage competition. Maybe not these Bongs. I often run into the Boastful Bong Brigade, especially during pujo and cringe when I hear them going on and on about their 'pedigrees'. Are you Maltese dogs? I have yet to attend a Bong-dominated function where the opening remarks have not included throwaway references like: 'Aamar dadu studied at Oxford, same year as Jawahar' or 'my great-grandfather's baari—if you can call it that—extended from one end of the street to the other.' … 'Our thakur-da was invited by the Queen to join her inner council of advisors.' … 'My grand-uncle was married to the princess of Pataliputra.' Listen you pompous old thing—if you are such a bore yourself, your forefathers must have been worse! Why do Bongs stubbornly live in the past? What's wrong with today? I feel like shouting: Speak for yourself—tell me what *you* do. I really don't care a fig what your great-grandfather did. Whatever he did do, poor fellow—he produced pathetic you!

Podey laath. The pronunciation is key (nasal, extended 'ponnnnnndey'). It translates to a kick on the backside. Lots of candidates for me to perform my well-aimed high kicks.

Abhijit walks in with his wife, economist and co-Nobel Laureate, Esther Duflo, their two gorgeous children—Mimi and Mimo—and Olivier. They come bearing the most unusual and delicious fruity cheese from Provence, where they've been holidaying. The kids are terrifyingly bright and giving our friends a complex. Mimi is a math wizard and Mimo has views on football that are far from kiddish. The kids aren't jet-lagged even though the family has been flying for hours and have come straight to dinner after dropping off their bags at the hotel. I'm keeping my fingers crossed the men don't get into the 'my fish is bigger than yours' kind of competition.

Maach and I share an uneasy relationship. There's a whole book right there. After forty years, I remain clueless and cannot tell the difference between rohu, hilsa, tilapia, topshe, parshe, nor do I go into an orgasmic trance buying bagda or golda chingri. All I know is I am supposed to buy fish that's smiling. These days I smile back and move on …

We have invited a few close friends who are keen to interact with not one but two Nobel Laureates in one room! Mr Dé is sporting a mint green dhuti with a dull gold paad or border, and preening away. I am dressed in Dimpy Gujral's plum-coloured caftan with autumn leaves floating all over it. The Banerjees are wearing Fab India–style soft, eco-friendly cotton clothes. Suddenly, I feel horribly over-dressed and gauche. Thank God, I avoided wearing plum-coloured lipstick!

The table is looking rather nice. I have brought out old silver bartans and they are looking fabulous! The Banerjees are warm, informal and friendly. Everyone wants to click pics. I wonder aloud if Abhijit finds it intrusive.

'He's used to being photographed ...' Mimi assures me.

Abhijit speaks indulgently to his children in Bong-accented French. I think the food has passed his test, but I'm not certain. The bhaja stuff and luchis are not emerging fast enough from the kitchen. Ashwin Sanghi and Devdutt Pattanaik are holding their own individual durbars with a fawning audience of lovely ladies in fine silks. At some point, Mr Dé produces a chocolate cake, makes a great speech and requests Abhijit, Esther, Mimi and Mimo to cut it. I'm not sure whether or not to start singing 'Congratulations and celebrations, I want the world to know how happy we can be...' Fortunately, Santosh, our regular bartender, offers me a fresh glass of white wine just then and I want to immediately give him a Nobel for discretion!

I remind Mr Dé the morning after that he had ordered a special cake made entirely out of sandesh in honour of Amitav Ghosh when he'd come home to dinner. Not comparing or anything—just sayin'!

—⁓—

'My mother always used to say, "The older you get, the better you get,
unless you're a banana."

—Betty White

It's Holi today—not my favourite festival. Even as a child I resented the liberties taken by strangers who'd happily smear my face with colours and drench me with coloured water filled in gleaming brass pichkaries. Those are gone—the brass pichkaries—replaced by plastic guns straight out of a video game. But it's also lunchtime and Mr Dé asks, 'Eggs and soup?'

'No, lasooni palak, dahi papdi chaat and gulab jamun. It's Holi! I know it isn't a popular Bengali festival … even so,' I say.

His eyes light up. 'Gulab jamuns? Hot, please …'

I mention that the meal has been ordered by Anandita since she felt her parents should not be eating eggs and soup as Holi lunch. She is right.

The conversation at the table is a bit strange. Or not so strange. Mr Dé, like all Bengalis, is a political expert and a closet revolutionary. He wants to talk about Ukraine and diss Joe Biden. He has views. Strong ones. I, on the other hand, want to discuss the texture of the velvety lasooni palak with shredded ginger on top. Anandita wants to talk about her sprained ankle. After listening to both for a while, I say in a good-natured sort of way, a tight smile stretching my facial muscles, 'When you are done … I want to get back to planning dinner. Kosha mangsho?'

Mr Dé takes the hint, looks injured, pushes back his chair and prepares to walk back to his study table to carry on his research into the war that is playing havoc with world markets. 'Do you know how many office spaces are vacant next door?' he asks testily.

I confess I don't but still ask, 'Because of Ukraine?'

He glares and continues walking. Anandita hobbles off to her room— more exaggerated than usual, just to make a point. I guess I have not been mother enough to fuss over her sprained ankle. I used to sprain my ankles routinely as a competitive athlete in school and college without my mother ever knowing. But we didn't have to deal with the war in Ukraine back then.

A few minutes later, Mr Dé returns to pat me affectionately on the head (my hair, wet and uncombed). I'm holding my breath. What if he asks me to rattle off the number of causalities in Kyiv or define my final position on Russia? But no. Mr Dé leans forward and says, 'Happy Holi! You are my Radha! The gulab jamuns were too good—but I ate just one.'

Mr Dé's attempting at an Omar Khayyam.

If I am Radha, then he is Krishna, right? Yes, right! Mr Dé's dak naam is Gopal. Back in Kolkata, his cousins still call him Gopal-da. The Krishna in him surfaces from time to time. And do remember—my given name is Anuradha!

—⁓—

For someone who grew up in a primarily vegetarian home, I am a voracious meat-eater today. I love mutton! Author and group director of Masala World, Camellia Panjabi, the lady who knows more about global foods and cuisines than anybody I know, tells me it's okay to like and eat mutton. Mutton. Not lamb. I had always thought it was the same thing! Remember that old snarky put down—mutton dressed as lamb? Mutton comes from a three-year-old animal, and lamb is usually a year old. These meats come from sheep. What we eat in India is typically goat meat. We rarely eat sheep meat. And even though goat meat has a term reserved for it (chevon), it is sold as 'mutton' here. I prefer goat over sheep—it's less smelly and leaner. And in my head, therefore, healthier. But I needed Camellia's informed view on this.

Oh no, my dear, she explains patiently, as we munch on chicken-mayo sandwiches, malai-chicken kebabs, chilly cheese toast and sev puri.

We are meeting Camellia after ages. Seated on the low, cane sofa is her other guest—Navin Chawla, former chief election commissioner of India and author. The mood is very 'Raj'. Navin being a Dilliwala, is behaving like one, greeting all and sundry who pass our table, whether or not he knows them. All the other tables in the vast, marble-floored veranda of Mumbai's Willingdon Club or 'Willy' as it is nicknamed—surely the snobbiest club in India—are taken. Around us, sit stately Parsi dowagers nibbling on vol-au-vents and tinkling the little brass bells on the table to summon bearers and ask for a fresh pot of pudina tea. Suddenly, there is a hush as God is spotted making his way to the gentleman's washroom. Some guests stand up and bow, like they are in the presence of Brit royalty and we are still in pre-Independence India. God has that effect on lesser mortals—I am fully fida over him myself, and am known to swoon when he's in the vicinity. I notice he is dressed impeccably in a pink linen shirt—as he passes our table, I stop myself from leaping into his arms and startling him.

God is the legendary 'Doc' who has saved more lives than anyone else I know. At more than ninety years of age, Dr Farokh Udwadia still makes male and female hearts go boom-boodi-boom each time he deigns to make eye contact. He remains the presiding deity at Breach Candy Hospital, close to Willy, and I worship him, like zillions of multi-generational fans.

I love the Willingdon Club. I am not a member but as a schoolgirl I would be taken to the swimming pool by my House Captain, the very wonderful Laila Talyarkhan. She wanted me to learn swimming, assuming wrongly that I would take to it like a fish. I didn't. I hated being in water and was scared of drowning—I still am. But I didn't tell her that then because I didn't want our visits to this posh club to come to an end. She would generously pack mutton sandwiches with a dash of English mustard for me each time, and I can still taste the slivers of perfectly roasted mutton which I'd greedily devour in the back seat of Laila's chauffeur-driven car when I got dropped home.

Mutton is a rich man's food—I still think of it like that.

'But lamb is far more expensive,' Camellia Panjabi smiles as she continues the lamb versus mutton debate, as one of the most successful restaurant owners in London, along with her sister Namita and her husband Ranjit Mathrani. They run the award-winning restaurants Chutney Mary, Amaya and Masala World. Like Laila, Camellia and Namita too are Queen Marians …

How lovely! Mutton has played a part in the evolution of my palate, thanks to our alma mater!

Eating mutton makes me feel I have made it to the *Forbes'* rich list! Back home, Mr Dé says, 'We should cut down on the mangsho ...'

He says to me each time Ansariji phones (once a week).

Ansariji is our muttonwala. We have never met but I know his voice and he knows mine. He also knows what the order is likely to be. Ansariji and I bond over mutton—the cuts (with or without boti), kheema lightly or finely ground, larger chops from a senior goat or baby chops which are tastier, what about some kaleji for sir? Or bone with marrow for soup? Anything for the dogs?

Ansariji also feels he has the absolute right to call me any time to ask, 'Aapka order ...?' I could be anywhere in the world but what does it matter to Ansariji; he does not follow boring time zone protocols. Neither does he apologize if I say I am thousands of miles away and it is 3 a.m. 'Agley haftey ... khuda hafiz,' he says and hangs up. Ansariji knows a loyal customer when he hears one. Since our phonewali mulaqat years ago at a gourmet friend's recommendation, I haven't looked beyond Ansariji. Never as much as flirted, forget straying. I know better.

Mangsho is very important to Bengali men—second only to fish. Chicken is rarely mentioned and hardly ever eaten. When all else fails, and the evening looks ominous, I bring on the mangsho to keep the peace. It's important to have an Ansariji in my life on speed dial—a man who knows his mangsho. So, it's okay if my phone screen lights up during an 'important' meeting, and the person next to me stares at the caller's name with a strange expression and then looks pointedly at me. The screen reads: *Ansari. Mangsho Man.*

According to the very finicky and ridiculously fastidious Bengalis who have eaten at our table (round and covered with a Jaipur block-printed tablecloth), there is no better kosha mangsho west of the Hooghly than Anil Das's special version Chez Dé. When we eat with guests, Anil is instructed to fry fluffy luchis and present them one by one, not five on a plate. The appearance of the luchis is of prime importance.

The perfect luchi can be no bigger than the size of a well-endowed woman's breast. It has to be light as air, spherical and golden (luchis have complexions too). We avoid luchis when we enjoy Anil's kosha mangsho. Mr Dé specifically asks for a slice of 'kacha ruti' (white untoasted bread) with thick raw onion discs and raw green chillies on the side. The chillies have to look perky and not tired, he insists. Why the 'no luchi' clause? Because the mention of anything deep fried generates an instant reaction as Mr Dé's left hand moves to his stomach and moves in a circular motion. He mentally calculates the calorie load by poking his belly and firmly shakes his head—'no luchi'.

Anil Das is the youngest of three brothers who have been working at our home in turns for over forty years. Sunil passed away a few years ago; Subhash started his own canteen in Navi Mumbai; and we inherited Anil, a genial, ever-smiling man, who insists on calling our favourite Goan prawn curry, 'Ganesh curry.'

This evening, Anil is beaming as he lowers his face mask and says, 'Boudi, bhalo news.' His son is finally getting married to his college sweetheart! Her parents have agreed after resisting the match for years. Why? Because of caste and financial differences. She is from the other coast and belongs to a different community, better educated than the boy, earning well and good-looking. Anil describes himself as 'acchut' and semi-literate. After struggling for decades, he managed to borrow enough money to get a tiny one-bedroom flat of his own in the back of beyond. This is where the newly-weds will begin their new life.

'Do the in-laws eat non-veg?' Mr Dé asks Anil. He said indeed they do. 'Problem solved! Feed them your special kosha mangsho and they'll forget everything else!'

That's the power of kosha mangsho done right!

It's thanks to the three Das brothers that I speak a mangled version of Bangla—since they don't speak Hindi, Marathi or English. 'Just heavily accented Bangla', which Mr Dé insists is more East Bengali than West. *Ami jaani na*. So long as we get authentic khaabar on the table, east, west, north, south hardly matters. I am not eating their accents. My detailed instructions in grammatically twisted but passable Bangla to Anil, Subhash and Sunil over the years have helped me impress the in-laws in Kolkata. It is their sweet nature and my eagerness to communicate that has frequently saved my neck. I still mix up 'dhokar dalna' (lentil cake made with chana dal and simmered in a gravy minus onion and garlic) with 'dimer dalna' (boiled eggs and potatoes in a thick, rich tomato-onion-ginger-garlic paste gravy) and always forget that 'daab chingri' requires tender green coconuts fresh off the palm tree, but it's okay. We still laugh and enjoy what appears on the dinner table. Anek dhanyabad! Mangled Bangla is better than no Bangla—theek achchey?

But back to mangsho! Uff! I have so many lovely and mad memories of bonding over mangsho. My children crave our ghar-ka-mangsho the most. We have a family friend who demands we cook an extra kilo for him alone when he comes to dinner. He rolls up his sleeves and gets down to business, taking his time to suck out the marrow from the bone—very noisily at that. It is an impressive mangsho performance and we always clap when he's done.

Mangsho has played a major romantic role in my prem kahaani and I remain eternally indebted. The first night I ate at Mr Dé's table (it was rectangular back then, and most undemocratic in the inflexibility of its seating plan), he grandly served me kosha mangsho and something else I had never tasted. The mangsho had been cooked by Bijoli Devi, a short, rotund cook who ruled the household after Stella—the mild-mannered Mangalorean resident cook at the time, who married Subramaniam, Mr Dé's Malayali chauffeur. Maybe she wooed 'Mani' with Mangalorean fish curry rice? Sweet Stella—she still sends us delicious prawn gassi with appams during Onam.

The hour was late. Most of the other guests at Mr Dé's sumptuous dinner party at home had left after enjoying Bijoli Devi's fine cooking. I was ready to leave as well. But Mr Dé would have none of it. He was the mighty host, and I was just another invitee at his banquet for over fifty high-profile guests.

'Stay!' he had commanded. 'You cannot leave without tasting the kosha mangsho.'

I had skipped dinner and was about to skip dessert and skip home by then. Most of the guests had left and I was done making pc with people I barely knew. I was halfway to the door when Mr Dé stopped me and added silkily, 'Besides, I am planning to serve you something special which I didn't offer the other guests.'

Uh oh. I held my breath. With impassioned Bongs you never know! Was the man propositioning?

Triumphantly, Mr Dé announced, 'It's called "kuler aachar".'

Frankly, it sounded slightly obscene. I didn't know then, what I know now—it's pretty pointless to argue with the main man. I stayed. I ate. And I guess I never left! Was it the mangsho or the man? Or was it the tangy kuler aachar—a seasonal pickle made from local berries with a specific tart aftertaste?

Forty years later, I'm not asking!

—m—

'I don't believe in aging. I believe in forever altering one's aspect to the sun.'

—Virginia Woolf

It's Gudi Padwa today, the Maharashtrian New Year, and in most Maharashtrian homes across the state, and wherever traditional Maharashtrians observe these age-old customs, a 'gudi' will be hung up prominently, often on a balcony. A gudi represents a flag or a symbol of Lord Brahma. It is a spring festival celebrating fertility and a good harvest. The gudi is an upturned lota in copper, brass or silver that's mounted on a pole, draped in silk with wheat or rice stalks and marigold garlands decorating it.

Our gudi has been ceremonially put up in Alibaug, at the entrance to the farmhouse. The gardener has decorated it prettily with garlands of flowers picked from the flower beds and potted flowering plants on the property. A colourful zari blouse piece bought in the local Chondi Bazaar, the nearest local market from our house, is placed on top, anchored to the pole with a tumbler. Our humble gudi looks really charming and I smile to myself seeing the blouse piece fluttering in the breeze.

At our city home, our lady-for-all-seasons, the ever-enthusiastic Pushpa, has prepared rawa sheera (also known as suji ka halwa), with ladles of pure homemade ghee, slivers of blanched almonds, diced cashew nuts, plump kishmish. She has enriched the sheera with strands of the best saffron, soaked in warm milk to release the flavour to its full potential. I like that Pushpa has taken initiative without waiting for me to wake up and instruct her. Pushpa is wearing new gold jewellery, recently purchased from her 'Bhishi' bonanza. Bhishi is a form of a group saving scheme devised by enterprising house-helps as a version of the fancier kitty party, which yields a 'bonus' when the contributor's turn comes. She wants the day off tomorrow to flaunt her gold ornaments to her family and collect a watch promised to her by a generous chacha. Pushpa is dressed in a new outfit (lime green and embroidered palazzos with a plain kurta). She's also wearing orange lipstick and kohl in her eyes. I feel ashamed. Here I am in a shabby caftan. I am still to bathe, which means till that is done, I cannot light a diya and say my prayers. My hair is uncombed and I regret not waking up early to observe the rituals in an appropriate manner. Nor have I got myself a new set of clothes, forget jewellery!

Mr Dé looks at the sheera and declares it's 'too dry'. Pushpa is asked to 'loosen it up' (through mime and broken Hinglish). She nods her head and quickly looks at me. I tell her to heat it again and add more ghee— that combo could loosen up a ball of concrete, let alone sheera. The last mangoes from the Alphonso peti are neatly cut and perfectly chilled. Why not! Tally ho! It's Gudi Padwa … Let's have it all! Isn't that what we pray for on this auspicious day—prosperity?

My secret wish is to join the gorgeously dressed Maharashtrian mulgis, the attractive young women of the community, dressed in traditional finery, prominent naths in place, complete with men's elaborate phetas and pagdis, as they roar down Girgaum's main street on heavy duty motorbikes. Mr Dé and I are attending a swish shaadi this evening. He wants me to wear a Nauvari sari in honour of Gudi Padwa. I tell him a nine-yard Paithani is a total waste of effort on this nouveau riche crowd. The ladies won't know a genuine Paithani or Patola from a polyester curtain. I'm being very supercilious and snobby and displaying my cultural/textile superiority.

'Wear it for me …' he says.

I duck the request. 'I don't have the right accessories. My Maharashtrian nath and thushi … so incomplete without those essential adornments.'

He nods and goes off to get his dhuti organized. He has his priorities in place. Dhutis before Paithanis.

Just then, I receive a 'Happy Gudi Padwa' call from Bhawana Somaaya, film journalist, critic, author and historian who was awarded the Padma Shri in 2017. Bhawana is my only friend who is not food-obsessed. She is food-indifferent. She cannot understand my passion for food, and I cannot understand her disinterest. We must meet over a dhokla and sort this out.

She often greets me with a cheerful, 'What's your news, Shobhaa Dé?'

To which I lamely respond, 'All theek … and yours, Bhawana Somaaya?'

We both laugh at our old, tired joke, and she says, 'Bhawana Somaaya does not sound as good as Shobhaa Dé!'

I don't contradict her. My children have wished me over WhatsApp. I guess they're too busy to call. Children are always busy. I recall my father's petulance when, in an accusatory tone, he'd say, 'Too busy writing, writing, writing to talk to your old father?' And I would get bugged. Bugged, not contrite. So, I say nothing to my own children even when I am dying to hear their voices. Today's parents have to train themselves to not show eagerness. No expectations, I remind myself. Often, I amuse myself reading those '10 Questions' style interviews with celebrities. A standard question is: 'Which is your most favourite possession?' Most reply, 'My children.' And I think, how dumb. Seriously! Children are not 'possessions'. You don't own children. Parents are lucky if their children actually tolerate them once they're old enough to do potty without help and brush their teeth on their own. So, remember—no expectations from children.

Bhawana tells me that exactly fifteen years ago I had advised her to move into her beautiful new home on Gudi Padwa.

'You won't find a better mahurat. Just do it. Say a small prayer before you enter, take a coconut with you, and a Ganeshji, put a toran on the front door, step in with joy and gratitude in your heart …' I had apparently told her.

I have forgotten that moment. But she has remembered. There is one more reason to celebrate Gudi Padwa this year—Bhawana has completed her new book about her extraordinary parents this morning. I'm so glad she is sharing it with me. During the course of our conversation, she recalls her days at the Government Law College (this was years before we met and became friends). I am stumped! Impressed! I didn't know Bhawana had a law degree! I knew about so many of her accomplishments, but not this!

'Wow!' I exclaim. 'I had no idea! What made you do law?'

She told me how particular her parents were about all their eight children excelling at academics—Bhawana being the youngest, was expected to keep up the family tradition. I commented that my family also invested heavily in making sure all four of us received the best education, except that I, being the youngest, was simply not interested in academics and refused to study further after acquiring a basic Bachelor of Arts degree from St. Xavier's College.

Bhawana promptly shoots back, 'Shobhaa Dé, you were always a rebel. I was anything but!'

Haiiiiii … What I would do for a law degree today! Imagine being a rebel without being Marlon Brando—khaali-peeli, faltu ka rebel.

> *'You know you're getting old when you stoop to tie your shoelaces and wonder what else you could do while you're down there.'*
>
> **—George Burns**

'How's the josh?' I yell, staring at my dishevelled self in the bathroom mirror.

This is crazy. What bloody josh? I am not Vicky Kaushal. But I do feel better after I shout at my image.

It's late evening. Murderously hot outside, but the tide is coming in and there is a mild, uncertain twilight wondering whether to turn into a full-blown dramatic lurid orange sky. Pushpa has been hard at work for hours in a beastly hot kitchen. I have asked her to make puran poli.

As I've mentioned before, technically, Pushpa is not a cook but that's just a small detail. She hates ironing but loves cooking and is always willing to give something new a go. Rolling out puran polis is a feat—more than just a culinary art. My mother and grandmother (Aie and Aji) rolled the perfect polis—paper thin, crisply baked on the outside and moist inside, the puran just lightly flavoured with crushed cardamom and sweetened with gur (jaggery). This is the Maharashtrian puran poli, delicate, soft and yielding like a silken handkerchief. It's eaten with homemade ghee (tup), and a spicy, thin gravy called 'kaath'. I eat mine with green mirchi aachar, and love the contradictory, quarrelsome flavours on my tongue.

Pushpa is looking worried. She needs Vicky Kaushal's josh. 'We don't have gur at home,' she says, a distraught expression on her face.

'Surely gur is available at the kirana store,' I say, a bit too sharply.

Pushpa looks crestfallen and assumes an injured air. Is she going to cry? I channel my inner Rajesh Khanna and mutter, 'Pushpa … I hate tears.'

Soon enough, the gur is procured and mission puran poli gets underway.

It's going to be a special, somewhat sentimental evening. I need josh and more. Our son Rana, his wife Radhi and their baby daughter, Samsara, are coming over to say goodbye before catching a flight to Singapore, where they are based. (Rana is a copy, data and SEO-based

70

creative director who lives between Singapore and Thailand, with Radhi, who is an aspiring expressive arts practitioner, a graphic designer by profession and who is taking a break from the screen world to raise a toddler. Radhika is the family's true 'artist'—a gifted painter, sculptor, writer and poet, with a masters in art history from the prestigious Faculty of Fine Arts, Baroda. Gifted and sensitive, beautiful and spiritual, there is much I can learn from her.) For the past two years, they had made Goa their home. Initially, because of the pandemic—like millions of young couples—they'd been caught off guard and got stuck! Our lockdown, Singapore's lockdown, the world reeling … all that. Finally, they had got an all-clear and were on their way to reclaim their old lives, and perhaps set out on a fresh journey which would take them to—I don't know—Costa Rica was one option, casually mentioned by Rana. The puran poli was a sweet send-off for them.

My josh is returning, and Pushpa seems to have plenty of her own after getting a gigantic lump of gur from the neighbourhood shop. I can smell the aroma of the chana dal being tempered with spicy garam masala for the kaath. And the puran is being given its final touches with green elaichi. I have opened a jar of the most velvety, grainy Gir Cow Full Moon ghee—a ghee so rich it's shameless. The marketing blurb says the ghee is made from cow's milk on a Purnima night, when it absorbs the rays of the moon. I believe every word.

The children and their child arrive and offer us ragi chips and cacao-coconut choccies without sugar. My heart sinks. My josh takes a hit! Who will eat the painstakingly made puran polis? Well … the dogs are eagerly waiting, going by the way Gong Li and Bijou are behaving around the tea trays. Samsara, with just two front teeth in her lower jaw, looks on in anticipation, a bit of drool escaping her open mouth. The moment is here!

Mr Dé glares. 'Oh, oh—no shingaras? What sort of an evening snack is this?' He launches into a long discourse about menfolk in Kolkata coming back to laden tables of assorted mishti and piping hot shingaras stuffed with phool kopi, matter and aaloo, crushed pepper being the main spice.

Pushpa nervously produces the first set of puran polis hot off the tawa. Radhi takes a bite, then two, then twenty! Ha! My josh is coming back. Baby Samsara spits out some and sucks on some. Rana disappears into his old room. That leaves me and a sceptical Mr Dé. I boldly offer him a puran poli. He insists on it being cut into half. 'What nonsense,' I mutter inaudibly. Who eats half a puran poli? Bong men who watch their weight! I offer the Full Moon ghee—but the spoon is not of the right size, he grumbles as he scoops up a tiny amount with a sliver of puran poli. He knows I am watching! He bites into the ghee-covered largish piece of Pushpa's offering.

Baat khatam! One more puran poli is instantly ordered for the sa'ab.

Pushpa is beaming. The baby is gurgling. Radhi is on her third poli. My josh is higher than Vicky's!

—⁓—

APRIL

'We don't grow older, we grow riper.'

—**Pablo Picasso**

I AM STARING AT TWO LARGE CARDBOARD CARTONS, BOTH FILLED with unripened fruit. One has chikoos from an organic farm in Gujarat. The other, mangoes from an organic farm in Maharashtra. Both look equally unappetizing.

For all these years, I have happily eaten chemically ripened hapus, chikoos, bananas, apples and strawberries. That is the taste I am accustomed to. Unlike my children, who closely examine expiry dates on everything and scrupulously avoid non-organically grown foods, I belong to a generation that ate what was given, half-afraid it won't be there tomorrow. This insecurity has not entirely left me.

There's a whole lot of food-induced guilt still left unacknowledged and buried in the recesses of childhood memories, when the arrival of a peti of mangoes at home was a huge, much-looked-out-for 'event', as Aie carefully separated the mangoes, keeping the ready-to-eat ones on top and covering the firm, green ones in old newspapers before tucking them back into the hay lining the peti. Each mango was sliced with precision, the two plump halves reserved for my father and brother (Tauba! Such blatant discrimination!). The girls were given the sides sliced off the centre stone, while the stone itself was taken by Aie. We made an occasion of the mango season and managed to convert every bit of the fruit into an edible something—chutney, pickle, spicy curries, basundi, Maharashtra's rich, milky sweet dish with mango bits blended into it. (Please note: thickening basundi with a can of condensed milk is a strict no-no.) Sometimes we got small cups of vanilla ice cream or fresh cream and squashed overripe mangoes into it. But it was the Sunday aamras–puri treat that the family looked forward to the most.

The cartons on my dining table remind me of how far I have come from that time, when a single mango was considered unattainable and priceless, when it had to be shared and enjoyed with other family members. Right now, I am wondering what I would do with the chikoos and the mangoes—gifts from growers who are hoping for a mention in my Insta story. I rarely eat mangoes these days—not only because of the calorie-overload, but because an angry pimple invariably pops up on my face almost instantly. Mr Dé enjoys his mangoes with dahi, while the children and their children gobble them up greedily at every meal during the season.

Now that I can 'afford' mangoes, they no longer appeal to me. I feel superior to the mango and not the other way around. The mango needs me; I don't need the mango. Such a strange and silly game between a fruit and a woman who is still coming to terms with childhood complexes, seven decades later. Hey Bhagwan—deprivation has a name: aam, amba, mango.

Later, biting into a crisp, air-fried ghugree and lingering over the texture of the filling (a deft mix of smashed green peas and finely diced French beans with bits of boiled potato to hold it all together), I silently thank Avantikka and think what a great blessing it is to receive food in the form of treats from a loving daughter. Someone who knows your weakness and is thoughtful enough to always, but always, bring a snack or two each time she visits. The same goes for Arundhati and Anandita—the girls are forever indulging me with delicious khaana. All three make sure their mother doesn't go hungry! For me, a doggy bag from them is far more valuable than a designer bag from Milan or Paris or London. Food, as I never tire of repeating, is love.

Last weekend, Avantikka came to our regular Sunday lunch with the season's first pairi mango (thin-skinned and not as pulpy as the better-known hapus) cooked as a shaak (a vegetable dish). This was my first taste of mango shaak, and I was most excited. I ate it greedily with just-off-the-tawa dosas.

Of course, during the aam season, ripe and raw mangoes go into nearly every preparation. Fresh chutneys, dals, prawn curries, pomfret gravies with red chillies and gur, with mustard seeds and hing. The combinations and possibilities are limitless and so enticing. Aam papdi (beaten and flattened sheets of dried ripe mango) is painstakingly made during the mango season and carefully preserved to be relished when mangoes go off the market. Such is our passion for mangoes, we are sure never to be stranded without them! If all else fails, there are jars of fresh mango pickles to keep us going. Maharashtrians pretend to dislike the sweet chundo pickle preferred by Gujjus, but I honestly believe chundo has not received its due in the culinary sweepstakes. Everything tastes better with the sticky, sweet and sour chundo, with a bold hint of roasted jeera. I know Gujjus who pack chundo sandwiches for long trips, since theplas are not considered cool snacks by their English-speaking kids. Avantikka never leaves her home without foil-packed theplas in her fashionable tote.

As I sit by the balcony at my usual chai hour, I take my time to eat Avantikka's ghugree. No, she hasn't made it herself—she cannot cook, and sheepishly admits as much, but has got it made through her building network of industrious young women who run modest businesses from their kitchens. The Ghugree Lady is a specialist—renowned for her expertise from Nepean Sea Road to Cuffe Parade. This 10-kilometre area pretty much circumscribes our world—we don't really know too many Mumbaikars beyond the Sea Link. On a tiny striped plate next to the ghugrees, sits an almond flour financier baked by Anandita. It is rich in taste and entirely irresistible. But I resist it even at the risk of offending her. I take a tiny nibble and compliment her. Daughters are competitive and sensitive. You cannot praise one and ignore the others. No way! What if, I ask myself, my daughters had married outside this charmed circle? Would we have stayed this connected, this close? Would the ghugrees have arrived with as much frequency? Would Arundhati have thought twice before sending another Gujju staple—undhiyu—at short notice?

Unlikely. Proximity, both emotional and physical, matters—and how!

—⚬—

'I do think that when it comes to aging, we're held to a different standard than men. Some guy said to me: "Don't you think you're too old to sing rock 'n' roll?" I said: "You'd better check with Mick Jagger."'

—Cher

I have been invited to culinary heaven. Italian super chef and restaurateur Massimo Bottura will be creating a very special meal for sixty privileged Mumbaikars at the posh St Regis Hotel. But before we get to the enormity of the invitation (gourmets have shelled out Rs 40k per seat to salivate over Bottura's inventive cuisine in their own city), a sheepish 'back story' first. I have left a somewhat miffed Mr Dé behind at our home in Alibaug, happily jumped on a speedboat and rushed back to Mumbai to keep my date with Massimo (I'm casually dropping his first name as though we went to school together in Modena, Italy).

Yesterday was Poila Boishakh—the Bong New Year. I sent 'Shubho Noboborsho' messages to all our relatives and phoned a few to wish them personally. My tongue still takes a while to negotiate the two words, and non-Bongs have no idea what I'm saying and think I'm drunk at 9 a.m. So much for my reputation. This day is celebrated with great fervour in Kolkata, but we are stuck in Mumbai, where people give us strange looks when we wish them and they don't know how to respond. Not that we did anything special to mark the new year at our home. No mishti. No nolen gurer sandesh, not even a tiny bite of Sprüngli's dark chocolate with noisettes.

Instead, we had taken a catamaran to Alibaug to celebrate a friend's birthday. Since the Birthday Boy lives in Delhi, is a strict vegetarian Tam–Brahm and it isn't *his* new year, just to be sensitive, we avoided mentioning it was ours. There were twenty-five Dilliwalas on the catamaran. The Delhi ladies were clad in very short, very trendy beachwear. I noticed their legs were untanned as compared to their arms and faces. They were carrying huge designer totes and wearing huge designer sunnies. The sandals from Italy were lovely and showed off their perfectly pedicured feet. The nails on their hands were made of gel and there was a great deal of complex art going on them. The men wore linen and Italian loafers. They were in a state of heightened excitement at the sight of the pre-monsoon sea, huge waves breaking against the stone steps of the magnificent Gateway of India. I thought how much we take our sweet Arabian Sea totally for granted—we barely notice it. And here were these well-heeled, middle-aged folks carrying on like they'd reached Marbella, not Mumbai. Much bubbly was consumed as everybody danced to Bollywood tracks and behaved like Deepika Padukone and Siddhanth Chaturvedi in *Gehraiyaan* (2022). Why not? Same location, same sea, same views of a receding Taj Mahal Palace Hotel. All the Dilliwalas were just fine—shamefully, me the veteran, senior citizen, card-holding Alibaug-er felt seasick!

Mr Dé repeatedly asked if I was sure I needed to be back for Bottura's feast the following night. I was wondering if he was feeling a little 'J', not because he was missing out on a memorable meal, but at the thought of the rather handsome chef known for his tantrums and creativity. I am certain I have to be back, I said firmly, adding I wouldn't miss this amazing opportunity, this once-in-a-lifetime experience, for anything in the world. We docked at the Mandwa Jetty and I nearly threw up—that would have marked a big first. An ugggh first. And the Dilliwalas would have laughed, even mocked me—the woman who is an Alibaug resident but cannot handle the short sea voyage!

The beachside party was a huge hit. By then I had not just found my sea legs, I wanted to show them off! Wait till you gasp at my hot moves, Dilliwalas, I said to myself, and broke into Ranveer Singh's 'Malhari' dance from *Bajirao Mastani* (2015). Come on—it was Poila Boishakh, the sky was clear, the moon was shining, the sea was glittering, the boats were bobbing. Go for it, gurrrrrl ... The smoked salmon was superb, and the Mexican chef who'd flown in from Goa was pretty dishy. Much merriment later, we got home at 2.30 a.m.

'You'll never make the speedboat tomorrow morning,' Mr Dé said. 'Forget that dinner. Cancel! The heat is terrible ... you may suffer a heat stroke! What's the point of rushing back? That too, for an Italian meal? Tell you what, I'll take you to Bottttt ... whatever's restaurant, in whichever town it's in ...'

'Modena ... Italy,' I said quickly. 'His restaurant is called Osteria Francescana. It is considered the best restaurant in the world.'

Silence. 'How old is this Botttt guy?'

'Not sure ... perhaps sixty-ish ...'

'Foreigners age really badly ... He may not be able to handle the heat in Mumbai, the ingredients won't travel well. You'll be wasting your time.'

Wisely, for a change, I did not argue.

The breakfast tray arrived in our room at 9 a.m. sharp.

Mr Dé said gleefully, 'Doubt you'll make the boat ...' I was already dressed and gathering my things. He pretended to be reading the papers. 'Do you want me to drop you to the jetty?'

Victory! Mr Dé had finally accepted that I was leaving! Now it was my turn to feel bad. 'Maybe it won't be such an amazing meal ...' I said lamely.

His smile became devilish. 'Remember, Wife, you chose the belly over the mind and the heart.'

Ouch! Low blow. I rushed out of the room before he struck again. I had to get my hair done, my sari needed ironing ... Oh gosh, there was so much to do before the grand evening! The meal had better be worth the preceding drama.

It's now the morning after and I'm hungry! Starved in fact! My tum-tum is growling furiously.

The world's most celebrated chef has left me feeling famished after a dramatic presentation of five miniscule courses, mainly consisting of multi-coloured foams, reductions and other molecular gimmicks. Should I brazenly fib to Mr Dé and rave over the black cod served on a plate decorated with colourful blotches of assorted coulis? A tribute to the English artist Damien Hirst. Or should I be upfront and brave and confess all to Mr Dé, who will no doubt gloat and say, 'Serves you right!'? Total loss of face!

He has already tried to pile on the guilt by sending cheesy messages throughout my dinner saying, 'I am really missing you … my raat-and-din champa flower.' Me, as a frangipani blooming giddily night and day? Okie! He has also sent pics of his chappals. Why? Because he wants to know whether to wear them to his poolside party. My recommendation is red suede loafers. There will be an Elvis Presley medley, and the blue ones are in Mumbai. Next comes a Monet poster. Yes, water lilies. And this message: 'What a wonderful place to share a glass of wine, maybe caviar, and listen to the author in my life …' He really knows how to turn the screw and make me feel bad. Before I can think of a response that's light and flirty and witty, Mr Dé is at it again. 'Eat heartily … and think of a man who listened to his future mother-in-law and bought a small bag to carry his future wife's small comb. Mankind has defined this act as Love, Commitment and Loyalty!'

Gosh! The Italian chef is really making him insecure and jealous!

To Mr Dé's immense satisfaction, my account of a really disappointing evening makes up for my ditching him in Alibaug. Going by his pictures, he certainly had a far better time than I did. He enjoyed great food, his favourite single malt, a Monte Cristo, live music, attentive female company. We were quits!

—〰—

'Old age is always fifteen years older than I am.'

—**Oliver Wendell Holmes**

Uff!

Not another Jayanti! Nobody knows whose birth anniversary is being celebrated today, and nobody cares. There's no shortage of 'jayantis' in India. Each year sees new additions to this list. Today marks yet another bank holiday and so all offices are shut (I have been informed there are fifteen bank holidays in August 2022—go figure!), and I am broke. Someone should have warned me! I can't withdraw money from my friendly neighbourhood bank and am down to exactly 65 bucks. The notes are glaring at me angrily … they need more company! Confession: I have never used an ATM and I don't possess a debit card. I'm convinced I will be mugged if I try to get money out of that machine or it will eat up my card. To make it worse, another long weekend has crept up. I hate long weekends.

I overhear boisterous neighbours saying, 'Let's celebrate Baisakhi, yaar …' But I am in Mumbai, not in the fertile fields of Punjab, wearing a phulkari dupatta and driving a tractor through sarson fields while my man dances a robust bhangra with other sturdy Panju farmers.

In fact, I am eating the best crabs on earth at Trishna—the only restaurant in India that really, really knows its crab. I mean, once you've eaten a Trishna crab, all other crabs are tadpoles. These Trishna crabs have a personality—they talk back to you if you stint on appreciation. I am proudly wearing the Trishna bib and demanding the biggest claw. After all, my son Aditya is paying, and the young team can hardly challenge the boss-man's mom in the crab round without losing.

I am staring slyly at Aditya as he orders lunch. He looks so in charge! A man! But in my over-indulgent, ridiculously 'proud mom' eyes, he is still the kid with the melting brown eyes who spoke little, cried a lot and generally got his way. Of course, he will over-order, I'm thinking. And he does.

Course after course arrives from the kitchen in waves, overwhelming us with tantalizing aromas and great visuals. Aditya has ticked off far too many items on the extensive menu in one go. The meal begins with Koliwada fish, chilly garlic squid, black pepper Hyderabadi fish tikka, fried lady fish, reshmi kebabs, paneer tikka, vegetable kebabs, butter naans—and these are just the starters. We wait for the 'voila!' moment—when live crabs are produced for the host's approval, depending on the weight and size of the catch that day. I try and appear extra knowledgeable by saying, 'Hope you have female crabs today—preferably with roe ...' They do. People at the table look suitably impressed. Along with the crab selection, it is important to specify the style—garlic-butter sauce, black bean sauce, tandoori masala? Deshelled or cooked whole? Do we want to work hard for our crab meat and crack the claws ourselves?

'We'll have all three,' Aditya declares.

Our bibs are in place.

There is also tadka dal, jeera rice and lasooni palak to add to the pigging-out party. And malai kulfi to follow. In under an hour, we have polished off every last morsel. Our food-stained bibs are a witness to the eating orgy. People at adjoining tables have rolled their eyes in disbelief. They are still staring. The old waiting staff at Trishna are gossiping away with me. I am watching in awe as Aditya settles the bill. My instinct is to treat Aditya as my little boy—for that's how I still see my first-born. I'm tempted to crack a lousy mom joke or two but I stop myself. This is his crew. He leads the team. They call him AD. My heart thumps audibly when I watch him at work. I conceal my pride by trying to be exaggeratedly casual, 'cool' and 'with it'. Truth is, I'm flattered each time I am included in their team-meets.

They have invited an alarmingly good-looking South African business associate from Cape Town, along with the gorgeous interior designer, Sussanne Khan, who is the creative force in Avās Wellness, this ambitious enterprise, which has kicked off with its unique villas, receiving a great deal of attention. Phillippe Fouche represents SAOTA, an award-winning

global architectural firm. AD and his team have got SAOTA on board for
their passion project in Alibaug.

Phillippe turns out to be an absolute charmer. I should make a good
impression. I start off just fine and mention my visit to Cape Town,
making a joke of the scary baboon attack that had left me half-dead
with fright. Fortunately, Phillippe smiles in complete understanding
and narrates an incident when his pregnant wife was roughed up on the
beach by an angry baboon who couldn't find any food in her beach bag.
One more baboon story and I'm done, I warn myself. Instead, I switch
to wildebeest and someone mentions Botswana where her son witnessed a
lion devouring one of these creatures. I gag on my crab claw and quickly
sip limbu paani. Phillippe then tells us about the strange behaviour of
animals during the pandemic, citing accounts of relatives in Cape Town
with beach houses that had CCTV cameras capturing footage of leopards
in their backyards chewing on penguins that had strayed in from the
dunes. I decide there and then to skip the kulfi.

Quickly, I change the topic to Mumbai's Art Deco promenade at
Marine Drive and compare it to Shanghai's famous Bund. This is just
a little motherly show-off to establish my credentials as a well-travelled
woman who knows her buildings and landmarks. All the others at the table
are thirty to forty years younger than me and I want to belong! Insecurity
is creeping up! Can't sound too old and from another era.

Aditya is busy ordering more food and going by the expression on
Phillippe's face we are doing well in the lunch department. It's 4.30 p.m.
and the restaurant needs to shut for a bit, before it reopens for dinner
service at 6 p.m. The senior manager at Trishna hastily produces finger
bowls and starts clearing the tables. No tea, no coffee, he informs sternly—
go across the road and have it there. Yes, Boss! Some leave while others
stay back and help the staff to sweep up, clean the kitchen and the tub
full of jumbo prawns. I hastily pick up my doggy bag—one portion of
sukha masala tisrya (clams) and two portions of prawn gassi (a spicy curry
from Karnataka) for Mr Dé's dinner. It's an old habit. If I relish eating
something somewhere I take some back for him.

Outside Trishna, there is the loud band-baajaa—no, not for Baisakhi, but the bloody jayanti of a 'mahaan aadmi' not many in the city know about. Loudspeakers blaring, an energetic group of young men set off to garland a statue nearby. I thought, weren't there prohibitory orders in Mumbai regarding the use of loudspeakers that disturb public peace?

'Oh, that's only for mosques ...' explained a young woman from Aditya's team casually.

Oh yes, of course! Silly me!

—⁂—

'Old people shouldn't eat health foods. They need all the preservatives they can get.'

—**Robert Orben**

The family experienced a tadgola moment yesterday. Half the members loved chilled, peeled tadgolas, while half had not heard of them.

Tadgolas are called 'ice apples' in angrezi. It is the juicy coastal fruit of the sugar palm tree found primarily in Maharashtra and Tamil Nadu. The texture is a bit like the lychee, but the joy is the surprise the fruit springs on the unsuspecting who bite into it, expecting nothing more than a bland, fleshy, mushy taste. And that's when the fun begins, especially if the fruit is tender. Squisshh ... out squirts a delicious, mildly flavoured liquid that fills the mouth with its slightly viscous juice. I have always loved the unexpectedness of that moment. Will this particular tadgola have a soft centre or will it be a bit too mature and rubbery?

The request to get tadgolas from Alibaug has come from me. Mr Dé is not always receptive to my Alibaug requests (garlands of white onions, for example) but this time he readily agrees and calls to triumphantly state the tadgola mission had been accomplished.

'I hope you've got plenty. The children are coming to lunch, and we must serve tadgolas ...' I say.

Pause. Bigger pause.

'How many tadgolas do you require?' he asks.

I am stumped by the question. 'Meaning what? I have to count? Are they being rationed? Is there a per person tadgola quota?' I am being testy and not liking this line of questioning at all.

Tadgolas remind me of the moonstones I admired in Galle, Sri Lanka, and wanted to eat on the spot, till the jeweller calmed me down and explained gently, 'Moonstones are not edible, Madam. But if you like them so much, why don't I show you a necklace?' I recall feeling crestfallen and buying the necklace, which I've never worn. Maybe I should try eating it. I admire the translucent beauty of both—moonstones and tadgolas. I want to make a necklace out of the tadgolas and wear it to the Met

Gala. Let the world know more about this incredible fruit … Imagine harbouring such weird thoughts and images when I am still to join the girls, who are on their third glass of a crisp white. Even without wine, those tadgolas are spinning inside my head. I instantly want to get into my Salvador Dali mode and paint them in a lurid way.

Anyway, Mr Dé sounds less grumpy when he tells me he will bring sixteen tadgolas—eight for himself.

Wisely, I keep mum and say sweetly, 'Oh, nice! The six of us will eat the other eight.'

Sarcasm wasted because he replies, 'Yes, that's fine.'

So begins the tadgola saga, with a divided family. The lot that likes the fruit thank me profusely as they pop tadgolas whole into their mouths, knowing there will be juice inside which will dribble down their chins. The others watch with a distinctively suspicious look. 'How does it taste? Any good?' one child asks.

I am keeping count. Now there are just six tadgolas left in the bowl and I don't want the plebs to waste even one. Mr Dé is keeping a close watch on the depleting numbers, possibly worried I may poach a few of his.

'Try one with vanilla ice cream,' I suggest to the children, who promptly put me in my place by saying, 'Why ruin vanilla ice cream?'

This tadgola story does not have a happy ending at all. Mr Dé decides to save his eight for breakfast. The next morning, a very worried looking Lakshmi comes to me and whispers, 'Mainey usko kaat diya …'

What? How could she cut tadgolas? Who chops up tadgolas? Well … Lakshmi is from Nepal while tadgolas are coastal creatures. She has never seen the fruit before. She didn't know she was supposed to peel them deftly, without puncturing the fruit and letting the juice flow out, and then leave them whole to chill in the ice tray before serving. Not her fault at all! I have failed as a housewife! Worse, I have let my husband down. Those eight precious tadgolas have been reduced to tiny chunks of nothingness. Mr Dé will be furious. I want to escape … But that will leave a quaking Lakshmi to face his wrath. Nooo! Lakshmi must be saved. I square my shoulders and wait for Mr Dé to discover the travesty.

Aha ... He peers at the unrecognizable, mutilated bits of tadgolas in an uncharacteristically mild way. He is thinking of Putin; I can tell. I distract him immediately by saying Zelensky is such a clown. He thrusts a fork absently into the tadgola bowl and picks up a chunk. It is being transferred to his mouth, while I hold my breath. No amount of Zelensky talk can save me now. Lakshmi hides in the kitchen, behind the dishwasher we never use.

What's this? Mr Dé has not noticed! He is going for a second chunk, and then a third ... Soon we are left with an empty bowl. And I, left with many puzzling questions that may never be answered. Has Mr Dé gargled with vodka? Is the war in Ukraine over? Or is he just happy to see me this morning?

—⚬—

'No man is ever old enough to know better.'

—Holbrook Jackson

I have the dishy Imran Khan on my mind today because there is turmoil across the border. He has just lost his job. The generals are growling. And the next prime minister of Pakistan just may be my beauteous writer–friend Tehmina Durrani's husband, Shehbaz Khan. Not sure whether to rejoice for Tehmina or feel sad for Imran, I recall the last time I met the First Lady-in-Waiting of Pakistan in her palatial home in Lahore (Shehbaz's ancestral home) for a lavish and mind-boggling high tea. And that reminds me that this evening is a major 'jal-khaabar' event at home.

I like the idea of jal-khaabar. The literal translation is 'water-food' or more colloquially, 'chai-paani' and 'chai-naashta'. It is a charming tradition when guests are invited, not for a meal, but mid-meal snacks—generally at teatime, around 5 p.m. Or around noon. Here's the thing: I grew up in an austere, frugal, typically Maharashtrian home in which snacking between meals was considered a superfluous, wasteful, decadent, self-indulgent 'bad habit'. Children were expected to adhere to consuming milk and biscuits if famished, and perhaps neatly unpeel and eat a generally overripe and spotted banana from a bunch lying on top of the refrigerator, protected by a mesh cover to keep fruit flies away. Maharashtrians are not known for either their generosity or hospitality (for a rich taste of both, go to Lahore or Amritsar or Kolkata), nor are we particularly people-friendly. We could be, infact, called people-phobic—suspicious, distrustful and caustic with anybody outside the family circle. Even more so, with those within! In fact, we stop just short of plain rudeness when we meet strangers. A faint, impatient frown appears between our brows, our eyes (often light and pretty) turn cold, the voice gets a frosty edge and we promptly turn away to discourage further interaction.

Guests are treated like a bit of a nuisance—like pesky, pushy intruders who have invaded a space that is so 'pure' that any contact with outsiders is likely to taint it. Faced with the inevitable (unwanted guests) a mini-family conclave is hastily organized to figure out how fast one can pack off the visitor. Then comes the major annoyance—what to serve the pest? It has to be cheap and easy. After all, the invaded space must be reclaimed as quickly as possible.

The solution?

Bare-bones hospitality. Nothing more than chai and plantains (always called plantains, never bananas). But before that, a glass of water, that too only after asking if the guests are indeed thirsty and looking for something to quench their parched throats. Most greetings go like this, 'Since you've come straight from home, you must have eaten?' Eyebrows are raised and looks exchanged if the guests actually say, 'Yes … water is welcome. And no, we have not eaten since our last meal hours ago … You see we have been on the road since morning delivering wedding cards.' Depending on the importance quotient (IQ!) of the guests, they are served water (refrigerated) in 'nice', unchipped glasses, if they come from a 'decent' background. If they are seen to be lower down in the social hierarchy, stainless steel tumblers (strictly no tray or paper napkins), are thrust towards them. The overripe bananas are kept on hold.

If the guests have some worthwhile reason to be at your home, the mandatory cup of tea is over-brewed with carefully calibrated pods of elaichi and last night's milk. Sugar is added on a rationed basis. These folks are spared the overripe bananas. They get the expensive variety (firm, unspotted and ready to eat). Unbreakable plates (melamine) are put to use. Spoons are optional, since the tea is pre-mixed, and nobody will dare ask for additional sugar. Biscuits? Only Parle-G, thank you. And take just one each, please.

If it is indeed an extra-special occasion—like a prospective groom's parents checking out the bride's living standards—poha studded with roasted peanuts is prepared and kept ready to serve, with freshly grated coconut and chopped kothmir as garnish, plus tiny pieces of lemon (so tiny, they are almost invisible). Why this tiny? Don't you know the price of limbus has gone up? And, maybe, tomato ketchup in a small plastic bowl (ketchup indicates it's a modern family that enjoys instant Maggi noodles on Sundays with a dollop of sticky, over-sweet ketchup). If the visitors are super super special, sheera made in homemade ghee, with slivers of almonds and kishmish, is served hot with lukewarm tea. Besan laddoos are a safe standby option, along with chaklis and thikhat sev. But this is rare and reserved for VVIPs.

Meanwhile, here I am, getting set for the Bong jal-khaabar for an arty couple Mr Dé and I both like a lot. Since I am yearning for Lahore and its legendary hospitality, where laden trolleys of elaborate snacks that could include quail samosas and galouti kebabs, along with other mouthwatering specialties, depending on the season, are rolled in by well-trained bearers, I am keen to pull out the stops for the youngish couple. Mr Dé reminds me they are not 'fussy', but I happen to know their hardcore carnivorous palates a little better. They enjoy their meats—anytime, anywhere. Aleti-paleti types who order bheja (brain) masala on toast without blinking. So, while our Pushpa is busy thinking of rubbish like chopped up leftover idlis with tadka on top (don't be so DM, darling, even if I could easily get away with it by calling the mess 'steamed lentil cakes, lightly stir-fried in extra virgin olive oil with freshly pounded south Indian spices as seasoning), my mind is more on chicken puffs and mince cutlets. Cold coffee, fruit tarts, mango slices with vanilla ice cream, tiramisu in shot glasses.

But dear Mr Dé's mind is elsewhere … He has worn his summer shirt (flower print, cotton) and bounced. This is one jal-khaabar I'm going to slave over and enjoy. I can hear Anuradha giggling: this ghati girl sure has moved up in life!

—m—

MAY

'The idea is to die young as late as possible.'

—**Ashley Montagu**

MAHARASHTRA DIWAS, OR MAHARASHTRA DAY, COINCIDES WITH May Day celebrated as Labour Day across the world. Being both a Maharashtrian and a mazdoor (labourer), it's a double whammy of a day for me and has to be celebrated with puran poli and basundi, considered 'appropriate' treats for the occasion. I sniff both, but don't taste. Just like those delusionary folks who claim they smoke but don't inhale. Being sugar-free for three years (wine is not 'sugar' sugar, okay?), my taste buds actually rebel when I place anything sweet on my tongue (words aren't included in the list of banned items).

This year's May Day fell on a Sunday, and I sat by the balcony window waiting for a sighting of the Eid moon. Depending on the crucial sighting, I was looking forward to an Eid lunch at home with the family two days later. The celebration had been initiated by Aru85 and involved critical planning, down to our festive Eid outfits—the women in shararas, the men in chikankari Lucknowi kurtas. Her two children and husband follow the Jain faith, so I have to factor in pure vegetarian elements in the lunch menu. Aru85 is a chicken-fanatic (she's put in a request for Anil's homemade chicken curry, chicken biryani and chicken kebabs), and Anil has been at it for hours.

A real biryani, according to food connoisseurs, requires chunks of tender mutton. Chicken biryani ain't biryani at all, say biryani lovers with a derisive laugh. If you are from Kolkata, the preference is for mutton biryani with gigantic pieces of meat on the bone and jumbo potatoes. Bongs prefer the Lucknowi version of India's most popular dish, with light masala, which is delicate and highly aromatic. Legend has it that the Nawab of Awadh (1847–56) invented this version of the famous Awadhi biryani when he was kinda broke and scaling back. He decided to bulk up the biryani for his soldiers by adding aloo. The royal treasury was facing issues but the hungry hordes had to be fed. When in doubt, give them carbs—old Chinese saying.

Biryani tops my personal list of treats. I eat red meat three times a week without guilt or shame. Avantikka relishes most meats, but her taste buds remain rooted in the Gujju food she grew up eating (she has offered to get air-fried ghugrees stuffed with green peas). Anandita hates chicken but loves lamb. Rana and his wife, Radhi (vegan), who live in Singapore and are moving to Thailand, aren't at the family lunch but Rana eats anything that moves and is unashamedly carnivorous. We don't know who their daughter Samsara will take after. As of now, her diet constitutes raw veggies, fruits and breast milk. Radhika, who lives in Kolkata with her young and handsome son Sudhir—all of five—will be missing the lunch too. For years now, she's been adhering to a simple vegetarian diet in respect to her spiritual calling. But I remember with a smile, that as a young girl she used to be partial to oysters and escargots. Sudhir is adventurous like his mother and unfussy about food. During our last visit to Kolkata, Sudhir had carefully picked what he wanted to eat at the legendary Flury's on Park Street. Aditya is finicky. Period. He judges whatever enters his fastidious mouth by its aroma/odour/smell. If it passes the smell test, it's consumed. If not—out it goes! Perhaps it's these hard-to-impress standards that have led him to launch successful restaurants and, recently, Thai and Vietnamese delivery kitchens. That leaves the equally quality-conscious Mr Dé. He has informed me that he will be skipping the Eid feast to get some pending work done at the office. Unusual. Oh—the five grandkids who will be showing up won't be eating any of the specially ordered Eid delicacies, their mothers have warned me in advance. I've told the mothers to order pizzas on Swiggy.

Meanwhile, the debate is still on—which biryani to order. I pick two reliable sources, and keep my fingers crossed. Both kitchens (Mughlai and Memon) are dominated by mothers who are superlative cooks, and whose clever children manage the business end of the home delivery service. 'Masalaesque' is my go-to biryani delivery kitchen. Rushail ('soul of the sun') Navani, half-Sindhi, half-Muslim, who's a crime and family litigation lawyer, markets the range of Mughlai biryanis prepared by Nasreen, his hardworking mother. I am partial to the moist and fragrant nalli biryani, drenched in korma and pure ghee. My favourites include Insiya Rangila's Memon-style samosas from her home in Bandra. My good friend, the snowy-haired Naazneen Karmali, former editor of *Business India* and currentl *Asia Wealth* editor and India editor of *Forbes Asia*, first recommended Insiya's samosas to me. Naazneen and her husband, Aqil, are serious gourmets, and Naazneen herself is a superb biryani-maker.

But back to our Eid lunch, I will be mother-hen and go cluck-cluck as I bite on a moist shammi kebab made at home, and listen to Begum Abida Parveen's plaintive 'Aaj jaaney ki zid na karo'. I hear it obsessively, at least ten times a day, and always go into a bit of a trance. It's playing inside my head right now. I'm tripping! But I stay Sufi-calm and watch the family eat. I feel satiated just watching my loved ones enjoying food. I allow my eyes to feast on them and take it all in little by little. I know what each one likes or dislikes so well. I miss those who aren't with us at the feast, and keep aside small portions for them—in absentia, as it were! Rana and Radhika have been living away for far too long.

Their palates may have adapted to their new adopted cities, but when they come home, it is intense Bong khabaar at every meal, and I make sure their favourites are always on the table—from aaloo posto to labda, chholar dal to begun bhaaja.

Despite being a generally confident person, my ego takes several hits when one of them makes even a light-hearted joke about the meal. Why am I so hypersensitive with the people I'm closest to? Why do I overreact and sulk even when no offence is intended? Hmm … I'm going to give this a long think as I tuck into the biryani which has just been delivered, with its purda intact and our family name in raised atta alphabet!

—※—

'You're only as old as the woman that you feel.'

—**Groucho Marx**

It's the last night of the bloody marvellous JLF Lit Fest at Soneva Fushi in the Maldives. I have just stepped off the Dolphin Cruise and started the Culinary Walk, before getting back to the main party zone for the night. Kutle Khan will sing 'Dama Dum Mast Kalandar' and I will go pagal. I know it! Then all the other delegates will stare and wonder how Mr Dé puts up with me.

It's been six days and six nights of one incredible experience after another. My dimaag cannot handle any more cerebral fodder. I am hungry, and slightly seasick. Also, somewhat dolphined out—all those clever mammals leaping in and out of the azure waters around our boat (authors on board!) at the world-famous Soneva Fushi resort, while a manganiar attempts to lure the playful creatures with the insistent beat of desi castanets (two untethered pieces of seasoned rosewood). The manganears are traditional folk musicians from Rajasthan whose songs are passed over generations oral history. Kutle Khan is a testament to this impressive lineage.

The choppy sea and those playful dolphins have made me hungry. I'm looking for instant gratification. 'These plump scallops are from Hokkaido ...' says Suvir Saran, celebrity chef, author (aur bahut kuch), to me, as Chef Shivek, the Soneva Fushi executive chef, gently drizzles a few drops of olive oil on a couple of scallops and asks, 'One or two?'

I greedily and shamelessly say, 'Three, please ...'

Suvir smiles his wicked smile and whispers, 'Don't worry, we can always share a few more with Katrina Kaif.'

We both giggle and stare pointedly at Chef Vardaan Marwah, Suvir's young and immensely talented protégé and business partner—they run a company called Cold Love which makes hand-churned, artisanal ice cream in Delhi. Vardaan is about to pout. The Kat moment is upon us! Okay. That's a private joke. Can't repeat. Suvir also instructs Shivek not to 'kill the flavour of the scallops by sprinkling chaat masala' on them.

Suvir and I are recent BFFs. Very, very recent. So many elements to deal with in this 'milaap'.

—⁓—

Confession: I had not heard of the celebrity chef with the Michelin star. He had earned his very valuable Michelin star as a chef in New York, where he was running Devi, a highly acclaimed restaurant that demonstrated what 'human connections can do for food'.[1] All this I discovered later. All I knew then was that he was going to be in conversation with my Ana Banana, at the first edition of the JLF at an out-of-this-world piece of heaven called Soneva Fushi. My interest in him was selfish—it was Anandita's debut on the big stage. His unusual book, titled *Instamatic*, looked terrific. I was super excited about being back at the JLF—this time as the mother of Anandita. Yes, yes, yes. I had my own well-curated sessions but her virgin experience on this prestigious platform was far more important. Not that Anandita was nervous. She was prepped, she had said confidently, and had asked me to calm down.

Suvir is all heart. And a lot of bheja. His wit and sharp observations reminded me of my cousin, Gautam Rajadhyaksha, India's best portrait photographer. In Suvir, I found another equally sensitive person I could talk to on any subject knowing he'd get it instantly and not judge me.

Suvir has serious competition the evening we meet at Villa 14, where Sanjoy, Ankur, Shams, Sharupa, Kritika, Pinky, the hard-working Teamworks gang, is expertly mixing cocktails and keeping the throats of thirsty authors lubricated enough to have sparkling conversations that are heaving like the choppy waters of the Indian Ocean, furiously rocking the boats at the jetty. Seriously, I have yet to see a better-knit, more integrated bunch of multitaskers than the Teamworks core team. Do they ever sleep?

1 Suvir Saran, 'How Devi in New York City showed what human connections can do for food', *The Indian Express*, 6 March 2022. https://indianexpress.com/article/express-sunday-eye/devi-new-york-city-restaurant-human-connections-suvir-saran-7800558/

Before one high-octane lit fest ends, they are off to set up the next one! As soon as former diplomat Gopal Gandhi walks in, barefoot (we are all barefoot, only his feet are far prettier than ours), holds out both his hands to greet me, I know I am a goner. Fully enamoured and behaving foolishly, I start blushing and what not. Chheee! Schoolgirl kahin ki! My dil is going dhak-dhak and I'm desperately channelling my inner Madhuri Dixit—only a far coyer version.

I'm done chatting with the soignee Cartier heiress, Francesca Cartier Brickel, and the beautiful Maharani of Baroda, Radhikaraje Gaekwad. Both fine and very bright ladies. Francesca is on a world tour promoting her plush book, *The Cartiers: The Untold Story of the Family Behind the Jewellery Empire*, while Radhika raje with her husband, Samarjit Singh, is attending as a keen environmentalist and tradition-keeper of Baroda's rich legacy. But it is our first day at the fest—there are other, equally dazzling personalities holding forth on topics that range from the emotional quotient of mathematics to the excretion of parrotfish which created the island we are sipping cocktails on. I rather like the imagery—aggressive, multihued parrotfish chomping on algae deep inside the coral and excreting tonnes of poop every day—enough to create Kunfunadhoo in the Baa Atoll. Imagine the colossal amount of parrotfish shit it has taken to create the biggest island resort across 1400 x 400 metres. So, all that pristine white powdery stuff I thought was sand was actually … Noooooo!

I'm staring at a poet wearing a cravat (did he forget to pack his linens?) and am gradually, but surely, zoning out when I hear someone squeal— Suvir is here. Laidback and friendly, he is working the room, oozing charm and compliments. Within minutes, we regress and start behaving like characters from an Enid Blyton book. Between Suvir and Gopal Gandhi, my heart has quite a workout to handle. Not sure what I would have done had art critic and art historian B.N. Goswamy not left on the first sea plane off the Soneva jetty. He is gone and Mr Dé is pretty cross; he had brought Goswamy's latest tome to get it signed by the divine scholar. Emails had been exchanged and Mr Dé's enthusiasm to reconnect with the art historian, after listening to him a couple of years ago in Jaipur, has been dampened. The drippy weather hasn't helped but the spicy crab at dinner consoled him sufficiently to smile benevolently at me and comment, 'Hardly a few hours here and tanned already!'

Feeling like 'the Girl from Ipanema', I sink my teeth into succulent lamb chops and hold one out for Mr Dé to sample. He firmly shakes his head, muttering something about going easy on red meat, and sugar, of course. His free hand strokes his tum-tum to check for any weight gain. Okay, so no pineapple ice cream with chillies then? I tempt and taunt. Mr Dé being a resolute, annoyingly determined sort of man, waves me away and starts a conversation on … Ukraine! (How did you guess?) … with a retired ambassador. I'm missing Suvir, but he himself is missing. He's been grabbed by several foodies who want a crash course on making the perfect gourmet khichdi in their home kitchens.

I'm still in a trance. Gopal Gandhi has assured me that my nakshatra naam—Anuradha—beautiful as it was, did not sufficiently capture my 'shobha'. Oh ho! Big question: Did the great man just kill my search for Anuradha? Gopal is kindness and refinement personified. Perhaps he is just making me feel better. Even his voice is kind and soft and sweet. He totally finishes me off when he tells me that he reads my columns regularly and admires my 'spunk'! Maar dala. Thoughtfully and with much deliberation, he adds, 'I may not agree with all that you write … But I respect the truth behind it.' I faint. Imagine—Mahatma Gandhi's grandson admiring my experiments with truth! Should I instantly make my peace with the very ordinary, very boring, very mundane, very pedestrian, very vanilla 'Shobhaa'? Bilkul nahi!! I need more wine, before we head out … I've noticed a glass of cranberry juice in Gopal Gandhi's delicate hand and hope it's been laced with a huge shot of vodka.

Earlier, PJ, the friendly general manager of the property, smiled broadly at me, while offering a glass of chilled rosé. Mistakenly, we had crashed his party instead of heading dutifully to Villa 14 for swigs of precious daaru. Seeing me visibly embarrassed, he offered a side show—eight or ten reef sharks swimming around the jetty, waiting for supper. In my excitement,

I nearly tumbled off my perch trying to spot fins. PJ assured me the sharks wouldn't bite even if I did fall into the unreal, transparent, swirling waters. Why, PJ? I am pretty delectable (to some!). Were the sharks that picky?

He had flashed a set of gleaming white teeth and whispered, 'These are vegetarian reef sharks ...'

Khallaas! I felt less rejected as we headed to Villa 14 with Sae, our beautiful Japanese barefoot butler.

My own sessions are scheduled over the next two days. At the first one, dearest Sanjoy Roy asks me about the 'Big O'. I want to say, forget the 'Big O', most Indian women have never even experienced the 'Small O' or any 'O' at all. But I spot the diplomat, politician and author Pavan Varma looking at me strangely and keep my reply tame and well behaved. My next session, 'Future Tense', features The Tharoor as moderator. Sitting in the audience, is darling Onyeka Nwelue, my Nigerian son, clad in a gold-bordered Kerala mundu, looking resplendent ... Like a king, Mr Dé comments. Nigerian son? Haan. Long story. He calls me 'Mom', and mom I remain to this gentle giant, an academic visitor at the African Studies Centre at Oxford.

After the session, lounging languorously on a colourful bean bag, wearing a printed Fab India shirt over floppy linen pants, is a dishy Croatian Prince. But, I find out about this royal lineage later. Oxford Don, Peter Frankopan, is at Soneva as a historian/author, not a gora rajkumar. He is having a bad hair day, he confesses on the beach with unreal twilight making him glow, and says he envies Shashi Tharoor his perfectly coiffed hair. Two vain, brainy guys worrying about their hair as a tropical gale threatens to ruin the evening's incredibly well-planned programme! Ha! The past and future of the planet can wait; this is far more serious.

Over the next few days, luxury of a specific kind—slow, deliberate, sustainable, pure—the way Sonu and Eva Shivdasani, the founders of Soneva Fushi, visualized it twenty-five years ago, takes on a new meaning. Sonu never stops thinking. He is single-minded about Soneva's vision, which Eva and he want to share with like-minded people from across the world. It is indeed an exceptional resort and I have been fortunate enough to have been Sonu's guest here a few times, along with my children. All of us have declared Soneva Fushi to be the most outstanding property on the planet. It's in all the finer details that say 'responsibility' towards preserving and conserving the earth's precious resources on multiple fronts. I admire these two visionaries for sticking to their convictions with a missionary zeal without the slightest compromise on the high standards they've established. It is these standards that have made both of them take a daring plunge by hosting the first edition of a sparkling and highly enlightening lit fest on their property, which, as most recognize, is by far the most valued lit fest property in the world. It is intimate enough to allow participants to speak and share stories about their lives and literary journeys inside a circle of trust, in a setting that is nothing short of heavenly.

Suvir and Katrina keep me entertained sufficiently to forget why we are all there in the first place. 'Bad puppies' becomes the favourite catch phrase, as we behave like delinquent brats, hoping nobody will notice. But absolutely nothing escapes Sanjoy Roy's vigilant eyes as he glares at us for daring to chat through the screening of *Slumdog Millionaire* (2008).

'Bad puppies,' he hisses, and we promptly shut up.

British mathematician Marcus du Sautoy has stolen the thunder from everyone—Shashi Tharoor, too! The wunderkind of mathematics has stunned one and all by participating in an energetic performance of 'Jai Ho!' from the same film, dressed in a chamki-chamki rani-pink outfit with a green turban bobbing away on top of his head. Is this the same man all of us are putting our money on as a future Nobel Laureate? You bet! I am ready to genuflect and say, 'Oh Master! You fill me with admiration and wonder …'

Two days before his cabaret (I think he wants to get into Bollywood as an 'item number'), we had risked life and limb to keep an appointment with the former President of the Maldives, Mohamed Nasheed, as a part of an outreach programme organized by JLF. Given the lashing rain and turbulent sea, I was pretty certain this was it! Goodbye, world! I asked Ana Banana to click a formal 'Farewell duniya' portrait, before the hungry manta rays impatiently circling the atoll claimed me. But I couldn't risk being dubbed a 'bad puppy' once again by Sanjoy, so off we went to keep our appointment with Nasheed, with Sanjoy's strict instructions, 'He's a friend of India … be nice!'

Marcus was dressed in red pants and a black tee for the outreach event. Fine, he's a certified genius. He could have come in a langot and gotten past the hefty security guys. I wore a demure salwar–kameez, my head covered with a dupatta. Sanjoy conducted our session with supreme authority and expertise. My comments and responses were chaste and 'shuddh'. There were zero references to sex, politics or religion. I was being a 'good puppy'. Marcus dazzled! What a presentation! Suddenly, a numbers-challenged woman (me!) was falling in love with complicated mathematical equations and suchlike!

Uske baad, to see the same genius aadmi, dancing to 'Jai Ho' (he'd sportingly rehearsed for just two hours with the team) was just too much. I went up and declared, 'Tussi God ho, God!'

Marcus smiled benignly and bowed. I could almost hear him think, 'Stupid cow! She can't count for nuts. And she just stated the obvious!' From 'Bad Puppy' to 'Incorrigible Puppy'.

P.S. Marcus my Jai Ho moves are better than yours.

'Mostly, what I have learned so far about aging, despite the creakiness of one's bones and cragginess of one's once-silken skin, is this: Do it. By all means, do it.'

—**Maya Angelou**

I'm startled when I hear the koel's plaintive call at 4.45 this morning. Had the koel forgotten what time it was? Or the month? The monsoons are still a couple of months away in Mumbai, and here's the monsoon bird telling us to gear up for what is Mumbai's worst or best season, depending on whether you are a poet like Gulzar or a commuter wading through flooded streets to catch the 5.35 a.m. fast from Virar.

I have a love–hate relationship with the monsoon, not being a romantic poet like Gulzar (I have the biggest crush on him! And we have a running joke each time we meet at a lit fest—we look at each other and ask, 'Shall we elope?'). But back to the koel's insistent call. I shoot out of bed and go to the window to look for the elusive bird, knowing all too well that it's next to impossible to catch a glimpse of it. I'm in the mood to tick off the wicked little thing for disturbing my sleep. I had drifted off at midnight after reading the last page of *The Book of Ichigo Ichie: The Art of Making the Most of Every Moment, the Japanese Way* written by two extraordinarily smart writers, Francesc Miralles and Hector Garcia, who have hit upon a winning mantra that is so compelling, the contents of the book stay in your mind long after you've finished the book. Since (shame on me!) I hadn't read their first, phenomenally successful international bestseller, *Ikigai*, I didn't really know what to expect. Now I do! Every moment in our life happens only once, and if we let it slip away, we lose it forever. This is really the essence of the phrase 'Ichigo Ichie'.

I was hooked from the prologue itself. Here's a bit of it: 'On the afternoon that, though we didn't yet know it, this book was about to be born, a storm was battering the narrow streets of Gion, in the heart of Kyoto—home of the last remaining geishas, among other mysteries ...' Uffff, yaaar! Ruko bhi, na? Aisey kaisey?

The koel's call has disturbed my attempt to achieve a Zen-like state. There's no going back to sleep, so I start to concentrate on 'listening', which the authors of *Ichigo Ichie* believe is a much-neglected practice in our day-to-day life. We hear, but rarely listen. They are right.

I listen to the water tanker pulling into our complex. I listen to the nightwatchmen from our building speaking in a heavily accented Bihari dialect to the watchmen in the adjoining tower. Their conversations make me think with enormous fondness of Lalu Prasad Yadav. I really liked the guy and enjoyed the photo ops of him milking cows in his backyard when he was chief minister of Bihar. I listen to the two building dogs barking at intruders (strays from the next block) in their territory. I listen to Gong Li's sonorous snores from her favourite spot near the front door. For such a tiny dog, she sure has a roar of a snore. I'm getting tired of listening. I try watching my breath—there is nothing to watch. Until now, I hadn't realized how tough it is to be 'in the moment' and not get restless.

I switch on the bedside light and go back to the book I have just finished. Yes, it's that kind of a book. You never really 'finish'-finish reading it. Randomly, I open it to 'The Beauty of Impermanence—Part 1. Kaika and Mankai'. 'Kaika' refers to a blossom—a kaika moment is when something unknown begins to blossom within us. When this shifts to the next phase and actual transformation takes place, that's mankai. So, ikigai + kaika + time = mankai.

Both words sound like Marathi. Japanese–Marathi. A strange marriage indeed. I read about the most anticipated annual ritual in Japan—when the sakura flowers blossom in springtime. Instantly, I'm reminded of Mr Dé and me on our sakura pilgrimage. I wish these two geniuses had written this jewel of a book four years earlier. It would have greatly enhanced our 'hanami' moment. Hanami, the authors tell us, means 'viewing of flowers'. Well, we had participated in the viewing of flowers with gusto, without understanding the delicacy and tenderness associated with the ritual.

In Japan, nearly everything is a ritual imbued with deep meaning. Donning a kimono, the elaborate tea ceremony, even the picnics under the cherry blossoms during the viewing which are thoughtfully planned by families and include specifics—a hanami bento, fried and grilled dishes, onigiri, salads, miso soup, sweets, saké and beer, and tea. We had noticed extended families quietly enjoying the picnic, with kids running around under the trees which were weighed down with flowers in full bloom. We had 'felt' it, but instinctively, and not with the required knowledge. Or else our appreciation and joy would have been doubly enhanced. My only major grouse with the book is that since each chapter, each page celebrates the sensual, I wonder why the writers have completely ignored sex. The one human act that engages all the senses simultaneously. Nothing is more 'in the moment' than an orgasm.

The book has my eyes, ears, heart. Now, each time I pick up my mug of morning tea, I will take my time to allow the fingertips to react to the heat of the porcelain mug (pale yellow, with green dragons, which I had bought from a Tibetan vendor next to the lake at Nainital). I will breathe in deeply and linger over the aroma of my favourite Darjeeling tea. My tongue will anticipate the thrill of the first sip ... Then, and only then, will I do the unthinkable and dunk hot buttered toast into it. Japanese meets Maharashtrian. I like the idea of making a centuries-old ritual uniquely my own. I will be in the moment and allow the melting butter to drip down from the sides of my mouth to my chin. I will not use a napkin to dab it—I will use my index finger to mop it all up and put the dribble back into my mouth. See? I'm so Ichigo Ichie already.

'I'm the sexiest I've ever been. And when I say that, I mean I feel the most myself.'

—Tracee Ellis Ross

Several behavioural changes during the pandemic have been noticed across the world. I know one major change in me—I can no longer air-kiss people I am familiar with but secretly loathe.

Never having been a touchy-feely person, hugging and kissing even my own children doesn't come naturally to me. It is a major thing for them. I have explained to them that I grew up in a family that could be described as emotionally stunted, or perhaps undemonstrative. There was zero sho-sha of affection, no matter what the occasion. Little Anuradha longed to be held and rocked to sleep but that rarely happened. I guess Aie used to be plain exhausted looking after four children and a demanding husband to make cuddle time for her youngest—me. Come to think of it, I never saw my parents hug, much less kiss! Baba was nuts about my mother and called her 'Babani' when he was in an exceptionally affectionate mood—that was about as far as any demo of love went. I didn't know people freely flung their arms around one another without feeling embarrassed and deeply self-conscious.

So, while I am greatly relieved to have finally quit the fake mwah-mwah club, I have started to long for a few genuine hugs from people I care about. I realize I have missed out on a great deal of warmth and tenderness as a young girl. When I stroke little Bijou while playing 'catch you, catch you, catch you' with her, I see her eyes as she looks at me, and I melt. There is so much trust and unfiltered affection in Bijou's expressive eyes. Her tiny paws hang on to my hands, reluctant to let me go ... She has become my baby (even though Anandita is her official Mom). When I hold Bijou and she clings to me, my maternal feelings get instantly aroused. It's such a reassuring, comforting experience to have a warm, little 'girl' cradled in my arms as I rock back and forth cooing gibberish to her. I thought I had lost those emotions a long time ago, once my children had grown up. But hey … my nazuk motherly feelings are alive and still there! Jai ho! I wish I had recognized my need to hold and be held much earlier.

It's going to be Mother's Day soon and, as with every year, I'm looking forward to spending time with my children and their children. Sometimes I forget that three of my four daughters are mothers themselves. I will be sharing them with their own kids! And I think back on the time I would be in bed with one of mine, sometimes two … one of them would stir, a plump arm would land on my face, hurt my nose but I wouldn't squeal in protest. I'd gently replace it and smile, grateful for the moment.

A few minutes from now, I shall take my favourite position by the balcony, seated in my favourite Bhavnagri chair with inlay work that I have recently reupholstered. It is just the right height, and I prefer the new salmon pink covers to the earlier olive green. There will be a beautiful sunset, I can already tell from the cloud formations on the horizon. My dear friend Olga will send me a text, 'Hello, Gorgeous! Isn't the sunset fantastic?' Two heart emojis.

Olga Tellis, the fiery activist journalist ('Call me reporter, not journalist'), and I have been friends for more than forty years. She can't see the sunset from her home in Colaba, near my favourite veggie market, but such is Olga's network of admirers across Mumbai, someone or the other will be on the terrace of a high-rise near the sea, probably risking life and limb, clicking pictures to send to Olga, who will then share them with me. She may stop talking to me after reading what I am going to say, but I am going right ahead and saying it: Olga Tellis is the femme fatale of political and business journalism. Who can forget her at press conferences at Mantralaya, dressed in mini-skirts, her feet in stilettos, her sloe eyes ringed with kohl, her mouth, a vivid shade of blood red, her loooooong nails polished in shades of the season. Olga loves her long nails and continues to keep them sharp and painted. It's a pity she no longer wears her risque gowns—but looks great in well-matched outfits with bright stoles. We meet often and she never forgets to bring me a bag of shelled walnuts. I love Olga—the last of a dying breed of tough, hard-nosed journos who never let go a hot biz story or political scoop.

Our dinner dates are limited these days—Olga is a vegetarian who shuns spicy food and eats early. She no longer enjoys her Old Monk with tepid water. Nevertheless, she indulges me while I tear into a steak or have my third glass of white.

  This evening I'm especially peckish. I'm anticipating interesting snacks on my tea tray. I like those to be a surprise. Let me guess … Pushpa has soaked moong and matki last night. Maybe she'll make bhel? Or if Mr Dé has his way, it will be crisp Melba toast cut into precise squares, which will be enjoyed with slivers of his favourite cheddar or stinky blue cheese. God help Pushpa if she forgets to place an assortment of cheeses, hard and soft, on the tray. If it's going to be a cheesy treat, I'm looking forward to the soft, crumbly one with cranberries—Bijou and Gong Li's favourite. What's teatime if these magical mellow moments can't be shared with the two tots who bring me so much joy?

—∞—

'Don't let aging get you down. It's too hard to get back up.'

—John Wagner

It's been declared the hottest day of the last two decades in Mumbai. My brain feels like melted Brie. Pushpa offers me chilled chaas with grated cucumber and a pinch of rock salt. There's a great deal of froth on the chaas, with a few chopped leaves of kothmir speckling it, like seaweed floating on monsoon waves. I receive a call from Agent Vishnu—no, neither does he work in Bollywood nor is he a polished spy like Saif Ali Khan whose *Agent Vinod* (2012) featured one of my favourite scenes and songs ('Pungi').

Agent Vishnu is my go-to person when I need a house help, like urgently! Like, yesterday. For more than a decade, Vishnu has managed to stall divorce proceedings at our home with his swift interventions. As the cliché goes, the most important person in an Indian household is the lady who works behind the scenes and makes sure everything is tickety-boo—we used to call them maids or ayahs in politically insensitive times. Now we refer to them as 'house helps'. Nothing much has changed besides the terminology. Unlike other neighbouring countries where there are hours and rules and minimum-wage laws in place, here in India we have been taking full advantage of underprivileged working folk ready to slave away at all hours, no questions asked.

Nobody refers to the house helps as 'servants' any longer. It is considered disrespectful and crass. So archaic and rude, we say. But old habits die hard, alas. If we don't watch ourselves, that awful, colonial word does slip out on occasion. We quickly cover up the gaffe and call them 'servies' like it's an endearment. The people who work in our homes know our secrets. They are aware of our insecurities and vulnerabilities. They are mute witnesses to our fights, squabbles, sulks and arguments. They watch from the sidelines as we go through family dramas, no-talking phases, divorce battles, abortions, arrests, tax raids … our drunken dancing to 'Kala Chasma' and 'Oo Antava'—everything! An occasional suicide, too. But we barely know anything about their lives outside our homes. We demand undying loyalty from them. As if loyalty can be guaranteed with a pay slip. We expect them to participate and rejoice with us. Mourn and grieve with us. Feel for us. But we will not have them sit at the table with us. We are prepared to share a lot with hired help—but not our meals.

I have not visited their families, even when some of them live close by. I may have met a few of their kids over the years when they've come with boxes of mithai after completing school. Do we know their spouses? No. We give Diwali gifts without knowing the person's likes and dislikes. Is that purple saree or yellow salwar suit bought over Amazon really suitable? Or do we feel 'they should be grateful for whatever they get'. What do their cramped rooms look like? Do they have proper bathrooms? They laugh at the money we spend on toilet paper. We hold our noses when we drive past their slums. As if our s**t smells of Dior. Do you ever wonder what saddens them? Have you ever caught them crying? Do you hug a 'servie' who is visibly distressed? Do we comfort them when they are down? Do we even 'see' them?

This goes beyond being 'enlightened employers' who take care of staff members financially, pay school fees for their kids, handle medical expenses, provide clothes and never stint on their food. We need them. Simple. But they see everything. And forget nothing.

Domesticity is overrated, we all agree. Keep it functional. Keep it calm. No dispute here, either. Right? How many of us achieve the enviable but totally elusive balance between managing a home and managing the 'other'—the 'other', which is always far more attractive and, frankly, less stressful than running a home. Most women, even from my mother's generation, resented the daily grind—wake up, organize meals, clean up, organize more meals, clean up again. Repeat. Show me one woman who swears she loves housework and I'll prove her a liar. I have an issue with the term 'homemaker' as well, though it does sound better than 'housewife'. Today's 'homemakers' are different with the men either sharing or at any rate participating in the dull, monotonous, tedious routine.

For the past week, I have been dealing with what is politely called 'maid issues'. I am stranded and upset. Agent Vishnu has not been able to come up with a single suitable candidate so far. All our conversations start with, 'Madam, ek ladies hai.' Ladies in the plural. I am not making this up, but one too-good-to-be-true maid left abruptly when her mother called to inform her that her young son had been badly bitten by a monkey. A monkey. Not a stray dog. Not a snake that had slithered into their village home from the fields. There was no question, she had to hurry back. I managed to buy her an airline ticket and she was gone. Poof! Her replacement arrived a few days later—calm, mature and literate enough to write dhobi lists in beautiful handwriting. She also got a call from her village. I groaned. Her eyes were red with crying for her dying mother. She showed me graphic shots as she FaceTimed a woman gasping for breath with an oxygen mask covering her face. I am not mean—so, I took her word for it that the patient was indeed her mother. One more airline ticket bought. The third called a few minutes ago to say her Ola had taken her to the wrong address—and, in any case, she had a better job offer and won't be joining. Maids have a power over all of us who depend on them, so that our 'other' can survive and, with luck, thrive. You can't say a thing after you know just how terrible their lives are. 'Uska aadmi kaam nahi karta … naukri gaya … Daaru chaalu.' Sounds familiar?

Well, the lockdown threw up several challenges—the absence of house help was one of the most serious ones. Getting live-in help these days is next to impossible in certain cities (Pune, for one). Even in Mumbai, most homes have switched to a tribe called chhootaks—freelancers who waltz in and out and handle specialized chores. For better or worse—go ahead and judge me—I have been used to relying on house help throughout my life. In my parents' home in Delhi, where I spent my early years, later moving to Mumbai, then Bombay, at age ten, we always had helpful, hard-working folks living with us. At the time, they were sturdy young chaps from Garhwal, who could do just about anything, except cooking, cleaning bathrooms and washing clothes. I didn't realize at the time, but those domestic tasks were caste-specific and these men were clear they weren't up for any of it. A neighbourhood dhobi took care of the laundry, a sweeper kept the loos clean and my mother did the main cooking, with a little help from the men with the cutting and chopping.

Our move to Mumbai (where I've lived since 1958) meant getting used to Mumbai's kaamwali bais and other such workers. Then came the 'maanas' tribe—male help—generally robust Maharashtrian villagers, who worked hard except on specific days when they had the licence to get drunk, Gatari Amavasya, for example, which is celebrated on the moonless night just before the holy month of Shravan starts. Most believers switch to pure vegetarian food for a month and abstain from drinking alcohol. 'Gatari' refers to 'gatar' (or gutter), according to popular thinking, since it's the last chance to booze up, eat like unbound carnivores, and land in a gutter, at the end of the drinking–eating orgy.

Till a few years ago, I used to be a good Saraswat Brahmin woman, and observe the stipulated Shravan Somwar fasts. Arundhati would be my fasting companion. I admit even that one day a week of strict fasting was pretty tough for both of us. Mostly, my body protested and I gave up, convinced my immunity levels had drastically dropped. A quick note: I did not fall into a gutter during Gatari Amavasya. Now it's too late—would have been a memorable experience for sure.

Now comes the Agent Vishnu lockdown story when I was desperate enough to hire any willing worker to help around the house. Any! The small army of chhootaks were banned entry by our vigilant building society committee, which now had a dedicated task force to enforce COVID-19 protocols. We had two live-ins, but they weren't used to the extra load without the chhootaks, and I didn't want them to fall sick. To add to the complications, we had to sack one of the live-ins (an Agent Vishnu protégé) because of a serious misdemeanour which could've landed him in jail. That left the industrious Tara, who had to quickly learn how to cook, since the cook was barred entry. We needed someone to help Tara. Agent Vishnu had just the person, he boasted. All relevant info about the new recruit was duly sent over WhatsApp. She sounded fine. Another Nepali girl, who'd work well under Tara's guidance, I figured. I was crazed enough by then to not ask too many questions—like, where she had worked previously. Basics! I told him to get her RT-PCR test done and bring a negative report with her.

When Sarika arrived, I was a bit startled by her over-glamourized appearance. She was dressed in fitted jeans and a snug tee, with a vivid shade of coral lipstick, neat eye make-up, and black nail varnish. Errrr—wrong address? I rechecked with Agent Vinod, and he assured me it was the same girl I had interviewed over the phone and approved.

Stop it, Dé, I scolded myself. *Stop judging her by her appearance. Besides, remember, you need her!*

For the first two or three weeks, Sarika was just fine. She worked well with Tara and I was able to write my book, which I was struggling to complete, in peace. Mr Dé was okay dealing with the new entrant. Soon, I start to hear Bollywood songs emanating at a high volume from the staff room late in the night. I figured Sarika enjoyed dhinchak music and ignored it. But hello! She was not merely listening to Bollywood songs; she was busy shooting videos of herself dancing to these hits. *Why not,* I thought. Most of us were looking for some fantasy land to escape into. Tara seemed amused enough, and it was none of my business what Sarika did once the lights were off and the kitchen closed. This went on till one day Tara came and shyly told me these videos of our resident dancing queen were being widely shared on their Nepali networks, and Sarika's husband was not amused by the attention his wife was receiving, especially in the comments section, where randoms were paying Sarika extravagant compliments and propositioning. Oh oh—trouble ahead. But how could I intervene?

Then came the hula-hoop incident. Manjeet (Honey Bunny), my lovely friend, had come over for Anandita's 'Come as your favourite celebrity' themed birthday party. It was during one of those short lockdown windows when one could invite twenty people home for sundowners and early dinners. Honey's party prop was a glittering hula hoop, for some odd reason. Sarika's eyes lit up at the sight of it but I was dumb enough to not make the connection. Honey decided to donate the hula hoop, figuring one of the grandkids would enjoy playing with it. Next thing we know, Sarika's hula hoop act was on YouTube! It was time to dig a little more. Tara was tight-lipped but definitely disapproving. Turned out Sarika was an out-of-job circus artist, whose hula hoop act was the highlight of the travelling circus, where her husband was employed as an electrician. She also performed various other acrobatic acts, during which she swung from a harness around her neck to a roar of applause. Sarika was a performer! If only she had told me! If only Agent Vishnu had been upfront.

That sultry siren Sarika was showbiz-obsessed became embarrassingly apparent when actor Rohit Bose Roy—who had set the small screen on fire as Rishabh Malhotra in *Swabhimaan* (1995-97), the first television soap to be telecast in India (it's a tie, according to experts; *Shanti* debuted around the same time)—came visiting. *Swabhimaan* was scripted by me and directed by Mahesh Bhatt. Rohit had called out of the blue (lockdown syndrome) and walked in for champers and gup-shup. Since the lockdown curfews were still in place, we'd figured we could easily kill a bottle or two before sundown. For the record, we consumed five! Sarika was clad in her fitted tangerine kurta, matching lip colour, smoky eye make-up for the big occasion. She was too thrilled to be welcoming a bona fide actor and star, and beamed at Rohit as soon as he walked in. Was it an audition? This was repeated each time she refilled his flute and lingered just a few seconds more than needed. He was very sweet, polite and indulgent, as he beamed back, giving Sarika the full Rishabh Malhotra gaze. Just before he stepped out, and I was seeing him off at the entrance, with Anandita rolling her eyes, Sarika jumped in and asked for a pic. No selfies, please. A proper posed click. Rohit at 6 foot 1 inch, folded his tall body in half, and put his arm around Sarika's trembling-with-excitement shoulders. Tara was biting her lower lip and looking cross. I'm sure Sarika couldn't wait to share the sweet images with her circus group. Why not? We all live for magical moments like this one to keep our spirits up. Lots of champagne definitely helps.

As soon as the lockdown restrictions were sufficiently relaxed, Sarika wanted to go back to the circus—she missed the animals, she said. She was used to sleeping next to them and enjoyed their company the most. She was the star of the circus, and her old employer wanted her back!

Occasionally, I miss Sarika's vibrant presence around the house. I miss her laughter and the sound of her dancing to her favourite song ('Piya tu ab toh aaja'), which was also her caller tune. I heard it five times today. It is hypnotic and I can understand why it appealed to a woman who is a born attention-seeker, almost an exhibitionist. I hope she is back where she belongs—centre stage under the big top. I hope the bright circus lights are on her supple body as she twists and twirls. I am sure deafening applause greets her death-defying acts as an acrobat. Some people are born for the spotlight—Sarika was one of them. Besides, all of us are closet performers … our lines and costumes keep changing depending on the audience. But the performance never stops.

After Sarika came Aruna, the beautician who pretended to be a cook because her husband worked with a man who sold momos and chicken manchurian at a roadside stall near a suburban station. Both had lost their jobs during the lockdown—beauty parlours were shut and so were roadside food stalls. She was one more recruit from Agent Vishnu's stable of people, and I have no complaints—she couldn't cook, but could she tweeze eyebrows and upper lips! Invaluable home facials and pedicures later, she was gone. Back to the parlour where she specialized in blackhead removal and threading. One thing she did manage to make brilliantly was momos with a burnt chilli-garlic garnish. Her husband had taught her well.

Our petite Tara had the last word, as she smiled sardonically and commented, 'Aapke ghar sirf kalakar, actors aur artists aatey hain kaam ke liye …'

So here I am, fretting away, making calls to friends, retired drivers, neighbours, old security guards, even strangers. The desperation in my voice is easily understood and accepted. Haven't we all been there? Our frenzied lives are controlled by 'didis' and 'chhuti bais'—why pretend? Agent Vishnu has stopped taking my calls. His 'ek ladies' was a no-show.

While we didn't have Agent Vishnus back then, and I didn't grow up with fancy didis who wore jeans and spoke English, my father's home was always fully staffed and my 'duties' were pretty limited. The family had unanimously declared me to be the best fryer-of-fish (plump, fresh, thickly sliced pomfrets, covered with turmeric and red chilli powder, some salt and perhaps a few drops of lemon juice). And a competent fryer-of-puris (the trick is to fry on a high flame with plenty of oil, drowning the puri till it rises like a perfectly shaped breast). I rolled out good chapattis, too—round and even. Occasionally, I went to the Dhobi Talao market to buy fresh vegetables and fruits, and to Sahakari Bhandar to get the month's groceries. I didn't resent any of this, not even laying the table with stainless steel thalis, katoris and water tumblers. I hated rinsing and scrubbing after. Or washing clothes—was happy hanging them up to dry. I still enjoy ironing, especially on an old-fashioned ironing board, with a pull-out arm for reaching creases on sleeves. I have done jhadoo–pochha in my time and would still do it without any issue or hesitation. None of this is tedious if you know how to manage your time. But none of this is enjoyable, either.

Which is why, I am waiting with an aarti ki thaali and boondi laddoos for the latest candidate to show up. Will I match her expectations? Will she approve of me? Fingers crossed I'll pass her test and not flunk the interview. Hang on—I need to apply lip colour, brush my hair, change out of my shabby caftan and look presentable. These days the didis arrive with near professional hair and make-up—enough to give our movie stars a complex. I hope she's okay with the green Thai curry and rice we are having for dinner. I'll let her know there's a Domino's nearby just in case she prefers pizza …

—⁓—

Ooops! I think I just flunked the interview. Ranju Devi from Bihar told me she's forty and has just returned to the city after marrying off her son. Seeing my startled expression, she hastily added, 'In our village, we get married by thirteen and have children by fourteen.' Seeing sweet Gong Li, wagging her tail furiously and saying 'Hello!', Ranju Devi made it clear she wouldn't walk her.

'If my gaonwalas find out I am a "kutteywali", they will scorn me and my husband,' she said.

So the hunt is back on … A certain Sapna is on her way from Juhu. She's asked if I'll pay for the Ola ride—450 bucks. I said I will not just pay for it; I will give her an early bird gift if she arrives before sundown. Maybe she is a retired trapeze artist? Agent Vishnu, now back in the game, has sent her details over WhatsApp. I see her face-to-face hours later, when I return from a movie and dinner date with Aditya. She is a 'dream girl' like her name suggests. Slim, smiling, polite. She dives to touch my feet when I meet her. I feel like Rabri Devi. Hope this one is a keeper.

We have national integration in our home … that's for sure! Subramaniam is from Kerala, Choudhary and Santosh from Bihar, Durgesh from UP, Anil from West Bengal, Pushpa from Andhra Pradesh, Majida from Maharashtra, Dhani Ram from UP, Sapna from Darjeeling. I like it!

—⊷—

JUNE

'You don't stop laughing when you grow old, you grow old when you stop laughing.'

—George Bernard Shaw

THE IDEA OF A GIRLS' NIGHT OUT (GNO) SENDS SHIVERS DOWN MY spine. Nothing ever goes according to plan—all of us drink like schoolgirls escaping a Girl Guides camp, and genuinely believe such an occasion is a licence to behave badly, starting with inappropriate outfits stolen from a teenager's closet. We seek the elusive bird of youth, which has flown the coop decades ago. We bravely assure ourselves—age is a number. Old is what you feel. Not how you look. I have just come back from a 'Spanish night' at which the paella was awful, but the mood was great. I danced. I drank. I met friends. I felt alive. Don't tell me the flamenco is beyond me! Just don't. Watch … as the march of the toreadors begins and I metamorphose into Carmen Amaya in an instant! Olé!

Ladies of a certain vintage start prepping for the big day (the GNO) weeks in advance—deep-tissue massages, caviar facials, Dead Sea salt scrubs, jade face-rollers, Korean skin serums made from sheep placenta, lip fillers, butt fillers, Botox and new hair. No jokes. Five different looks are kept on standby, with compatible, skin-toned body-shapers (boned stomach support important). The jewellery, handbag and footwear selection takes a week—these are key decisions and cannot be taken lightly. A visit to the bank locker is a must, but only after the final outfit has been frozen and the hair and make-up (HMU, as the movie stars call it) artists booked. Women fight over these talented folk like blood-thirsty gladiators in Ridley Scott's brilliant *The Last Duel* (2021). Which car to arrive in at the venue, is another major problem—at the moment, foxy ladies like to drive up at the wheel of a convertible Mini Cooper, which has been declared the 'it' car that goes with the 'it' bag. It is imperative to declare loudly, 'Thank God there are no men around!', which is a blatant lie. Who doesn't like the attention? Besides, it's obviously elitist—the waiting staff, and most of the other service staff, are all men. And they have eyes.

I went along for a girls' night out yesterday, pretending it's a huge headache—but how could I say no to the persuasive hostess? That, too, on her birthday? Secretly, I was most excited but also nervous—the other ninety-nine gorgeous ladies of the city on her list of 100 invitees were much, much younger and seriously loaded. I knew most of them, of course, but hadn't met them in years. To go or not to go. Avantikka solved the conundrum instantly.

'Mom …' she said, 'just wear a caftan and beads and collect me at 9.30 p.m.'

I am good at taking instructions from my children. I went on a treasure hunt, trying to locate the paper bag which contained a burnt ochre satin silk batik Yolanda caftan I had bought on an impulse from a sweet saleslady at Colombo's Bandaranaike International Airport six months ago and forgotten all about. I stared at the crushed and crumpled ball of golden silk, which had been lying in neglect for months under a heavy wooden ledge in the bedroom. How can I wear this rag, I asked Avantikka, after clicking a few pictures.

'The colour will look great on you. Keep the make-up really light and soft—no black eye pencil, just halka brown eyeliner, heavy mascara and nude lipstick.' Click. Call over.

Only a foolish mother would challenge a better-informed daughter in such matters. Avantikka is the creative director at a leading lifestyle magazine. She oversees ultra-stylized, super glamourous shoots with top Bollywood stars and biz leaders. If they listen to her and follow her directions, who am I to question her?

Her other instructions were equally clear: 'And, Mom … it is *not* a lit-fest party. Please don't wear your lit-fest look this evening.'

Hurt and rejected, I timidly asked, 'What's wrong with my lit-fest look?'

She answered quickly, 'It's meant for lit fests—Fab India skirts and mismatched arty tops. This is a glam party …'

Her crystal-clear brief was noted and absorbed. I went in search of my multi-string faux pearls (good quality; bought in the Chinese pearl market in Hong Kong). I couldn't find them in their usual place. Of course! Anandita had 'borrowed' them for her birthday dinner and forgotten to return them. Gingerly, I took the plastic wrapping off a new eye-make-up box I had recently bought from a busy pharmacy behind the Shiva temple on Colaba Causeway. The pharmacy caters to a predominantly Arab clientele since Arab tourists prefer this area when they visit Mumbai to shop for weddings in the Gulf. The sales ladies at the pharmacy wear hijabs and prefer to converse in Arabic. I relied on sign language and managed to buy an eye pencil in soft brown, a mascara wand in dark brown, a brownish lip pencil and pressed powder in a neutral shade. All the products were from Lakmé, not Guerlain. This is the most amount of make-up I'd bought in five years. The GNO had better be worth all these monumental efforts to dress for it. An hour or so later, I checked my made-up face in the elevator mirror—was it 'soft' enough?

I rang Choudhury to bring the car round. Raghavendra Choudhary's been with us in Mumbai for forty years. But only physically. In spirit he has never left his village in Bihar. He often educates me in Maithili, a sweet and rich language. Thanks to him I know all about the *Garuda Purana*. Devdutt Pattanaik—you have competition! To Choudhary's credit, it must be said that he has accurately predicted the results of every recent election in his state. Prannoy Roy should instantly hire Choudhary.

What do you know! It turned out to be a brilliant party and I had the most fun channelling my inner Zorba the Greek while hoping I wasn't looking like Anthony Quinn in drag. I danced my feet off (shod in lizard-skin block heels) and felt energized. In other words, I felt young! My old, pre-pandemic self was alive and well and kicking up its heels, dancing with a beautiful young Greek girl in a backless blue gown, which was very Santorini, while in reality she was from Salonika. I liked the energetic restaurant hostess who helped guests smash clay plates on the dance floor, even as she danced with the invitees. A pony-tailed Greek God was at the feet of the birthday girl, urging her to join him, as the DJ switched to playing Bollywood tracks and 'Badtameez Dil' got the ladies panting (heat, weight, lust).

Avantikka was drinking champagne with her friends. I was listening intently to a gorgeous socialite of yesteryears as she talked earnestly about my 'legacy' for women like her. 'You freed us,' she pouted. I did? From what or whom? I wanted to be freed as well—from the uncomfortable grip of the body shaper which had kept my stomach firmly in place under the golden-hued caftan but was cruelly cutting into my post-pandemic thighs.

It was time to summon Choudhary and head home, hoping he wouldn't mention Lalu Prasad Yadav or Akhilesh Yadav during the half-hour drive at that hour. There's only so much I can take.

—⁂—

'For the unlearned, old age is winter; for the learned, it is the season of the harvest.'

—Hasidic saying

I'm feeling uncharacteristically sapped of my standard josh. The left knee is acting up again and I'm angry with it. In the old days, one stern conversation with a delinquent body part used to be sufficient to take care of the problem. I'm a firm believer in the old mind-over-matter approach to health problems. This knee has always been naughty and disobedient. Just like Aie's left knee, which she would absently tap or massage while talking to me, seated in her corner of the rexine upholstered sofa, watching but not really watching Doordarshan.

I'm missing Aie a lot this evening, driving back from a quick meeting in Aditya's new office at Churchgate. The workers were at it, and the place was full of dust, with a sharp smell of paint mixed with toxic fumes from God knows what. Despite that, I, the proud mother, had stood there gagging, gazing at the mess through the partially opened door, and saying, 'The light is lovely in this space—look at the trees outside! Gulmohur in full bloom.'

Aditya is leaving on a longish trip a few hours from now and, as always, I am missing him already. He has instructed a staff member to make sure the silver Ganesh moorti I'd given him for good luck, now placed next to the computer screen, is never without fresh flowers during his absence. 'White or yellow?' the man asks. 'Both,' my son answers.

My heart always feels a few kilos heavier when my children travel. Aditya is off to Madrid, not some remote, dangerous, godforsaken outpost. Even so. Avantikka has been in Phuket with her family for ten days. It feels like ten years. Arundhati is here, but not here—mad busy with her demanding jewellery pop-up. Anandita is here. And she's right *here*, if you know what I mean. Radhika is painting, sculpting and writing poetry in Kolkata and not taking calls. Rana is blissed out in Koh Samui, his new home. I don't ask, 'For how long?' I'm scared of the answer.

The babies who are in Mumbai (Aryaman and Ayesha) have their own packed schedules. Raju Sir is my biggest competitor. He has conducted fun gym camps for the bachchas for years. He used to be a scrawny, cheerful trainer. Today, he resembles a movie star, with a 'hot' wife as co-trainer. I don't stand a chance with these two monopolizing my grandkids' free time. Even so, I try and tempt Aishu-Paishu to spend the afternoon with 'Mrs Naani', as she refers to me. It turns out wonderfully well—we respect each other's silences. She lies next to me on the bed and 'reads' from her favourite book, making up stories as she goes along. At the moment she's fascinated by baboons, and I don't want to ruin her fantasy by telling her my Cape Town baboon stories. It's a warm summer afternoon—and here we are, two independent-minded females, separated by seventy-one years but perfectly in sync. I recall Mr Dé's comment when he came back waving Ayesha's janam patri (horoscope) soon after her birth.

He was frowning. 'It's all good, right? Nothing to worry about?'

'Well, there is something slightly troubling—the punditji said our granddaughter takes after her naani—similar traits.'

So…? Troubling? Hell, no! Exciting? Ya!

'When will the rain come?' Ayesha asks, staring at the dark clouds outside the window.

I smile and say nothing. Aishu-Paishu is fast asleep already!

Mumbai anticipates the monsoons in its own unique way. There's dread and excitement in the air as we stare at the changing sky and comment authoritatively, 'If the rains have hit Kerala yesterday, then we'll get them in another four days.' We are as wrong as the weather experts. The gulmohurs giddily nodding across Mumbai make me long for something—possibly the past. I come home and listen to 'Pasoori' on YouTube for the hundredth time. It's Coke Studio's fourteenth season and the deeply subversive ballad 'Pasoori'—a Punjabi and Urdu superhit single by Pakistani singers Ali Sethi and Shae Gill—has broken all previous records. This song goes well with the gulmohurs. And gulmohurs always make me cry. They transport me to Malabar Hill during my college days, when I would persuade a love-struck youth (not always callow), to accompany me on a gulmohur-viewing expedition. Sometimes, I'd be a pillion rider, enjoying the wind making my waist-length hair whip the poor fellow's face (no helmets back then). Sometimes, I would place my hands around his waist. At other times, they'd be on his shoulders. Occasionally, I'd take the BEST bus along Marine Drive and walk up to Malabar Hill from the Babulnath temple.

This evening, Aditya has promised to stop by at the temple and pray to Sreenathji before leaving for Madrid. Neeleshbhai, the gentle-mannered pujari, will greet Aditya with a big smile and say a special prayer. Aditya will close his eyes, bend his head low and seek Sreenathji's blessings. In all likelihood, he'll be remembering his Ba—the woman who gave him the kind of unconditional love only a grandmother showers on a beloved grandchild. I know he misses her every day ... even if he never speaks about it. I know I can never compensate enough for the intensity of love he received from Ba, when I wasn't there for him. This evening I want to be Aditya's Ba.

Perhaps that's why I am crying.

—⁓—

I'm alone, even though there are five people at home right now. Being and feeling alone has little to do with who's around and who isn't. Staring at the waves crashing against the shore, I listen to Jacques Brel. 'Ne me quitte pas,' Brel intones, his voice not sonorous, but wracked with sadness. Why am I listening to Brel and making myself even more miserable? Okay, let me try a mood elevator. I switch to Nusrat Fateh Ali Khan and 'Mere rashq-e-qamar'. I start laughing at myself. For years I used to think the 'qamar' in the song referred to a woman's slender waist ('kamar' in Hindi)! I had no idea what the words meant, but I loved the song. 'Rashq-e-qamar' roughly translates to 'envy of the moon'. The ghazal–qawwali was originally written by the Urdu poet Fana Buland Shehri and subsequently reworked by lyricist Manoj Muntashir.

I'm looking at the pre-monsoon clouds scudding across the bay, plump and heavily pregnant with rain that won't drench the city but will continue to make its way further up. My eyes are filling up again, but the tears don't fall—like clouds that are possessive about their still-to-be-unleashed rain. Across the walking path and close to the shanty towns by the edge of the grey-black sea, I spot more gulmohur trees—even they are refusing to shed the last of the flowers. José Feliciano is next up on my playlist. 'Listen to the pouring rain … listen to it fall …' he sings. '… and with every drop of rain, I will love you more …'

Suddenly, I am transported to a car parked at Breach Candy. I'm twenty-two years old, and possibly in love (never sure about that one!). Love is such a tricky animal. There are far too many bewildering definitions of love. I have still to script my own. The implications of romantic love have always terrified me. Feliciano and uncertain love go well together. Before I start crying again, I switch moods with deliberation and ask Pushpa to get me kebabs. Yes, the homemade ones that are permanently stocked in the deep freezer.

She looks surprised. 'But sa'ab doesn't want kebabs with his tea …' she says reproachfully.

I stick my chin out and answer, 'That's okay. I do.'

Mr Dé has specific teatime snack rituals. He likes to eat jhal muri, with freshly sprouted brown chana, sarson tel and bits of crunchy narkol (coconut). Each time jhal muri is served, he turns up his nose and says, 'Not like Kolkata … In my college days we used to go to …' I turn instantly deaf.

Being neither a Kolkata woman (thank God!) nor a Boxwallah memsaab (a bigger and louder 'thank God'!), I'm happiest with poha or upma or egg-mayo finger sandwiches. But today, I am craving kebabs. Ten minutes later, I am biting into delicious ghar ka kebabs, soaked in ghee— but still feeling sorry for myself. Mercifully, the kebabs have distracted me. There's no sadness on earth that a plate of moist and non-greasy kebabs can't fix quickly. I go back to 'Pasoori' and even attempt to watch the 'Kamli' video with Katrina Kaif's incredible dance moves. That's better.

The clouds have disappeared. The gulmohurs are still there, dancing away. I am particularly attached to a freak gulmohur tree which defiantly blooms throughout the year, like it's mocking the seasons. It stands at the corner of the road, right in front of my bank. We greet each other with formal nods each time I visit the slow and sluggish branch of this nationalized bank. I refuse to move my account to a modern, smarter bank where I'll have a dedicated 'relationship manager'. I can't handle any more relationships in my overcrowded life.

I send Aditya a fake-cheerful text and ask him to take care of his protective-Bhagwan chain, which has pendants of Balaji, Hanumanji, Ganeshji and Shreenathji's emerald padukas. He sends me a thumbs-up emoji. I feel terrible I am not Ba.

—˗˗—

Peut être sounds so much better than 'perhaps'. The former is poetic, filled with yearning and possibilities. I'm looking back at some of my more dramatic 'peut être' moments—not with regret, but a certain wistfulness. What if I had run off to Alaska? Stayed on in New York? Made Washington, DC my home? Considered London? Moved to Paris? So many choices, so many spontaneous but hard decisions, and then the realization—'this was meant to be'. Isn't that how we console ourselves and overcome grief, come to terms with disappointment, rationalize, compromise?

My mood is sombre as I take an ancient elevator to Knead, a trendy vegetarian, chef-led cafe near Mumbai's oldest synagogue at Kala Ghoda. I am meeting the family, those still in Mumbai, for a brisk lunch. My mood is still tres peut être. It is also 'a la peubelle' (throw it into 'the dustbin'). I want to throw a lot of people into a gigantic dustbin. They are so rubbishy—it's a wonder I let them into my life in the first place.

My grandson, Aryaman, who is five, stares at his mother (Arundhati) and asks, 'Mama, are you crying?' He has a worried look on his sweet face and has stopped eating the mushroom burger he has ordered, after looking crestfallen that there is no sparkling water on the menu. Like his father, Sahil, and grandfather, Yogesh, he loves sparkling water.

Arundhati hastily wipes her tears, composes herself, and answers, 'No … I'm fine … not crying.'

Aryaman's troubled eyes haven't left his mother's face, so I say gently, 'Darling, Mama is crying because she is really, really tired, not because she is sad. Sometimes we cry because we feel exhausted.'

Aryaman looks relieved and goes back to his burger. Arundhati reaches out and holds my hand. No words are exchanged. Little Aishu-Paishu is busy eating bits of croissant ('Butter on the side, pleassshhh,' she's requested) and doesn't seem all that concerned. But I am! Concerned. It's that dratted peut être raising its head again. I am not concerned per se about Arundhati's tears because I know it's fatigue finding a release, and nothing worse. She has had an unbelievably tiring week and I get it. All she needs is a short, good cry to feel okay. I am more concerned about me! When was the last time I cried? Let the tears roll? Why have I always hidden my tears? Felt ashamed of letting anybody see me cry? Even worse—why do I permit myself 'angry' tears when I resist shedding sentimental ones?

My children are the only ones before whom I can cry aaram se—sans shame. Mr Dé behaves like he has not seen my tears. Maybe he considers tears 'useless'. Maybe he feels tears need a solid justification. Maybe my tears weaken me in his eyes. He turns away rather than face me when I tear up. Why? Does he think I am Wonder Woman? Indestructible and made from reinforced steel? Sometimes when my tears are on tap, Mr Dé looks on with faintly disguised impatience and waits for me to compose myself before eye contact is made. Ditto for Baba, my father, who didn't encourage any of us to cry, since he himself didn't.

Denying tears is an act of passive cruelty. My tear ducts often speak to me and say it's okay to weep. But I hide and cry. And when that happens I always remember my father's disapproving expression. The only time

I saw tears in my father's eyes was when he recalled his childhood. He was blessed in that his ninety-eight years were far from emotionally or physically crippling. Besides, he had all his four children around him till the very end. These days, I find myself praying I have all of mine next to me as well when the time comes.

—ᛥ—

Last night, I woke up with a start at 4.30 a.m. with 'raindrops' on my face. What? The monsoons are here already? And have forced the rainclouds into my room for a rain dance? I was semi-dazed and still occupying the half-finished dream—a very satisfying one at that, involving food. The drops were for real. It was the air conditioner dripping again. Time to call Aslam for an unscheduled servicing of the unit.

Well ... Aslam, the regular AC servicing mechanic, has just sauntered in and is staring balefully at me. He looks genuinely concerned when he asks, 'Madam, why does this happen only to your AC?'

Good question. I reply, 'Let's ask the AC directly. There must be a reason. The AC definitely doesn't like me.'

Aslam nods his head in complete agreement (what did I ever do to Aslam?) and sticks his head out of the sliding windows to look for a beehive that could be causing the problem. Beehive? Well, it did happen in the distant past, when Aslam was far younger, and unable to detect why the old AC was acting funny. It was only after he'd risked life and limb, and clambered onto the ledge outside, that he'd found the culprit—bees and a huge hive which was growing, by the nano-second as it were.

Aslam had scurried back into the room, visibly scared. How and why did the blessed bees keep picking my AC, I'd asked Aslam. 'Of all the ACs in all the towns in all the world ... the bees had flown into mine ...,' I'd said paraphrasing my favourite line from *Casablanca* (1942). I suspected a conspiracy. If political parties can't sting you directly, they send bees. We managed to get rid of the bees by lighting incense sticks on the windowsill (a trick I had quickly Googled). My conscience was clear. I had not hampered the all-important pollination process in any way. The human race was not in danger of extinction. And the bees peacefully abandoned the hive soon after. We got five jars of honey as a return gift.

Today happens to be World Environment Day. I cannot even think of harming any creature without inviting nature's wrath, so I hope there's no beehive behind the leaking AC this time. It is murderously hot, and a fresh heatwave is expected according to our weather team (though its mostly wrong in its predictions). Aslam assures me there are no bees lurking around. But it could be—equally bad—a dead pigeon or rat. Oh great! We like variety. Aslam smiles ruefully. He has been our AC man forever. In and out of bedrooms without anybody experiencing the slightest embarrassment. Dishabille? That too. Aslam has seen me in faded caftans, my hair piled up on top of my head in an untidy bathroom bun, my face smeared with goop—sometimes a fruit pack, but most times malai with a few lime drops. I look a sight—almost ghoulish. But it doesn't bother me and if Aslam notices, there is nothing to indicate he is in deep shock. This makes me wonder if he has seen a lot worse in other homes where he's a regular. 'Aslam's Adventures' could be an entertaining mini-series. Maybe I should pitch it to Netflix.

Meanwhile, Gong Li and Bijou aren't too happy with the intrusion and are standing outside the bedroom barking at Aslam. There are some regulars to our home who have just never succeeded in winning these two divas over. Aslam is one of them. But Babita isn't. She was here for my Sunday massage last evening, and before I could greet her Gong Li had settled at her feet and started snoring.

Babita, blunt as ever, told me, 'Bhabhi ... you have definitely lost weight. But just a little. Please lose some more ...'

Thanks, darling, just as I was feeling reasonably good about myself after giving up dahi and dates (I used to eat one after brekkie every morning). Maharashtrians have a thing about eating lots of dahi. My father ate dahi thrice a day. Mr Dé eats dahi twice a day, sometimes three times if we are going out and he's likely to have a couple of drinks ('probiotic yogurt lines the system'). I used to enjoy well-set dahi myself till Babita gave me a complex and I figured it could be the dahi that's adding to the weight gain, considering I am off sugar, wheat and rice. (The things we do for vanity!)

Crushed and demoralized, I want Gong Li to be less friendly, and maybe nick Babita's ankle for hurting my feelings. I definitely don't want to discuss my breasts this time, that much I know. I am sulking, and Babita should leave me and my bulges alone. I had never imagined dahi and breasts could be connected in such a bizarre way.

—⁓—

'Try to keep your soul young and quivering right up to old age ...'
                                                    —**George Sand**

Mr Dé is in the grip of Rafa fever. So much so that he has suspended thinking about the menu for the next meal. He is living, dreaming, breathing, eating Rafa—the ultimate tennis God. Beyond G.O.A.T. Beyond *my* G.O.A.T—Roger Federer. It's a unique status Rafa has acquired after his spectacular win at Roland-Garros—a record of records. Fourteen is an awesome number. Such is Mr Dé's love and admiration for the tennis legend, he's taken off for Alibaug with a one-point objective—to watch the French Open Men's Finals without anyone around. That means me. It will be just him, the TV screen and Rafa. His devotion is touching.

I am feeling left out. He has asked, half-heartedly, whether I'd like to join him at the farm, swiftly adding, 'But I will be busy watching the finals, so ...'

I get the memo, and promptly back off, much to the man's relief. I can bet he has it all planned to the last micro detail—a quick but intense work-out before his afternoon nap, followed by tea and toast in the library, then the move to the living room to watch his God demolish the young Casper Ruud. Djokovic has been vanquished and packed off in the quarter-finals. The Russian Zverev has done himself in during the semi-finals. But just look at Rafa's noble gesture, packing his opponent's bag after Zverev's injury! Who can say anything at this stage about Ruud? He could spring a surprise or two and, God forbid, beat Rafa. Banish the thought, you disbelievers. Besides, Rafa is dealing with a chronic foot injury and still soldiering on! Look at the man's determination! I have received thirty-four forwards on Rafa by now, meticulously culled from multiple sources. I am Rafa-ed out. But I can visualize Mr Dé praying fervently at the small shrine in the bedroom, offering all the deities beautiful blossoms freshly picked from the garden and placed in a tiny silver thali on the marble-topped table where our Gods reside. He will repeat his plea a few times, eyes tightly shut, hands joined in prayer. All this for a stranger he has never met, does not know and is unlikely to ever meet. Mr Dé is a strange man.

I say nothing but I am glad I have stayed back and caught up with myself. I wonder what Mr Dé will eat (major!), and he says he'll go to the stylish The Deli a few minutes from the farm and pick up some lasagne. Huh? He doesn't like pasta. Nor is he crazy about Italian food. I get it! He wants his entire being to be focused on Rafa—no distractions allowed. Durgesh, our teddy bear of a cook in Alibaug, can relax and just serve the lasagne when asked. Mr Dé won't drink his favourite malt, either—unless Rafa wins. For days leading up to the finals, I have heard nothing but him singing hosannas—the tennis legend is more blessed than I am! Mr Dé gushes about his humility, courage and grace. How he is Aristotle and Confucius rolled into one, wise and philosophical. Even Rafa's wife can't be this obsessed! Mr Dé definitely won't eat his lasagne if the match carries on and on for hours. He'll starve but not let Rafa down by impolitely eating between sets. I'm amused and a little jealous. I can't recall any such sacrifice made for me or the children! Fortunately, his hero bags the title and life resumes its normal course and pattern.

'What have you organized for dinner when I get back on Tuesday?'

Errrr ... It's Sunday night. I don't plan this far ahead. Sorry! But by Monday morning, I am slavishly planning a Dé-style menu for Tuesday's dinner. Rogan josh with sheermal roti—Irani flatbread flavoured with saffron and rubbed with milk—should do it. Or maybe not. Mr Dé will abruptly and sharply remind me to avoid red meat, though he has happily digested Durgesh's mutton gravy in Alibaug without putting up a protest. Why is he being difficult about dinner on this specific Tuesday when we enjoy eating mutton every other day? Maybe he is doing it just to bug me. Had I said it's going to be grilled fish on Tuesday, he'd probably have sniffed and said, 'I had fish for lunch ...'

I consider writing a letter to Rafa to complain about my rogan josh dinner plan getting canned because of him. If he is all that Mr Dé thinks he is, he will apologize to me. On camera. At the next Grand Slam.

Important lesson: Never ask a man a question which has no logical answer. Well, rogan josh it will be—I want to eat it! But just in case that becomes an issue, I request Raju, the substitute cook at Cuffe Parade, to make malai chingri as a stand by. He's not Anil and he's not Bong. He will use powdered coconut to make the all-important gravy, and of course the taste and consistency will be foul. It's that or asking Pushpa to step in. Bigger disaster—hers will resemble and taste like an Andhra tiffin version of Bengali prawn curry. Maybe an evening at the movies watching *Downton Abbey: A New Era* (2022) prior to dinner will soften the blow. Mr Dé is back and I have dutifully eaten a Lotus Biscoff (too sweet!) bought by Mr Dé from The Deli. Grandly, he'd waved two packets at me and announced, 'Especially for you!'

Mucho gracias, signor! Surreptitiously, I shared a few with Gong Li, who loves Lotus bikkis. Fingers crossed, the evening will go swimmingly well …

But it doesn't. The movie is terrific but dinner isn't. Raju has done the unthinkable—he's chopped up the pui shaak which I had planned for dinner! Off with the man's head! What sort of a cook does that to pui shaak?

'A Bihari cook,' I say.

Mr Dé's face is a black cloud of rage as he summons Lakshmi and Pushpa to demand an explanation for this travesty. 'Were you present in the kitchen when Raju chopped up the pui shaak?' he asks.

The two girls exchange looks and sheepishly confess they had indeed been but a few inches from the chopping board when Raju massacred the shaak.

'Why didn't you stop him?'

Sensibly, they keep quiet. They aren't Bengali either. How would they know it's a sacrilege to treat pui shaak like lowly palak? There's just one way to get through this terrible dinner—add Tabasco to everything, pui shaak included, but most of all to Raju's insipid malai chingri. Maybe it's time for Mr Dé to go back to his place of birth and enjoy the perfectly cut pui shaak of his childhood.

'As soon as you feel too old to do a thing, do it.'

—Margaret Deland

Arundhati's toes are turning black and blue. She's just jammed them into the heavy door of Aishu-Paishu's room while trying to negotiate a peace treaty with Ayesha and Aryaman. She calls crying. Suddenly, my thirty-six-year-old daughter has regressed to her own daughter's age (three). 'Same toes, Mom! And the same foot! Third time I've hurt myself badly in the same place,' she sobs.

I make clucking noises and suggest she ice the sore toes.

'I'm doing exactly that!' she snaps.

Try another approach to comfort her, I tell myself. Don't offer helpful tips and advice. Just let her cry. We all need that from time to time. I try a different tactic to soothe her. 'Come over right away. I can send the car. I'll organize cold coffee and chicken curry ...' By now, I'm pleading. 'Or I can rush there?'

Aru softens. 'I think I'll just go get an X-ray done at Bhatia Hospital, then take a call.'

An hour later, she texts to say she's feeling better, and the X-ray shows a mild something. It's not a fracture.

'So ... are you coming for chicken and coffee?' Both are ready, by the way.

Aru breezily says, 'Thanks, Mom, but no. I'd signed up for a deep-breathing class ... talk later.'

'Of course, darling,' I say. 'No problem. Don't put your weight on the sore toes. Love you.'

'It's been ages since you said that to me—"love you"!' Aru says sharply.

Oh dear. Instant defensiveness kicks in. 'No, it isn't.' But Aru's deep-breathing class has started. She needs to hang up, and I need to breathe deeply myself.

Minutes later, Avantikka wants to know what time I'm coming over for chai-nashta. At her home, the Raju residence, chai-nashta is a big thing. It is elaborately served by Sonal, who, I think, actually dreams of becoming a movie star and, yes, is better-looking than most actresses. By the time I get to Avantikka's, the three kids have left to play in the newly restored area of the society known as the Plaza. I spot Anasuya Devi with her football, and she waves out to me. When I walk into the large living room, I find Pramod, Avantikka's husband, working on his laptop though he simultaneously listens keenly to our chatter laced with gossip (a bit of hot Bollywood goss never kills anyone).

'The rains will be here at 3 a.m.,' Pramod announces confidently.

Wow! Very precise! He grins and quotes a weather website which is generally reliable to the last microsecond. Meanwhile, I'm surveying the low table with trays of keema kebabs coated in almond flour, ghugrees filled with mashed green peas, creamy hummus and lavash, assorted pastries (brought by Arundhati), and delicious corn khichdi with tadka and plenty of hing! Not exactly a teddy bear's picnic. We pig out and gossip some more. The children come back to excitedly share that the neighbour's dog is going to be mated the next day. 'They are getting married and having puppies soon.' Don't tell me the kids are involved in the mating ceremony, I say. Eyes roll. I hold my tongue.

Going by Pramod's weather forecast earlier, I expect to see grey skies when I wake up the next morning. Instead, I see patches of bright blue, with fluffy white clouds rising above treetop level, and my heart instantly soars. This is like the 'abroadwala' sky, I think, as I idly watch my neighbour feeding cats in the compound downstairs. I associate beautiful blue skies with the English countryside, especially at this time of the year. In Mumbai, the skies are always muddy and dull, but not half as bad as the skies over Delhi. Even our annual winged visitors—the pink flamingoes and Siberian cranes—will soon flee the polluted mudflats and creeks where they dutifully arrive to spend a few weeks, delighting Mumbaikars, before flying home. But today is today—one of those 'the sky is blue and I love you' kind of days. And I'm not feeling loved at all. If anything, I'm feeling neglected and taken for granted. Perhaps my congested nose, scratchy throat and bodyache are making me petulant and sulky. It's not often that I fall sick, but when I do, I expect a little fuss, a little pampering, a little 'laad'. I don't think it's an unreasonable expectation.

Mr Dé barely looks at my unhappy face before asking on auto-pilot, 'Slept well? Rested?'

I want to yell, 'Can you not see my red puffy eyes or that I have lost my voice?' But I say nothing at all. No point. Women who talk about their health are dubbed 'attention-seeking ... nags ... whiners'. No use stating the obvious. Either the person whose sympathy you seek is interested, or not. The 'not' is unambiguous. And I'm not thick-skinned.

He is back to sending forwards/analysis/research to his group of like-minded friends. The Ukraine war is still raging. Do I stand a chance? Naah. I don't normally care for these things but today I'm feeling martyred and brimming with self-pity, and so I ask Pushpa to make me her special kaadha (hot water with ginger, honey, turmeric, cloves, pepper and cinnamon). I have no taste in my mouth, and my head is feeling like a bulldozer just hit it. I try reading the newspapers—my eyes hurt.

'Mom—it could be COVID. Please get yourself tested,' Arundhati texts me. She is genuinely concerned.

No chance! I'm scared. What if it is COVID-19? 'I'm not testing,' I reply testily, 'because I know it isn't COVID. The symptoms are different ...' It's time to eat a few macadamia nuts, and two dried apricots.

The blue sky has taken me back to this time last year when, during the same month, the lockdown had been relaxed but not lifted. Exactly a year ago, I'd looked up at a bright blue patch of sky, after picking up ridiculously expensive imported cheeses, muesli with exotic dried fruits, seeded crackers and other luxury treats from a fancy outlet near our home. I'd thrown away a monstrous amount of money on snacks nobody was dying to consume, but on some illogical level splurging like this made me feel good momentarily. There was nothing else really to spend on, and there was nowhere to go. Walking along the aisles of Nature's Basket, selecting sherry vinegars and first-pressed extra virgin olive oils neatly stacked above various brands of Italian pastas, helped me to escape from the reality of COVID-19. That bit of blue sky reminded me there was still hope for life and for a better tomorrow. The sun was low behind the tall IDBI Tower in the same neighbourhood complex as the upmarket grocery store, its slanting rays casting pretty shadows on the deserted car park. The eerie stillness, the tomb-like silence in what has always been a buzzing business hub, made me feel intensely alone. There were just two or three masked and gloved security guards around. Fear was in everyone's eyes. Even though I had stopped watching the news, there was no escaping the wails of ambulance sirens as they raced through empty streets, carrying helpless patients gasping for breath. And then there was that patch of cornflower blue sky to look up at and derive strength from.

I see the exact same sky today. A year has gone by, and we seem to have forgotten the horror, trauma and tragedy of COVID-19. Blue skies help to remind me that there is always hope and a sense of renewal as we gradually but surely pull through.

—⚅—

'Darling, the home kit showed it isn't COVID,' I call and assure Arundhati.

'Are you sure you did it properly, Mom? Did you push the swab stick to the back of your throat, and twirl it four or five times? And did you insert it into both nostrils? Remember, these home kits aren't 100 per cent accurate. Get an RT-PCR done tomorrow in case you aren't feeling better.'

Sure. The swilling of the swab stick made it sound like a perfect martini was being made inside my painful throat. I was glad Anandita and I did the damn test. And, for now, we are COVID-19-free. The children are expressing concern in their own individual style.

Aditya is on his way to Washington, DC. He calls just before take-off, 'Your voice is sounding stronger, Mom.'

It is? If he says so ... okay. 'Call the moment you land. Send lots of pics. Hope you are staying with friends and not in some dodgy hotel,' I say, trying to sound more cheerful than I'm feeling. I sometimes forget Aditya is forty-six years old.

This illness has made me weepy. Inwardly, I am crying a little. I'm crying over Aditya's graduation in Boston (1997). I couldn't sleep last night going over the memory of that trip. I had blurred out so many details that 'didn't suit me'. But so many years later, I can clearly see and understand what it is about that graduation weekend that continues to trouble me. I wish I had made the trip on my own—that's it. I wish I had spoken up and said, 'Look—I need to do this solo.' But back then I was a bit too timid to assert myself the way I can today. I'd gone along with a family plan, rationalizing it was better than not making it at all for my son's big day. He looked overjoyed when we met, but in my heart there was a deep sense of loss. Something—someone—was missing. Aditya's father. I didn't mention it. Nor did Aditya. But neither of us could ignore his absence. We have never spoken about that weekend, come to think of it. Maybe it's too painful to revisit. There are nights when I lie awake thinking how different life would have been had my choices at the time been less punishing for all. It is to Aditya's credit that he has never made me feel less of a mother because of that one decision that turned so many lives upside down. Neither has Avantikka, and I owe them both more than just gratitude for the consistent love they have so generously given me, without once making me feel wretched about the most traumatic, tumultuous period in all our lives.

I now really want to weep. I go to the bathroom and cry my heart out. But my tears embarrass me. What am I crying about? I'm not sure. Suddenly, I want to stop being 'strong' and 'capable' and 'in charge'. I want to be vulnerable and defenceless and demanding. I want to be fussed over and pampered and taken care of. I want hugs and caresses and sweet, comforting words. I go back to the window to look for that patch of blue. It's gone. Pramod is right. The rain will be here soon. I take a deep breath—I definitely don't have COVID-19. Maybe I should get myself gaudily painted acrylic nails like Cardi B to cheer me up since nothing else seems to work.

—ᴡᴡ—

The sky is sending me mixed signals—help. It's like a false pregnancy. Tell me, O Sky—monsoon or no monsoon?

It's only June, but the sunsets are mimicking October cloud formations, vivid twilight and all. Such a show-off, this sky! We've had the dramatic monsoon announcement from the rain gods, with thunder and lightning keeping me awake last night. It is Bijou's first monsoon and she is baffled with what's going on outside Anandita's windows. I can hear her howling, while Gong Li snores through the storm. Dark clouds are racing through my mind as well. The heavy-duty antibiotics are disrupting my brain and creating absolute havoc with my routine. Mr Dé's cryptic text arrives, 'I want macher jhol for dinner …' Red alert!

I'm meeting my lovely girlfriends, and will miss giving him company while he critically deconstructs Raju's version of macher jhol. Will the raw banana be cut in the right way? What about the panch phoron? Does Raju even know what constitutes panch phoron? Umm … yes, he so does. It is available at the nearest kiranawala in branded packets. At any rate, Anil is on standby, next to his phone in Kolkata, just in case Raju gets chopped up and finely diced like fried mocha (banana flowers). I overhear their daily consultations as Raju dials Anil to take specific instructions, one hand stirring dal, the other holding the mobile phone, before it falls into a kadhai of smoking hot oil. We make no concessions in this house. We take no hostages. The raw, green banana has to stay firm and not get mushy, while the fish cooks in a thin, turmeric and panch phoron gravy, with chunks of cauliflower and large potato wedges swimming in it. Chopped drumsticks may be added but won't be missed if they're skipped. And yes, the length of the drumsticks cannot exceed two-and-a-half inches.

Hey Bhagwan. Just as I'm getting ready I hear a scorching comment, 'Carrots in macher jhol? Has he lost his mind?' Mr Dé explodes.

Crushing and cruel! I know. How dare anybody take liberties with macher jhol? I hastily slip into a glam caftan, apply Ruby Woo on my lips and run out of the front door … Cannot keep the green-eyed beauty Leetu or the blue-haired Raisa waiting! We have a couple of bottles of red over a long and leisurely dinner, meticulously prepared and served by Leetu (with a little help from her Man Friday, Amit). We are meeting for the first time since the pandemic and there is *much* to discuss. But first, we devour scrumptious avocado toast, bruschetta, thin-crust pizza, cold cucumber soup, pasta and baby lamb chops. I wickedly laugh at the thought of Mr Dé grumpily eating macher jhol with carrots and go back to our delicious meal with even more delicious gossip!

As a peace offering, I take him freshly baked baklavas stuffed with pistachios from Hurrem's near Flora Fountain. It is a charming Turkish restaurant where Turkish chefs prepare translucent, wafer-thin pastry sheets for the baklavas that disappear as quickly as they emerge from the kitchen. Mr Dé launches into the history of the Ottoman empire, and the life of Hurrem Sultan, the powerful wife of Suleiman the Magnificent, of the era known as the Sultanate of Women. This discourse is delivered as soon as he takes the first bite but my mind is elsewhere—earrings or no earrings?

—◊—

'I have reached an age when, if someone tells me to wear socks, I don't have to.'

—Albert Einstein

'When I was growing up, there was no such thing as Father's Day, Mother's Day, Children's Day … all this nonsense,' Mr Dé says in a rather superior tone.

Before he resorts to making red-red eyes at us, I assure him we won't celebrate-celebrate, but just meet up and hang together at home.

'Make payesh …' he throws at me before heading off to read B.N. Goswamy's latest tome.

Payesh has to be served on all birthdays and other bhalo occasions—wedding anniversaries, births, new job—and the payesh has to match the one in Mr Dé's Ma's kitchen. Of course, it never comes close. We have yet to pass Mr Dé's payesh test. To start with, he flips out when the staff calls it kheer.

'Payesh is payesh—why do they keep calling it kheer? Can they not tell the difference?' Errrrr … Is there a difference, Mr Dé? Tell us, we are ignorant non-Bengalis.

I answer sharply, 'No, they can't.' It has taken me four decades of acknowledging there is even a difference! Come on, both have milk, sugar/jaggery, cardamom, slivers of almonds, kishmish. Ki farak penda? Wrong question. Payesh is an elevated, supremely sophisticated sweet dish, according to Bongs, best relished with luchis ('For heaven's sake, don't call them "puris"'). And yes—payesh has cooked rice in it, not vermicelli. It has to be cooked just so. Not over-cooked. A particular strain of rice—Gobindobhog, not basmati. Nolen gurer payesh is worthy enough to be served to the gods, but even without nolen gur, payesh has to possess just the right balance of everything. Nolen gur tastes like treacle and is a seasonal specialty also called 'jhola gur'. It is jaggery made from the first flush of juices from the date palm (khejur) tree. To me, it tastes exactly like the Sri Lankan treacle. Blasphemy!

Would payesh work with the Father's Day lunch menu? I mean, we'd all agreed on Chinese from Royal China. Jeff, the very polished and friendly manager at Royal China, has been instructed several times about the flaming fish. Yes, it would, Mr Dé states firmly. Apparently, payesh goes with everything. Besides, we also have mangoes with vanilla ice cream—we do, right? We do. The pre-lunch beverage demand was for gin cocktails.

'Count how many Sepoys we have in stock and make sure to order fresh grapefruit,' Mr Dé says as he stares at the bottles of Sepoy tonic water lined up on the bar. He's very possessive and particular about his stock of Sepoys. Yes, he counts each bottle. Maybe he even labels each one. He is not looking terribly pleased—has someone been drinking his Sepoys on the sly? What about juniper berries? Yup. Right here. In a jar on the bar. 'Where are my gin glasses? I see just five—where's the sixth?' Mr Dé thunders. Broken and disposed of! But I keep mum and shrug.

The friendly neighbourhood fruitwala sends two grapefruits to the house just as the doorbell rings. They are here—Arundhati, Sahil, Aryaman and Ayesha. And we are still looking for the sixth gin glass. Wide-mouthed, with a rim, and a large bowl. There's something not quite right with the ice, Arundhati says, staring at her drink. This is not looking good. I want to pick up the bottle of gin and glug it down. Not a very promising start to Father's Day ... But aah—there's nothing a few glasses of gin cannot improve and enhance in a gorgeous way. Besides, coincidentally enough, three of them (Mr Dé, Aru and Anandita) are dressed in fire engine red—Lal Salaam, everyone! Cin Cin ...

Royal China delivers our lunch on time. But wait—where's the tofu? What? It wasn't ordered? What will Sahil eat? The ladies of the family do one thing exceedingly well—we think on our feet. While we keep Sahil distracted by discussing Munich and cars, the tofu mysteriously makes its way home and to the dining table. Don't ask. The son-in-law gets his favourite dish, while Aryaman and Aisha tackle edamame dim sums and forget all about French fries, their current favourite accompaniment with every meal.

The late afternoon sun breaks through the pre-monsoon clouds and I say, 'Golden light! I love it! Happy Father's Day!'

Aru looks out and says, 'It's not golden … it's white.'

Definitely no more gin for Aru85!

I am waiting for my head to clear and thinking of carefully and cautiously curating a new list of 'special days' from next year's family get-togethers before we start getting on each other's nerves even more. Family gatherings have changed over the years. Naturally! But so have we. All of us are older … and busier. Stress on several fronts has insidiously crept in and disrupted the family balance, one way or the other.

Nothing should be forced—least of all celebrations. Formality and rules should not dictate our fun decisions. We should meet when the mood is right, and everyone is in a happy space. So many conflicts surface when the timing of such intimate interactions goes hopelessly wrong. Without a warning, someone says something in an unguarded moment, and boom! The atmosphere gets instantly vitiated and the happy occasion turns into a nightmare. So avoidable! We are all dealing with our own issues—some stated, others suppressed. All it needs is one spark for tempers to flare. One small comment—and oops! There goes the party.

We've had our share of birthdays that have backfired badly. Anniversaries that reminded us of some unpleasantness. Festivals that opened old wounds. It's time to be sensible and cut our losses. Much as we love to spend time together, maybe the moment has come to take stock and do only that which makes everyone smile and relax. So here's a resolution for the year to come. No more 'duty' celebrations that could end disastrously. Salut!

—⁓—

JULY

'There is a fountain of youth: it is your mind, your talents, the creativity you bring to your life and the lives of people you love. When you learn to tap this source, you will truly have defeated age.'

—Sophia Loren

IT'S BEEN ELEVEN YEARS SINCE THE ARTIST M.F. HUSAIN PASSED AWAY in London. It's his death anniversary today. Raisa, his beautiful daughter, who's looking more and more like him as she grows older, sends me two wonderful photographs of her beloved Baba and me. Raisa, along with her younger brother, Owais, are the custodians of Husain Sa'ab's legacy and estate. It is a huge responsibility, but Raisa who is as soft-spoken as her father, discharges it with grace and dignity. The world of international art has dramatically changed, with cryptocurrency and NFTs altering the broader implications of worth and value in the mysterious world of art. Anandita gifts the family a set of cute tees with an Andy Warhol–style image of Husain Sa'ab on it. Quirky and fun—would the man who was always so ahead of the curve have approved?

I often think of Husain Sa'ab these days ... Perhaps it has something to do with the weather and adrak chai. He was an erratic and frequent visitor to our home during the monsoons, turning up unexpectedly, to my absolute delight, generally around 5 p.m. and demanding, 'Where's my tea?' I rarely saw Husain Sa'ab eat a full meal, even though he had a fussy, fastidious palate and was a superlative cook. Consuming food made him restless, impatient, like the act of sitting at a table, chatting companionably and taking the trouble to let the hand travel from the plate to the mouth, was already a waste of time. Instead of a fork or spoon, the hand could so easily have held a paintbrush! Often, he would stop eating mid-meal and pull out a black felt pen, his mind hungrier than his stomach and his fingers itching to draw. I've spent many afternoons with him at assorted coffee shops, when he has left his meal untouched and started drawing on paper napkins, table mats, tablecloths, serviettes. He would do this casually, effortlessly, easily … like he was doodling in an absent-minded way. But the lines were faultless, ceaseless, sure and unerring as he continued chatting, his fingers moving steadily over the surface of whichever material he could find at that moment. Waiters, managers, restaurant guests, would watch in wonder and marvel, awestruck by his genius. He'd look up and do one of two things—if he was in a generous mood, he would give the drawing to whoever was at the table; at other times, he'd carefully fold the paper napkin and place it in his jacket pocket.

Across the world, there are hundreds of lucky recipients who own a bit of Husain, just because they happened to be at his table or in his vicinity when he was drawing. Husain Sa'ab could—and did—draw anywhere. Sitting at a roadside dhaba or in an airport lounge—his mind and hands were perpetually at work on images that seemed to burst out of his lithe being. Even in his eighties, Husain Sa'ab was a very attractive man, and he knew it. I have seen women and men drooling over him and craving his attention. His personality was his best artwork.

Chai was what kept him going; he once told me he drank twenty cups a day and that he was very particular about the taste. Adrak chai was not a preference, but he made a concession when he came home during the rains for a cuppa and was happy to share my ginger-chai. He noticed every little thing and made a joke out of what he observed—caustic, witty, sharp and frequently cruel. He told me how Madhuri Dixit, his muse for years, graciously and patiently brewed tea eight times in her kitchen in Denver, Colorado, when he 'dropped in' to see her, after travelling thousands of miles.

'Madhuri knew I was particular about my chai. When she served the first cup, she studied my face and could tell I wasn't satisfied … She is a perfectionist! She told me not to feel embarrassed … she'd keep brewing tea till she got it right and I was happy with it.' His eyes changed. He seemed far away as he sighed, 'Even the simple act of lifting a cup from a shelf and placing it on a table was so graceful. I have never seen so much beauty and natural grace in any other woman … every tiny movement of hers is mesmerizing to watch.'

This interlude at her home in America, where one of India's most extraordinary female stars was then living a suburban life as a doctor's wife, displeased her devotee. Husain Sa'ab couldn't quite accept the sight of an apsara he worshipped going to the neighbourhood mall to buy groceries, pushing a cart like an ordinary hausfrau, with a toddler in tow. To him, she was the eternal enchantress—Chandramukhi from *Devdas* (2002). Not Dr Nene's lovely wife dressed in baggy track pants and sneakers.

As a dedicated gourmet, who immersed himself on rare occasions in the art of cooking the perfect Bohri lasan kheema, Husain Sa'ab was invariably 'in the moment', listening to his favourite qawwali while prepping. It was nothing short of a major production, involving the entire family and staff. It was also pure theatre! Watching him create the complex kheema, layer by layer, was like watching a blank canvas getting covered up with the maestro's sure strokes.

This particular Bohri specialty is covered with a carpet of tender green garlic shoots. Watching Husain Sa'ab cook was like spying on a court painter working on a masterpiece. He cooked the way he painted—with the same level of concentration, not faltering or taking a break, except really briefly to recharge with a small cup of hot tea, before going right back to his unfinished task.

The Bohri lasan kheema is a seasonal dish and gets cooked during the brief week or so when fresh garlic appears in vegetable markets and the stalks are sold at a pretty price by only those vendors who stock limbus, fresh ginger, spring onions, mirchis, adrak, kothmir and kadi patta. The beautiful, delicate, bright green garlic stalks can be spotted during late spring and early summer, when one can mistake them for skinny spring onion, even leeks. The aroma of fresh garlic is distinct, and it is this that gets enhanced when, just before the specialty is ready to serve, a few raw eggs are cracked over the garlic carpet, with a ladle of smoking hot ghee being poured in a steady stream, allowing the eggs to sizzle, bubble, coagulate and cook.

I used to watch Husain Sa'ab bending low over the spicy, fragrant kheema, folding his long frame gracefully, before reaching for the ladle of smoking ghee. His movements were panther-like and equally noiseless. The ghee would be poured slowly over the raw eggs, till they'd start hardening, with the sizzle of the hot ghee meeting the cheerful egg yolks and soaking into the cool garlic shoots below, before gradually releasing irresistible, complex aromas, as we waited impatiently to be served this unique delicacy.

Rich, perfectly cooked Bohri-style biryani and Raisa's patiently stirred sheer korma were Eid feasts we greatly looked forward to during Husain Sa'ab's lifetime. Family traditions are precious—thanks to the surviving members who still respect and honour them. Sharing special repasts during festivals was once a non-negotiable 'duty' in so many families, regardless of their financial status ... I don't see it happening these days. And I plead guilty, too. No more Diwali 'faraal' thaalis or Sankranti laddoos (til with gur) sent to friends and family. Today, it's about impersonal but pricey statement baskets of exotic, imported fruits, or hand-rolled dark chocolate boxes that get exchanged. Barter! Khair ... woh bhi ek zamana tha ...

I just glanced up and looked at my portrait painted by Husain Sa'ab. Did I just catch it winking? I miss him. I miss our conversations ... I go in search of him and, to my joy and delight, find him easily in old albums containing countless photos clicked on different occasions. We have hundreds of albums in our family. We love our photographs! The one I am looking for has a series of candid pictures of Husain Sa'ab taken in the small room next to the living room, which show Arundhati aged two, parked on Husian Sa'ab's lap. It must have been Dusshera or Diwali, given the festive clothes she's dressed in. Arundhati is wearing a colourful gajji silk chaniya–choli, her belly button visible, while Husain Sa'ab is looking magnificent in layered whites. The two of them are laughing. His beard in this photograph is long and well-groomed, not trimmed and trendy as during his later years. It made me stop and think about how long I had known him. A really long time! I knew him when he was 55, 65, 75, 85 and, by a miraculous off chance, I was at his hospital bed a few hours before he passed away.

What was Husain Sa'ab's khwaish, as he lay propped up against huge pillows on a sterile hospital bed in London? Falooda! Not any falooda, but the one from Badshah Cold Drink, the juice centre in Crawford Market, Mumbai. It was this specific rich, creamy falooda, with just the right mix of vermicelli (falooda sev), beej (sabja seeds), ice cream and rose syrup that Husain Sa'ab was craving, even as his breath was getting shorter and shorter and emerging strenuously in sharp gasps from a very congested chest. I smiled, listening to his request and looked at Owais, his loving youngest son, as he promised his father he'd go look for falooda at an Indian or Pakistani restaurant in the vicinity. But Husain Sa'ab would have none of it. It had to be falooda from Badshah or nothing! That was the quintessential Husain Sa'ab—hard to please, harder to impress, impossible to placate … till the very end.

—m—

'Don't be defeatist, dear. It's very middle class.'
—Dowager Countess, *Downton Abbey*

I have butterflies in my tum tum. This is rather unusual for someone who deals with almost anything and everything with a shrug. I wake up feeling unprepared for the eight-day trip ahead. I've packed my silver-grey Samsonite without investing much thought into what I was throwing into it. The trip is to Thailand. More specifically to the island of Koh Samui, which our son Rana and his wife Radhi have made their temporary residence till they figure out their long-term plans. We are travelling there to celebrate our granddaughter Samsara's first birthday.

It is not a hectic plan, given how laidback all three of them are, having picked a 'free' lifestyle for themselves, away from urban tensions and pressures. They like their beach life way too deeply. Rana and Radhi send photos of sunsets as seen from their balcony that could easily be converted into posters for Thailand Tourism. Rana's 'workspace' is a beach shack from where he coordinates demanding creative assignments for two international agencies, one in Singapore and the other in America, and runs a successful poster business of his own.

Radhi and Rana are very clear about their life goals—and those are distinctly different from my own, very middle-class ones. I seek security—financial, emotional and cerebral. They seek a way of life that I can only describe as 'unburdened'. No creature comforts as I understand them. Their 'possessions', Rana has explained, should ideally fit into a backpack. A few shorts, cotton shirts from Fab India, that's it. No furniture, no 'bangla-gaadi'—just basics. No putting down roots either. And lots of bonding time with one another amid vast open spaces around them. As I mentioned earlier, their next stop could be Costa Rica—Rana is busy researching the options. Formal schooling for Samsara isn't a major concern either. She will be a child of nature, learn as she goes along. As her parents have pointed out gently, 'This is the new way of educating kids. So many of our friends are adopting this method. Children are studying … but differently. The important thing is we need to be happy, breathing clean air and Samsara needs to be with nature.'

It took me a while to figure it out. Initially, I was stumped. And worried. I was thinking in narrow *Jungle Book* terms. Samsara as Mowgli. But no! They are right! She will be far more in tune with tomorrow and how fortunate is she to be born to progressive, far-thinking parents, not bogged down by conventional choices the way my generation was, and still is. Bravo! I'm saying to myself as I pack Anokhi shirts, shorts and Sri Lankan cotton nighties into my suitcase. Yes, these will easily fit into a backpack!

Our trip to Koh Samui isn't exclusively about being loving grandparents and nothing else. I'm going back after twenty years. The last visit was unforgettable for more than one reason. I had planned a family and friends' holiday having been drawn to something called a 'Full Moon Rave' at Ko Pha Ngan, a nearby island. I had zero idea what a 'rave' meant, thinking it to be an innocuous music festival on the beach at Phi Phi—something like an oriental Woodstock. If the children were in the know, they didn't let on, but were most excited to go and so we went! Never mind the details …

This trip was same-same but different. The island has totally changed from what I can see from the websites. There are great restaurants and resorts along the beach. We are staying in one that's not too far from Rana and Radhi's temp home. I have included sarongs, and daringly even a couple of bikinis for our private beach moments. As always, I have asked my well-travelled friends for insider tips on where to eat. On his part, Mr Dé has pulled out an old diary in which he's got a Thai friend to carefully write the names of local specialties. Now all he has to do is flash it at a shack with friendly owners for us to savour off-the-menu delicacies. Or at least that's the hope!

No cannnnn, la!

Thailand is no longer the place of lovely memories. Rather, we are no longer age-compatible with what the country offers. And I'm not talking about sandwich massages and other sleazy delights. My knees protest before my heart can react. My body reminds me over and over again that holidays of this kind are not as enticing as they used to be even five years ago. Starting with the long walks at airports. For the very first time, I opt for a wheelchair when we land in Bangkok to catch the connection to Koh Samui. The hideous hour, time difference, lack of sleep and a vague sense of trepidation seize me as I tighten the seatbelt before take-off. This is just the start of many eye openers.

Ambitiously and enthusiastically, I have signed up for an eight-hour excursion to the protected Angthong Marine Park—an archipelago of over forty-two islands with crystal-clear waters and vivid coral. 'I can do this!' I tell myself, as I clamber into the speed boat and nearly lose my balance. No, you can't, a little voice from deep within says. The crew notices my difficulty getting on and off the boat, and sweetly start calling me 'Mama'. Now that's a first! I'm dressed in black shorts, proudly showing off my latest, pale-yellow Birkenstocks, cool cat eye shades, neon scarf with pom-poms and my favourite 'I Dream in India' Art Chives tote. Me? Mama?

Later, it's a 'no' from me for hiking, snorkelling or swimming. Then, I think, what the hell am I doing on the excursion? Aah—kayaking! This I can manage!

'Mama, I come with you ...' says a tiny, wiry man, and off we go. Yes, it's fun. Sort of. My knees buckle when we get to the shore and I kick myself for undertaking this stupid excursion, more suited to the fit, toned thirty-somethings in bikinis and swimming trunks, who are leaping on and off the speedboat with admirable dexterity. And this is just day three of the trip. I do a quick rethink about some of the other plans, and nervously leave for Bangkok after enjoying downtime with Baby Samsara and her proud parents.

Rana is right about the clean air in Koh Samui. And several other things in life.

On the short flight from Koh Samui to Bangkok, I review my time with the trio based on the idyllic island. They've made it their home for now. Would I have ever considered such a radical decision no matter how much in love I was? Highly unlikely. My practical self always scores over the romantic. Yes, that has cost me a lot. Most of the old loves are dead. We never did get the chance for closure. Faded letters and photographs bring a bittersweet smile to my lips when they pop up unexpectedly. And here are these two raising a happy little girl in an unknown environment. Their friends are like them—idealistic wanderers. They too are raising young children in a foreign land. I met Russians, Ukrainians, Americans, British and French—all neighbours and FB friends. All of them strangely connected in a destination that is thousands of miles away from their original home. They have made a new home and will discover many more such in the future. Their concept of home itself is entirely different. They don't need to put down roots in order to flower.

Impermanence is attractive and compelling. I look at this mélange of strangers, newly linked to one another, as they chat around the pool and enjoy watermelon juice served out of plastic jerry cans. Everything is disposable in their lives—paper glasses, paper plates, plastic cutlery. The food is basic desi vegetarian (Radhi is vegan but occasionally eats eggs), aloo tikkis and vegetable pulao. Filling. Not fancy. Naked toddlers run around the small pool, while young mothers unselfconsciously pop out a breast from inside their floral bikini tops to feed hungry infants. This is a scene straight out of a movie waiting to be made, and I'm busy absorbing and learning. Can gorgeous sunsets really make up for family, tradition and identity?

'Yes,' says Rana emphatically, as we stroll back after a satisfying dinner at a popular bar/cafe.

We'd both enjoyed a couple of Aperol Spritzes. Radhi had left earlier with the baby. I'm speaking candidly to a forty-nine-year-old son like he's twenty-four and still finding his feet in the big bad world. To his credit, he indulges me as I offer 'advice' and lecture him on security, education, investments, savings. My middle-class self is in overdrive.

Mr Dé, ever the sensible parent, is deliberately trailing and enjoying the sea breeze. Earlier, he had told me, 'Children always do what they want to do … Who listens? I refuse to give advice these days.'

I tell Rana to speak Bangla to his little girl, while Radhi continues to speak Gujarati. 'Your Bangla is so good, Rana. Samsara should learn both languages.'

He nods. Maybe Samsara will be fluent in Thai.

Staying out of children's lives is a very Western concept. I can't do it. I'm often told by them that I'm an 'over-involved' mother. Hello! What nonsense. How can a mother be under-involved? Or how does a mother calibrate exactly how much to involve herself without breaking invisible barriers and upsetting her kids? My mother knew the micro-details of my life—a life so different from hers. I wanted her to know everything—no secrets, no filters. It worked for us, so, this concept of a hands-off approach to parenting doesn't sit well with me.

I see Rana and Radhi consciously discarding the trappings—and traps—of a life that does not appeal to them. I don't understand their choices, and I'm trying not to judge them. In my mind, they belong to the 'hippie' generation I grew up in. Everything, my friend, is 'blowin' in the wind…' Including the answers they seem to have found and I am still looking for.

———~~~———

All the great restaurants and bars I've diligently researched are waiting for us when we land in Bangkok. But we don't make it to even one! We don't indulge ourselves with mango and sticky rice treats, nor do we trek to Sky Bar and Sirocco to admire glittering city views or revisit favourite haunts like the Mandarin Oriental Hotel on the river. Sadly, even the Tea Room at the Erawan Hotel, which used to serve the best dim sums in Thailand, is under renovation. Shopping at Central World—more a mini-city than a mall—involves walking for miles looking for a specific store in a distant zone of the shopping mall. Every time we think of venturing out of the Grand Hyatt to discover a new restaurant, we groan, change our minds at the last minute, and make our way to the popular bar in the hotel's basement instead. Imagine, being in Bangkok and ordering pizzas! Imagine drinking draft beer in a hotel bar filled with local ladies of the night flirting outrageously with rich Aussie patrons. Imagine opting for a bowl of ramen in a mall for lunch! Pathetic or what?

But so many realities become apparent during this one short trip. I know what I can no longer undertake or enjoy. The body is not in sync with the mind's desires. My physical energy level is unable to match up to my mood. I huff and puff when I emerge from the aircraft and walk towards Immigration. My legs and arms protest non-stop. Even my eyes feel tired as I idly survey new collections of luxury brands gleaming away in glitzy airport boutiques. It wasn't all that long ago that I'd hit the road running at a new destination, without bothering to catch my breath or worry about jet lag. A quick shower, and I'd be out and about, eager to explore and enjoy myself.

Bangkok provides a timely reality check. The covered skywalks and elevated sky trains that connect the city are the best ways to bypass frenetic traffic snarls, but these convenient systems still need climbing up flights of steep stairs since there are very few escalators and far too many people. Combine that with eyesight issues—I need glasses only for reading, so they aren't always parked on my nose or readily accessible. Reading signages, scrutinizing labels on items while shopping or even getting in and out of tuk-tuks pose major challenges. So does pressing the right button for your floor in a hotel elevator while struggling to find your key card inside a cluttered handbag—that's a major excavation. Then comes the trauma of screwing up the eyes to read menus or boarding cards—nightmarish.

Even worse is getting lost in a gigantic airport terminal after misreading the large signs guiding passengers to the right zone. Ufff! Scary. Almost as tension-filled as leaving a credit card or a passport or boarding pass on a perfume counter at a duty-free shop and then forgetting which one it was! And losing hats, caps, sunnies and scarves routinely on the beach ... Oh yes! Happens all the time. But hey—travel continues to remain my number one thrill. Fine—no more bungee jumping for me. I can live with that. But who says I can't go to Buenos Aires to learn the tango from the best-looking dancer in Argentina, preferably with slicked back hair tied in a ponytail. A young Antonio Banderas–type. Antonio is in his sixties now. Chalega, boss! As for my planned Morocco trip—wait till I get to Marrakesh, baby!

'You can be young without money but you can't be old without it.'
　　　　　　　　　　　　　　　　　—***Cat on a Hot Tin Roof***

Are we glad to be back in aamchi Mumbai! I've ordered Anil to make chicken biryani for dinner without realizing it's World Biryani Day. Had I known that before Anil entered the kitchen, I would have switched from chicken to mutton. Mr Dé does not recognize chicken biryani as a legit offering but it's too late.

Besides, Anil is back after a month. He now has a bahu, a daughter-in-law who touches his feet and calls him Baba. He is beaming as he boasts, 'Khub shundor holo.' Anil is a free man now. A proud father who has seen both his children married off into 'decent' families. Duty done. He is keen to describe the Mumbai arm of the celebrations—a grand reception hosted by the bride's family for over 500 people at a suburban marriage hall with a huge garden, where an elaborate multi-course, multi-cuisine buffet was served. I notice Anil's hair and moustache are dyed tar black and he has kept the top two buttons of his bush-shirt open to reveal a shiny, gold chain. He fingers it shyly and says it's a gift from the in-laws. With Anil in such a great mood, I'm feeling a lot more confident about the chicken-biryani-that-is-not-a-biryani making it to the dining table without an instant uproar or violent protest.

It's Sunday and the atmosphere at home is dull. Not mellow. Dull.

I am bored to death and least interested in whichever Wimbledon match is being played. The weather matches my sadela mood—it's that in-between monsoon weather—wet, slushy and pointless. Rain, dammit, or let the sun shine! Uncertainty is so unsexy, whether it's about the temperamental rains or a clumsy seduction.

I sit by the window, gloomily looking out at the fishing boats anchored in the bay. Last year was different. There was a reason to be gloomy; COVID-19 had crippled the world. We could all indulge our suppressed angst, legitimize frustration, throw tantrums, blame innocents, rage, rave and rant—we had an alibi. The virus could be blamed for several personal failings. This year is different—there are no safety nets. I'm upset and hurting over several issues. I like to 'have it out' as they say. Why keep it suppressed within when a good old no-holds-barred, gloves-off war is an option? But that requires a sparring partner, willing to take what comes with the turf—insults, accusations, taunts, wounds. What could be better than that, I ask myself, as soggy leaves and wet crows are the only visuals distracting me from the overall greyness that is slyly seeping inside my cranium.

I am still sore, hurting and seething within.

I'm not sure the chicken biryani will elevate my mood. As a back-up, I ask Anil to make malai chingri because nobody does it better. Pushpa, solicitous as ever, asks if she should cook me a little jeera-khichdi on the side—just in case. All these non-compatible food items presented on the dining table are bound to generate adverse comments. But tonight I don't give a damn! Enough pandering. If these odd dishes offer comfort, I shall dig into them minus explanation or apology. The 'mood menu' right now is a lot like this eccentric food combo—a smorgasbord of conflicting emotions. If one dish doesn't work, I shall still have two more to satiate the hunger.

But the 'other' emotional hunger is far more demanding. It is asking for too much! Conversation and reconciliation. But not of the tired, old variety. There are times when one has to bring it on, not back off. Hold one's ground and not flinch. I'm tired of holding back. Because I was raised to think women have to give in. Submit. Silence is better than confrontation. This is the old me. Not assertive enough. The latest version is saying: Do it! Go for it! Speak up! If not now, then when? Table what needs to be tabled. Don't hesitate. Don't postpone. The pattern needs to be broken and replaced with new templates.

I have a voracious appetite for self-punishment. It's selective, of course. And it does not involve martyrdom. Just a reluctance to engage with angry people. Anger is very unsexy. Right now, I'm thoughtful-angry as opposed to angry-angry. As Avantikka often reminds me, 'Ma, you overthink! Let it go or do something about it.' Perhaps my overthinking is connected to the after-effects of a commercial Hindi movie I watched last night …

Anandita had naughtily shot a candid reel of me laughing hysterically through *Jug Jugg Jeeyo* (2022) and wondered what exactly I found so amusing. I'd told her in my best movie critic voice that the premise was bold and very today (a young couple based in Toronto comes back to Patiala for a family wedding, wanting to announce their divorce, only to be confronted by a bombshell—the parents want a divorce too!). Hmm … food for thought. The otherwise mediocre movie definitely had a few sterling, thought-provoking moments. No wonder it was declared a hit.

Sensing my post-movie despondency that evening, Anandita accurately gauges the mood-meter as my dead eyes look nowhere and gives me a mini-lecture in her strict voice. 'You know what, Mama … You are a real sucker.'

Did my youngest child just tick me off? She isn't done though. 'Any rando who speaks nicely and says sweet, flattering things to you—bas—you fall for it, and agree to do ridiculous things for the person. People take advantage of you all the time! Stop being so damn naive. Learn to see through people.'

Family too?

Activist and classical dancer Mallika Sarabhai's message arrives just then. Mental (and useless) self-flagellation is set aside as I read her text message about her forthcoming book with a terrific title—*In Free Fall*. Will I endorse it? Of course, I reply. Ask Renuka Chatterjee (my book editor in the distant past, now hers) to send me a hard copy. I hate reading PDFs and vastly prefer physical books. Mallika reminds me that we have known each other for forty years. I was her mother's friend to start with, and had been to Darpana Academy of Performing Arts in Ahmedabad established by Mrinalini Sarabhai and Vikram Sarabhai in 1949. I enjoyed meeting the indomitable, feisty 'Amma'. I have watched three generations of Sarabhais on stage and admired all that they stand for in a nation that is rapidly and pointedly overlooking cultural icons who don't subscribe to its current thinking.

I'm delighted she's asked me to launch her book in her hometown. Mallika has faced the brunt of taking on the present government boldly and fearlessly after the Godhra massacre of 2002. In the book, she describes it thus: 'What followed was a well-planned carnage of the Muslims that altered Gujarat forever.' Mallika is a proud Gujarati who continues to fight the establishment, even after paying a huge price for her moral and political belief systems. She has battled ill health, alcoholism, bulimia, anorexia, tobacco addiction and worse over the years.[2] The book chronicles her courageous attempts to heal herself. I admire her for being honest and fair towards all the people in her life. She does not shy away from admitting she remains estranged from her daughter Anahita—their relationship is like a slow-festering wound.[3] It makes me think about my own wounds. How have I dealt with them?

By playing ostrich for the most part, I have to admit.

Now I'm asking myself if applying Pushpa's khichdi directly on those wounds might ease the familiar pain. If the khichdi experiment works, I'll explore other, equally creative healing techniques. Like lasagne, or crème brûlée for minor bruises and scrapes.

—m—

---

2 Nandini Oza, '"Often I play music loudly in my room and just dance": Mallika Sarabhai in new book', *The Week*, 2 October 2022. https://www.theweek.in/theweek/leisure/2022/09/25/often-i-play-music-loudly-in-my-room-and-just-dance-mallika-sarabhai-in-new-book.html

3 Nandini Oza, '"Often I play music loudly in my room and just dance": Mallika Sarabhai in new book', *The Week*, 2 October 2022. https://www.theweek.in/theweek/leisure/2022/09/25/often-i-play-music-loudly-in-my-room-and-just-dance-mallika-sarabhai-in-new-book.html

'Count your age by friends, not years. Count your life by smiles, not tears.'

—John Lennon

I am kicked that I have so many unusual friends in my life. Friends like Yusf Bhai from Srinagar.

His voice this morning is cheerful and eager. 'Namaste, Sister, I am coming to Bombay next week … What can I bring for you and your lovely daughters? You please don't feel shy, Sister, you just tell me … And also, guide me—what shall I get for Dé Bhaisa'ab? I'm planning to bring home-cooked wazwan … Don't say "no". It will be my pleasure.'

Yusf Bhai is an established shawl and carpet merchant, and a very fine Kashmiri gentleman from another zamana. I first met him in Lahore fifteen years ago at a friend's home and thought he was Pakistani. We were at the friend's grand mansion in the poshest part of one of the most fascinating cities in the world. It was late afternoon and mild, pale sunlight was streaming in through the French windows, making her silverware glisten like gold. There was a handsome gentleman standing deferentially near her chintz-covered sofa, a stunning canvas by Pakistan's most famous artist behind him. Every corner of this magnificent drawing room was filled with significant art objects of great value—bronze sculptures and marble statues. She was dressed in her trademark silk tunic (shell pink) with a delicately embroidered toosh shawl thrown carelessly over her slim shoulders. I had interrupted a meeting with the gentleman in the room. Clearly, she was one of his most valuable customers and patron.

I watched the beautiful begum as she surveyed his many and varied wares, spread over her beautiful Persian carpet. After a while, she turned to me and graciously offered to negotiate with Yusf Bhai on my behalf in case I liked anything. Oh my God, I gasped. How could I say I liked everything? I really did. What was there not to like? His shawls were exquisite. I cradled a beauty close to my face to feel its softness. But I certainly could afford nothing, going by the prices I'd overheard.

My friend lowered her voice to a whisper, 'Toosh … we only wear toosh in Lahore. It's legal here.'

For the non-initiates, toosh is the shortened version of 'shahtoosh'. It is made of the fine hair on the underbelly and chest of the Tibetan chiru or Tibetan antelope, an animal found only in Ladakh and some parts of Jammu and Kashmir. 'Shahtoosh' translates to 'king of wools'. Due to rampant poaching, India has banned the trade of shahtoosh. But the ameer memsaabs of Delhi happily flaunt their tooshes in winter and claim they have inherited them much before the ban kicked in and forbade trade. Like hell!

At the begum's salon in Lahore, the whole scene was out of a Muzaffar Ali film, each detail perfectly crafted. Yusf Bhai was clad in a loose salwar with a long shirt, his ruddy complexion glowing in anticipation of a big sale. Minutes later, a wooden trolley was wheeled in by two maids whose eyes stayed lowered as the lady of the house instructed them to serve tea to the 'mehmaan from Hindustan'.

This was no ordinary high tea—it was a lavish profusion of rich snacks, from keema samosas to mutton chops, chicken sandwiches to fish fillets. There was ghee-soaked halwa covered with neatly sliced badam, silver bowls filled with pistachios, pine nuts and cashews, baskets filled with fresh fruit, silver trays with Swiss chocolates and plump, seedless Ajwa dates.

I tried not to look too impressed. 'Oh, we serve tea the same way in India … yes, yes, all these wonderful preparations, and many more items for vegetarians … why exclude them?' I didn't actually say all this, of course, but faked a casual attitude, as the sweet maids surveyed me through the corner of their eyes. They were young girls, and it's possible I was the first 'Hindustani mohtarma' they'd seen at close quarters. I was dressed in a sari, and was wearing a bindi, leaving little room for doubt. I smiled at them as they shyly offered me an old English porcelain plate with a flower design on the edges. Wedgwood? The serviettes were starched and prettily embroidered.

Yusf Bhai had discreetly taken off to the other room, where he was served tea separately by male servants. Even though I didn't buy his shawls or carpets, we became friends and exchanged phone numbers. He told me he travelled across the border frequently and had clients in London and Dubai, who only trusted his taste and advice while buying those exquisite, fabulously priced shawls. He certainly had the eye and knowledge; he was soft-spoken and refined, kind and elegant in his manners. I never expected to meet him again. We said Khuda Hafiz, and I was gone.

Five years or so later, I received a call from Yusf Bhai saying he wanted to bring me wazwan from his home in Srinagar, since he was coming to Mumbai to catch a flight to Dubai. I was delighted to be in touch with him again and invited him over. He arrived late one afternoon, bearing boxes and boxes of the most delicious Kashmiri food I have ever tasted. From tabak maaz (baby ribs) to gustaba (meatballs in a rich, saffron-flavoured gravy) to a stewed apricot dessert. I was overwhelmed and wanted to hug him but stopped myself (tauba!). For the girls, he'd brought colourful phirans with delicate embroidery, and for Dé Bhaisa'ab, a pashmina scarf in deep maroon. There were two 'pools' (pinches) of the Valley's best and most expensive saffron, besides akhrot and dried peaches.

He then opened his suitcase and took out the most gorgeous tilla-kaam jamas, jamevar and toosh shawls, and velvet phirans with real gold and silver thread embroidery on the yoke and sleeves. His eyes shore with pride as he gently pulled out one piece after another. 'Sister, please see this one … it will suit you.'

I finally succumbed and bought a pashmina shawl. Each time I wear it, I recall my sweet dosti with Yusf Bhai. A few days from now, he'll be here. I have begged of him not to bring the wazwan but he sounded hurt when I mentioned this. Okay, okay, just bring one portion of tabak, I said, pointing out there aren't many takers for rich food at home these days.

'Okay, Sister, but I have kept a special embroidered chador just for Dé Bhaisa'ab,' he said.

Dé Bhaisa'ab was impressed enough by Yusf Bhai's old-world manners to order a carpet. Not just any carpet, mind you. He wanted a portrait of us woven into the shikar design. Gulp! Like he was Shah Jahan and I, Mumtaz Mahal. Guess what? A year later it was delivered home! Like

Mogambo, Mr Dé, khush hua—I was deeply embarrassed and suggested we hide it. But no! There it is in full public view hanging on the wall of the passage that leads from the living room to the front door. Fortunately, not too many people have noticed our mugs in the carpet. Or maybe they've been too polite to comment.

Dear, dear Yusf Bhai with his kind eyes and soft voice. He represents the best of the best—Kashmiri traders who know the arts and crafts of their beautiful state, who have the 'pehchaan' and the pride to showcase their beauty to the world, whose refinement is of the highest level … I feel lucky to have broken bread with him—the stranger I met in a land across the border, a friend I thought I had lost during those long years of strife in the Valley. May Allah always look after my brother Yusf.

AUGUST

'To find joy in work is to discover the fountain of youth.'
—Pearl S. Buck

MANUSCRIPTS ARE LIKE NEGLECTED LOVERS. THEY SULK. AND accuse. And get jealous. They demand every bit of the writer. Every micro-second. Every waking moment. They even lay claim to dreams. Every heartbeat belongs to the possessive manuscript. Every emotion too. Manuscripts are monsters. Bloodsucking vampires. They snatch every bit of you … Drain you … Kill you.

I plead guilty writing this. It was as hard on me too, staying away for this long and pretending I wasn't aching. There was travel. There was family. There were 'duties' and 'obligations'. I'm sure countless women writers face (and have faced) the same dilemmas—being forced to choose between their work and their lives. Silently accused of neglecting loved ones. Reminded from time to time about priorities. This may explain why so many writers who have opted for marriage and children over a solitary single-and-unhappy-to-mingle lifestyle, feel submerged under guilt. Martyrdom is but a hair's breadth away.

I have spent a week feeling low and beating myself up, even though I haven't really done anything 'bad' for this level of self-censure. Ah yes—I did take time off on a Sunday to attend a friend's fiftieth birthday brunch for an hour. A whole hour! And that included travel time. But it was I who had spontaneously organized a family lunch the same afternoon and forgotten all about the birthday brunch! Idhar bhi guilt, udhar bhi guilt.

I came back hurriedly from the friend's fancy celebration, quite annoyed by the frequent calls demanding, 'When will you get home?' Normally, I boldly and airily say, 'As soon as I am done.' This time I was worried the lunch order wasn't properly taken care of—there wouldn't be enough veg food on the table, pizzas for the kids wouldn't arrive on time, and we'd discover there are no limbus in the fridge in case limbu paani was requested. I walked in looking flustered and apologetic, instead of cheery and nonchalant. Big mistake—wrong signalling! I switched to breezy.

The kids were busy playing 'kitchen-kitchen' and barely looked up to say, 'Hi, Nani!'

'Did you get your fries, popcorn and pizzas?' I asked them.

They replied brightly, 'No, Nani. We ate ghee-rice with wafers. Also, dahi-rice with wafers.'

I gulped and rushed into the kitchen to check on the rest of the food. Yes, it was all there—Club Chinese. Check! How wrong can one go with that? Guess again! When it was served at the table it turned out to be inedible. And there were just two unappetizing vegetarian dishes. The angry glares had turned into mutterings. I felt worse. Even though I had 'delegated' efficiently before taking the hour off. This wasn't fair! How many women have been in this situation? Hands up! I see hundreds of hands.

Unfortunately for me, writing was and will always be viewed as a 'pastime' even by those who should know better (hint: family!). Then there are others who take one look at me and think, 'What? This one? A writer? Isn't she a famous socialite? Did you see her highlighted hair?' Oh, yessss! I intend to keep highlighting my hair as long as I have hair on my head. May opt for a few purple streaks too. 'Wisdom greys'? Not for me. Don't need wisdom and definitely don't need greys.

Over fifty years of steady and consistent writing later, I still have to confront the disbelief and offhand attitude of people who have never written a sentence in their lives. 'Must be fun, na? Writing in your spare time?'

Spare time?

Since I never discuss my work or writing process, I usually make light of it ('*Oh yes, I write now and then. It's nothing, really. Just placing one word after another … you should also try it. So easy, so relaxing … as good as hot yoga or pilates. Poora poora timepass. Workout for the mind. Haha …*'). Damn! Would the beauteous and multi-talented Tishani Doshi ever say something as dumb about her work? There is a subtle art of bragging classily. Clearly, it's beyond me. Naturally, these sweet darlings who ask me about my 'pastime' take my word for it and probably think I'm the desi version of Hank Ketcham in an exotic caftan.

Take the conversation at the fancy-shancy brunch I had abandoned. It revolved around the vivid colours of my floaty outfit. And everybody wanted to know about my special diet and exercise routine. Both non-existent. But who believed me? I could hear their thoughts: the bitch is lying. My mouth was full of creamy pasta at this point, so I just smiled with my eyes and kept mum. Next, I was asked detailed questions about celebrity love sagas—like the Lalit Modi–Sushmita Sen scoop, which I know as much or as little about as those asking searching questions about the viral tweet from Lalit Modi that launched a thousand memes.

Makes me wonder … Is it just me? My silly attitude? My compulsive need to underplay the most significant part of my identity—writing? How do I tell these people what writing means to me. It is my breath! There isn't a moment when I am not writing. I write in my sleep. I write under a shower. I write as I eat. I write during and after sex. I write when I speak. I write even when I am not writing. And yet I continue to undermine my most sacred passion.

A few days later, ten eager ladies in shiny branded outfits descend on me at a friend's birthday party in a sexy new restaurant to ask about the latest news. I feel like the bureau chief of ANI and stop myself just in time before giving them an update on the British politician Rishi Sunak and his chances of becoming the prime minister of Britain, quite forgetting Sunak scoops are not what they want.

'We've heard all sorts of things about Ranveer Singh's wild sartorial choices ...' A lady clad head-to-toe in brightly patterned Versace (did *she* raid Ranveer's wardrobe?) ask, before another lady carrying a baby pink limited edition Chanel bag interrupts, 'Please don't say anything mean about Ranveer ... he's a Sindhi! Like most of us here ...'

Like I hadn't guessed, looking at all the Hong Kong–style diamonds blinding me like flashbulbs. I took my time to bite into the honey-soaked baked Brie, before replying, 'He looks very happy with his wardrobe and sexual choices ...'

The women look crestfallen. That's the thing. I should have enjoyed the avocado toast and left. But no! I felt obliged to entertain and perform a dumb pantomime by talking amusingly about the weekend's premiere episode of *Koffee with Karan* and praising Ranveer's mimicry of his colleagues and rival superstars like Hrithik Roshan and Aamir Khan. I go to the ludicrous extent of mimicking Ranveer's mimicry, since I am pretty good as a mimic myself. Not satisfied with my own 'performance' and feeling like I have shortchanged my avid listeners, I offer my services as a photographer, since the man hired for the job seems clueless and wants to shoot selfies with me instead of covering the party. Worse, I provide an unasked-for masterclass in modelling and posing for the camera, besides handing out tips on hair and skin care. Before anybody asks me about Alia Bhatt's pregnancy and Katrina Kaif's birthday in the Maldives, I flee. I am not Alia's gynae. How the hell would I know?

Please note: I am not being supercilious or snarky. But I am screwed. No matter which topic comes up at social gatherings, I find myself in a spot. Political opinions are the worst. Women stare and men clam up— what's she talking about? Why is she bringing politics into everything? Because, you dummies, politics is everything! There is no such thing as being apolitical. Every act of ours, personal and professional, is deeply political—where we live, who we marry, what we eat or don't eat, what we drink or don't drink, what we wear, whom we make friends with, whom we shun, where we worship ... what we hold sacred. There are three topics women are expected to avoid discussing—sex, politics, humour. Yes, even today. I mentally tell myself to take a few tips from other writers and co-authors who loftily enter a room and don't waste a minute on anyone or anything unrelated to their obsession—themselves.

Yes, most writers are nauseatingly narcissistic. The hustling, name dropping and undisguised bragging make me squirm. This behaviour is not just tolerated but condoned, even encouraged by those who believe writers are a special breed and must be treated with reverence. Or shunned. I ask myself: What sort of a writer am I? Which category do I fall into? And, in any case, what is it that we writers really do? We start with one word, then add one more and one more till a sentence emerges. Followed by more sentences. Paragraphs. Chapters. We spend our lives piling on words. Why make such a big deal out of it? Do our words save lives? No. Possibly, they save us.

Those ladies in their designer clothes, Louboutin high heels and Bulgari Serpentine watches are in a far better space than I could ever be. God knows what they make of my life ... they stare at my Zara dress in awe. They ask about my humble handcrafted straw bag with a bright pink tassel from Koh Samui and genuinely admire it. My silver chains, bracelets and rings fascinate them. 'You put yourself together nicely,' one of them comments while I sip a strong cappuccino. There isn't a false note I can detect ... So what if they didn't read books? They read human beings. And I'm happy I got to step into their world for those two hours. I hope they'll invite me again ...

—∞—

Here I am, after having driven around in circles for miles and miles. The beautiful Nandana Dev Sen is in Mumbai to launch *Acrobat*, a slim volume of poems written by her late mother, the wonderful writer and academic Nabaneeta Dev Sen. The poems have been sensitively translated into English from Bangla by Nandana, who has flown in from New

York with her husband John Makinson (adored by Mr Dé and me, and affectionately addressed as Jamai Babu). Their energetic seven-year-old daughter Meghla is with them, and Nandana has warned me that she is a handful.

It's pouring sheets and sheets outside. I need a cuppa. I also need to pee before we start the two-hour session. Both options are unavailable. On-stage, I can't focus on the poems or the guests waiting to hear Nandana recite them. But I stop myself from displaying either discomfort or dismay, as I gamely read out three poems myself and keep my legs crossed … please, please, please, let me not think about peeing!

I see several people I know in the small audience and smile broadly. Among the invitees is a 'well-known media personality' as she frequently describes herself. We nod at each other. There is a demand for the poetry reading to continue after the stated time and I'm certain my bladder will disobey. It's been five hours since I left home and I'm asking myself a perfectly legit question: What the hell am I doing here?

Soon, it's time for us to step off the low stage and walk to a bookstore close by where the lovely Nandana will sign her mother's book for fans and admirers. Great! But my bladder comes first and I really want to leave immediately, get myself a roadside cutting chai, since there was nothing on offer at the venue. We've posed for publicity pics and I'm tired of being polite. I ask for a hand to help me down four or five steps. The self-declared 'media personality' is beaming as she walks up to me. I smile back in a friendly sort of way—we have known each other for about fifty years, after all.

She starts off with a cheery, 'Good to see you, Shobhaa …', and before I can respond, she adds gleefully, 'So glad to see you need help to climb down steps these days!'

End of conversation. That's it! What was that about, I think to myself as I all but run to the nearest washroom. This woman had expressed her delight at my predicament and mocked my busted knee!

I go to the bookshop to say goodbye to John and Nandana who insist we do a few more pictures for Instagram. John tells me proudly, 'Nandana has a huge following on Instagram.' Okay, John, I say. I'm happy for her.

A young author strolls into the bookshop with his beautiful bride. He barely wishes anyone—he is too busy scouring the bookshelves. Wow! What a committed book lover, I think. I am wrong. A sales assistant comes up to ask, 'Are you looking for a specific book, Sir? Can I help you?'

The man shoots him a dirty look and replies, 'Yes. I am looking for *my* book ... I don't see it displayed prominently!'

I burst out laughing (pee stop done, I'm more relaxed), and say, 'Are you serious?'

He is! He glares at me and then quickly remembers to smile.

I add unnecessarily, 'I have never walked into a bookshop searching for my own book ...'

'That's because you are Shobhaa Dé,' he replies tartly. 'Not all of us are that fortunate to find our books stocked in every bookshop we enter.'

Touché or what? I am pretty taken aback but make light of it. He's young, eager and ambitious. Hota hai!

Jaaney do. Clearly, this is not my evening.

I decide to drive to my daughter's glam event which is being held in a fancy carpet showroom. She isn't expecting me. The moment I walk in, I know I am at the right place. Avantikka's eyes light up and she rushes to hug me. 'What a lovely surprise, Ma! Let me get you a drink. There's no wine—sorry! But great cocktails. Try a whisky sour—it's yummy!'

It is! I'm super glad I made that detour.

—∞—

'Every year should teach you something valuable; whether you get the lesson is up to you. Every year brings you closer to expressing your whole and healed self.'

—**Oprah Winfrey**

It's 12 August 2022. Salman Rushdie has been brutally attacked this morning. I get the news flashes in rapid bursts and am shell-shocked. No! This can't be happening, I say to myself, as Pushpa brings me chai and Gong Li waddles up for her morning massage. Flashback time: An incredible night on the lawns of The Chambers at the Taj Mahal Palace Hotel, when he was visiting Mumbai after sixteen years with the 'Easy Exotic' (Whoa! It's the name of her low-fat cookbook!) celeb chef and actor, Padma Lakshmi. Salman was/is my hero. This was my do-or-die moment. I had cherished every word and sentence we shared on the occasion.

But right now I am frozen with grief and outraged by the audacity of the attack. Nothing registers as I absorb the clinical details of the horrific stabbing on stage in Chautauqua, New York. For several minutes after the news breaks, I remain numb and speechless, tears streaming down my cheeks. That the attack took place thirty-three years after the fatwa was issued against Salman, made it even more demonic. The news trickling in has been scanty and inadequate. I still don't know whether he's dead or alive. There are reports he could lose an eye and perhaps the use of his arm. Dear God! No! Spare Salman. I think of him as one of the world's most important writers—erudite, gutsy, deeply human. I want him to live! Selfishly … for myself. And for readers across the world who admire and love him. I feel proprietorial. He is 'our' genius, our original Bombay Boy, and that will never change.

It was this emotion I mined during that famous dinner that was hosted by Adi and Parmeshwar Godrej for a few of their close friends. Forget the six-course meal and the rare wines that were served, my exclusive focus was Salman.

'Do you mind …? I want to sit next to my boyfriend,' Padma Lakshmi said to me, her eyes glittering and her smile a bit too wide.

'Yes … I do mind!' I answered boldly, adding, 'You live with him, you will be spending the night with him after this dinner ends while we only have this short time with a writer we admire … A Bombay Boy, who's in our shared city after ages … So … terribly sorry, but I'm not moving.'

Padma Lakshmi's eyes stopped glittering. It was left to Parmeshwar (our generous hostess, seated on Rushdie's right; I was on his left) to defuse a potential catfight by her quick intervention. 'Darling, let's wait for dessert to be served, and we can all play musical chairs …' she said.

Brilliant! Dessert? What dessert? Salman Rushdie was the main course plus the dessert. Who cares what else was being served? Padma Lakshmi, pouting sulkily, went back to her designated place at the dining table and pretended to be interested in the two invitees on either side of her.

Such bad manners, I thought. I was at a sit-down dinner for no more than sixteen friends. Our long table overlooked the historic Gateway of India, bathed in warm light. All of us were behaving like Rushdie groupies, dying to engage him in conversation. All of us, but his girlfriend at the time (they married in 2004 and divorced in 2007).

I had managed to get Salman's attention long enough to have a decent conversation that was charming, attentive and engaging. We talked about Bombay/Mumbai, of course, and the people we both knew. I was flattered out of my skull that he had read my work! And even if he was merely fibbing by paying me these wonderful compliments—I was okay with it! No! I was over the moon! He was a regular reader of *Stardust*, he confessed, and loved the mirch-masala style, the wit and barbs, the irreverence, and the play on desi words. He mentioned my use of 'Hinglish' and how it registered strongly with him while he was writing *Midnight's Children*. I wanted to hug him there and then—but Padma Lakshmi seated right across the both of us, dreamily gazed at him non-stop. Salman was being indulgent and wicked, charmingly insisting he was in India primarily as Padma's boyfriend. He proudly pointed out that while Padma had nineteen projects in her kitty, he was doing nothing but tagging along. Her quote, 'The combination of the two of us is very seductive …', kept coming back to me.

The news has upset me terribly. Well … for all of us have Salman Rushdie stories, it's amazing and wonderful how every single story is positive! Nobody has a nasty word for the writer. His multiple interviews show him in the best possible light, answering the toughest questions calmly and with a smile. Such a shame that not too many people in India expressed sympathy, forget solidarity, for a writer who, in his own inimitable way, had put Bombay/Mumbai on the global literary map.

I have prayed for Salman's recovery every day. He is alive but, we have learnt, that the attack has left him without sight in one eye and the use of a hand. What a price for a writer to pay for being himself.

—ᨪ—

'There is nothing more aging than misery.'

—Michelle Pfeiffer

'Madamji, Bhagwan has done big galti with you,' the wild-eyed jyotish with an untamed beard and bright orange tilak says to me, while a few indifferent mules stand still on the edge of a precipice overlooking the famous Lingmala waterfall near Panchgani, a hill station in southeast Mumbai.

We are at a village named Bhilar, where every home boasts of a mini library. I am distracted by a huge billboard that states as much and feel very impressed, thinking, 'Must tell Sanjoy and gang to host a JLF edition in Bhilar. That way, we could all spend happy days in Panchgani and sing "Strawberry Fields Forever".'

The jyotish is right there—uncomfortably close—and I know I am being conned. The smooth-talking astrologer has me! Even though I have been pre-warned by Mumbai friends. 'Panchgani astrologers are like the mafia—too clever—they know which tourists to target. Watch out!' And yet ... Chhhhay! Such a bloody sucker I am! Stupid woman—c'est moi.

Pretending not to be interested in Bhagwan's big galti, I start to walk away, a gigantic roasted corn cob with red mirchi powder and rough salt in my hand. The jyotish instinctively knows he has found his victim for the day and follows me to the car. 'Give me one, two minutes, Madamji ... just to study your face. Myself, Joshi astrologer. I am a third-generation face reader from Kolhapur.'

I continue to resist.

He touches the Pandharpur mala of tulsi beads around his neck, closes his eyes and fake-prays. Then, he asks dramatically, 'Do you want me to break it to prove my faith?'

I sign up instantly. I don't want to risk a jyotish's curse on a family holiday. Besides, my ancestors came from Kolhapur and we are a few kilometres from Satara, my birthplace. It is a divine sign. Maybe he is going to establish his credentials and win me over by telling me he knows from the shape of my eyebrows that I was born under the Anuradha nakshatra ... Everything would have been just fine had my parents named me Anuradha. But then the big galti happened when my name got changed to the pedestrian Shobha (with the single 'a' at that!). Maybe he was the mysterious psychic who was going to redefine my future!

I turn to face him and bluntly ask, 'How much?'

'Not much ...' he answers but I persist. He shuffles his feet, looks away at the dark rain clouds rolling in ominously and says, '₹300.'

I quickly calculate and figure that I've just spent thrice that amount on popcorn at a multiplex. Here is a jyotish from the land of my ancestors who is about to unlock a deep and dark secret. I indicate he should go for it. The mules draw closer and so do a few idle bystanders.

He starts by saying, 'Madamji, you should have been a man but by mistake you were born female. Your mind works like a man's. You take independent decisions like men do. You are not afraid of anyone. You are clear-headed and have been firm from a very young age. You stand up against the world but do not bend under pressure. You care for your parivaar more than you care for yourself. People take great advantage of you. Nobody returns loans—and you don't hold that against the person. You overthink and are too stressed. You must give your brain a rest ...'

Instantly, I want to give Joshi the jyotish ₹3000, not ₹300. My eyes are moist. He has softened me up good and proper. The mules and bystanders move in closer still. They are expecting more drama. My parivaar is getting impatient (the jyotish is right—they are taking advantage of my goodness!). We have a long trek ahead of us. Seeing that his victim is about to slip away just before the kill, he quickly offers to read my palm and make 'accurate predictions'. I can see Choudhary, our loyal chauffeur, shaking his head vigorously.

Once again, I ask, 'How much?'

'People like yourself—badey-badey log—give me lakhs ...' the wily jyotish says.

He obviously approves of my car. I'm not such a bewakoof also. I tell him in my best man-manner and voice, 'I'll give you a thousand—take it or leave it.'

He grabs it.

Later, everyone laughs at me. I am being roundly mocked in the bar of Brightlands, a lovely resort in Mahabaleshwar, where we've stopped for lunch and are digging into garlic-butter naan and reshmi chicken kebabs. Avantikka is on her second gin-tonic. Anandita is enjoying a rosé; Pramod, his beer. And me? Miserably sipping limbu-paani.

'Just have a glass of Chardonnay ... you'll forget all this jyotish nonsense,' Avantikka advises.

Arundhati agrees, a glass of white in her hand. The kids are running around the property, and I should be in great spirits myself but the jyotish has succeeded in putting a keeda inside my bheja. I want to drive back and clobber him. A man would have done just that. And he *did* say I am basically a man in a woman's body because of Bhagwan's big galti. I could show him!

Instead, I order a Chardonnay. Quietly sipping it, I consider a makeover. I have the prince of couturiers, Raghavendra Rathore, on speed dial. Maybe he could customize a couple of louche smoking jackets and formal bandhgalas for my next big gender-neutral move?

—◆—

'When it comes to staying young, a mind-lift beats a face-lift any day.'

—Marty Buccella

My feelings about Bollywood and actors are … are … mixed, at best. But I have always liked Mr Perfectionist, Aamir Khan. He is pretty radical in the choices (professional and personal) he has made and I appreciate his guts. We are not 'friends'. (Friendship is a big word. Friendship and showbiz make strange bedfellows.) However, when we do meet, I enjoy talking to him. He reads a lot, is interested in several subjects beyond Bollywood, and he gets into a great deal of trouble. To me, that is the best part. By refusing to follow the pack and remain politically correct, Aamir Khan has paid a price. His last film (*Laal Singh Chaddha*, 2022) was targeted by those who disapprove of his views, and the knives are frequently out for the man who holds on to his way of thinking regardless of the outcome. Aamir Khan is his own man.

So, when Mr Perfectionist sends me a message inviting two far-from-perfect people (me and Mr Dé) to dinner at his Pali Hill home, I am game. Of course! Yes! We both like Aamir Khan and adore his ex, Kiran Rao. The last time we met Aamir was at the launch of Jolie's—the posh, members-only club launched by Aryaman Birla, the handsome cricketer-turned-businessman, son of Kumar Mangalam and Neerja Birla.

It was fashionably dark on the lawns that evening and the music was pumping. We couldn't really talk … Aamir who was with his daughter, Ira, said he had to rush home to help his son Azaad with his homework, being a single parent now. I was impressed.

Earlier, he had spontaneously come to our home to a dinner in honour of Amitav Ghosh (they are good friends) after a book launch at which I had been in conversation with the erudite Ghosh. I like people who don't have hang ups and childish ego issues about 'not being invited formally, so how can I possibly come?' Aamir is not one of them. We met at the end of the well-attended event and I asked Aamir about his dinner plans. He candidly said he had none. 'Come have dinner with us at home,' I had suggested. And he did. At our residence, he ate and drank heartily, posed with the staff sportingly and behaved like a 'normal' guy—not a Bollywood superstar.

This time we were going to his home. Driving to Bandra, we got hopelessly lost, being 'townies' with zero idea of what happens across the Sea Link. Disgraceful! After a great deal of discussion, we'd decided to take a fresh strawberry cake with us, and not a predictable bottle of wine. Azaad would be there, Aamir had said, and possibly, Kiran too, who'd join us if she was free. Great. It's a zero-agenda meeting. No matlab. No occasion. No reason. Just!

Unlike other very grand, noisily glitzy, overtly ostentatious homes of his contemporaries, Aamir continues to live in the same building in which he grew up. He now owns most of it. But, like he said simply, 'I like my family to live close to me—my first wife and our two children reside down the road; Kiran has the floor above and is in and out of this home, where I live with Azaad. My mother lives on another floor ...'

Just then his son Junaid joins us and offers to fetch drinks. Aamir lights up a Sherlock Holmes type pipe, asks for a can of Coke and mixes himself a tall drink with dark rum. Azaad is frighteningly articulate and bright, and Aamir talks to him like an equal. At some point, Kiran walks in and reminds Aamir about a screening in the theatre downstairs. But first—the feast!

Here's a family that takes its food seriously—shabaash! Kiran supervises the arrangements as the staff brings out degchis and platters from the kitchen with piping hot ghar ka khaana. The enticing aromas of exotic spices make me forget all the smart and brilliant things I have planned to share this evening—who knows when Aamir might invite us again? His mother's biryani with a secret ingredient is discussed at length. So is an unusual vegetarian house specialty with mushy potatoes slow cooked in pure ghee. Kebabs? Oh, the many and wondrous versions! Parochialism is in full play as Kiran and Mr Dé converse animatedly in Bangla while extolling the virtues of rolls from Kolkata's Nizam's Restaurant.

The meal has been meticulously planned by Aamir, down to the rich sheera studded with dry fruits. The dishes travel around the table on a lazy Susan as we adopt a fikar-not attitude and tuck in unselfconsciously. Nothing else matters but the tastes dancing on our tongues. It's time to cut the cake before Azaad goes to bed. Azaad instantly transforms into a little boy at the sight of the fresh strawberries, while Kiran cuts a slice for him and reminds Aamir once again that his crew is waiting in the theatre downstairs. Definitely not the right moment to make an impressive-sounding statement about movies I have not seen. We have discussed books, family, food and the brilliant Dr Rajesh Parikh, India's first neuropsychiatrist—a mutual friend. It's a good note to part on … Before Kiran once again … Never mind …

—∿—

SEPTEMBER

'If you worry, you die. If you don't worry, you also die.
So why worry?'

—Mike Horn

I MISS THE MONSOON CLOUDS DRIFTING ACROSS THE WESTERN Ghats. I miss the waterfalls and the lush greenery. I see nothing. My tears are obscuring the glorious vistas as I choke them back and fan myself furiously in an AC car which is already a bit too cold. I notice Choudhary's expression in the rear-view mirror. His brows are deeply creased, and he keeps repeating 'Hari Om' under his breath. The invocation is not for the treacherous, accident-prone hairpin bends of the Khandala–Lonavala stretch. It's for me. I'm running away from a situation I have little control over. It's not a question of who is at fault. Something has tripped. There's been a short circuit inside my heart. My emotions feel electrocuted. I'm battered and drained within. All I want is to flee … think … feel … believe … But how am I going to synchronize my steps with the new rhythm of an unknown experiment?

I'm driving to Pune with just a large carton of books, two paintings, a small suitcase packed with a few clothes, my old-fashioned laptop, writing pads, desk calendar, multigrain bread, biscuits, bottles of champagne and an empty heart. Arundhati calls just then to check if I'm okay as Choudhary drives cautiously up the Ghats, but my words are getting stuck in my throat and my angry tears stay put, refusing to leave my eyes. I've always faced issues with unshed tears. Something to do with not wanting to be labelled a cry baby as a kid. This is freaky as I'm not used to being 'not in control', regardless of circumstances. And what are these terrible circumstances? Nothing unknown or new has transpired. So why the pain?

'Everything has a season.' Aru85 sends me a link with these words after we disconnect the forty-minute call. Aru, the 'proper' Jane Austen woman, is genuinely concerned. She sends me a link of an online motivational speaker who suggests I get hold of 'muslin handkerchiefs' to symbolize my present state of fragility. Where on earth will I find muslin kerchiefs in Pune? I am more a box of disposable tissues kind of person and, in any case, I've never used kerchiefs. The other message talks of 'emotional labour' and goes on to say women are burdened with more than their share of it in a 'patriarchal society'. Tell me something I don't know, darling motivational genius whose identity I don't know! 'Women are socially conditioned to remain silent …' Oh yeah? So, all I need to do is get hold of soft muslin handkerchiefs? 11 inches x 8 inches, the cue board reads. Is this motivational lady a vendor of muslin kerchiefs, I wonder cynically. Or am I being a caustic super bitch? Again? But the thought-provoking line, 'Everything has a season', stays with me, and I feel deeply grateful to Arundhati for sharing it. I am soothed by her deep concern and assure her I will be just fine—need a little downtime, that's all. Bloody liar!

By the time I cross the misty, romantic, dangerous Ghats and reach Pune safely, my eyes are dry. My voice is back. The season is changing … I can feel it. There is a sense of optimism as I say to myself, 'Let's see how it goes … Something good has to come out of this trip.'

The first thing I do after opening the door to my apartment is significant—I rush to chill a bottle of champagne in one of the two refrigerators (the children call it 'the booze fridge'). The place is looking neat and tidy, but sadly three balcony plants have shrivelled up and died. But look, there are fresh new leaves on the ficus, the palms are looking healthy, a cluster of fragrant champa blossoms are about to bloom, the rubber tree has grown, so has the Christmas tree. There is life happening right there on the balcony! And hello! Here's Vaishali, with her light brown dancing eyes, strong white teeth, a gleaming gold mangalsutra around her neck, waiting impatiently to get to work, help me put away the groceries and other samaan, while chattering non-stop in rustic Marathi. She is calling me Aunty with so much affection—and we've just met! Pune has worked its charm on me yet again, so there's no point wallowing in more gloom and doom.

Yes, it's the first time ever that I'm here on my own, unaccompanied by any family members. But so what? Like I had defiantly said to Aru85, 'I have never shunned risks or challenges … this is one more. Your mother always rises … worry not.'

It's time to dip a freshly baked almond biscotti from Theobroma into a steaming cuppa, and sip it slowly on the balcony, while Vaishali kneads atta for chapatis, briskly chops up palak, pumpkin and bhindi, all the while talking to her young son who is soon appearing for the killer tenth standard exam. I spray on some Lavender Mist from Forest Essentials and feel instantly desirable. A touch of MAC's deep red Ruby Woo lip colour takes care of the remnants of any wilted feelings still lingering … Come on, Pune, are you ready for me? I am totally ready for you!

—⁂—

Getting into the Pune rhythm has taken me four days. I am meticulously maintaining my Pune Diaries. Sad to report, but the entries so far are all about 'kaamwali bais'. The days begin and end with the question: Will the bai turn up tomorrow?

In Pune, one is at their mercy. They arrive in shifts, dressed like Phoolan Devis, with just their eyes showing from behind firmly tied head scarves. You can offer them the fees Deepika Padukone charges per endorsement, beg them to stay 24x7 in a comfortable room with an attached loo of their own, but that is not an option. Not here in Pune. Nothing to do with money, they say, but a woman's place is in her home, with her family. The bais sign the evening roster and check into their kholis, incredibly modest dwelling places no bigger than shabby, cramped holes in the wall located in filthy warrens. It's a matter of izzat. Married or unmarried, a Pune bai cannot stay overnight at an employer's home. There are industrious bais who start their day at 5 a.m., cooking for young couples who leave home by 6.30 a.m. with their packed dabbas. The keys to several apartments stay with the bais; it's a matter of trust. Nobody I know has been robbed by a bai in Pune. Well ... I have pleaded with and cajoled the few who showed up, thanks to the network of enterprising ladies who are my neighbours. They are happy to work till 6 p.m. After that it's bye-bye, Aunty.

As I write, I am alone in my apartment. The morning bai has come and gone. The afternoon bai may or may not turn up. Vaishali had promised, 'Ek ladies aayegi ... Sushila Tai.' Not a single ladies turned up. It's a Sunday. Their schoolgoing children need them around. So do the useless, drunken husbands. Heavy jeans of teenage sons have to be washed, along with clothes carelessly discarded by grown daughters who attend college. The kholi has to be swept and thoroughly scrubbed, the week's rations organized, and then the next week's routine begins again ...

But some good has come out of my Pune experiment. I have finally learnt how to use most of the fancy gadgets in my 'fully loaded' apartment after a crash course in appliances from my son-in-law Pramod. I managed to heat last night's leftovers in the Korean microwave, load the German dishwasher, get the Japanese washing machine going and sync my iPhone to the laptop to locate the mysterious hotspot (sounds so erogenous, like looking for the G-spot!). In a while, I shall get the English electric kettle to heat enough water for my cuppa. No leaf tea, please—it's going to be teabags from now on ... so much more convenient. Darjeeling or English Breakfast. I can sense myself changing, adapting, learning and coping. All of it, most positive, given that I have never lived on my own in seventy-five years. Not once! I wonder why.

It's a pretty good feeling and time certainly does not hang heavy as everyone had warned me. That's my big takeaway. Time is not weighing me down; I am luxuriating in it. A new routine is gradually replacing the older, far more regimented one. I have discovered several secret strengths which I know will only empower me further, moving forward. Oh … my own company is not too bad either! Nor is eating alone at a large dining table set for one. Whoever said it 'sounds depressing' can go to hell! I am enjoying the space I had lovingly created three years ago … entirely on a whim. It's a space I'd be foolish not to make the most of—I love it! I mentally thank Sagar Chordia (a prominent Pune builder who, along with his older brother Atul, have been my main connect to Pune for thirty years) and Vicky Nagrani (managing director of Rock Realty) who had made this apartment a reality. (Oh, The Chordias are also on Donald Trump's speed dial. They are the promoters of the twenty-three-storey Trump Towers condominium in Pune, and I got to meet 'The Donald' in 2016 at a reception in his honour when the project was launched.)

My Pune apartment is a far cry from a luxe condo in the posh Trump Towers, but it's lovely! It was acquired blindly over WhatsApp videos sent by Vicky, who did me the great courtesy of not laughing out loud when I entrusted him with the job of buying the apartment without my ever having seen it in person! I liked what I saw in his videos, okay?

No wonder I experience a special thrill—let's call it a frisson—the moment I walk in. I stop myself and ask, 'Is this place really mine? What a cute powder room!'

Right now, I am looking out through the large window of the dining area of my modern sixteenth-floor apartment and admiring the low hills around Pune. Rain clouds are lingering over the ancient Aravalli ridges and hiding a few low peaks. I haven't switched on the fan even once during the daytime, and that in itself is a liberation of sorts. I'm reading reports about the scorcher of a summer in England and other parts of Europe, and smiling. The asphalt roads are melting under people's shoes, and tourists are jumping into the fountains at Trafalgar Square. Elsewhere, in France, forest fires are lighting up the night sky, and a few people have died of heatstrokes in Spain. Come to Pune, mates, and share a cold artisanal beer with me!

—m—

The electrician calls to say he's not coming because it is Nag Panchami. I've never understood why we worship snakes on Nag Panchami. But I do know (thanks to a great piece by Devdutt Pattanaik explaining its significance) that it's not about doing puja to snakes or feeding them milk (they don't drink milk) but rather it is a festival that marks Lord Krishna's victory over Kaliya Nag, the dreaded, multihooded snake who resided in the Yamuna. In Maharashtra, black sesame laddoos are made at home and fed to the Nag devta. Housewives avoid cooking in iron vessels and farmers refrain from ploughing the field fearing a snake may get killed. Some families create snake idols out of clay and worship them. Since our family is not among the snake worshippers, I really am clueless about the do's and don'ts of Nag Panchami when I open the door for the bais who arrive bright and early, dressed to their teeth. Both are wearing vibrantly coloured, nine-yard kashta saris where the drape goes between the legs, much like a dhoti. Vaishali in magenta with a deep purple and gold border, Sujata in haldi-yellow with an orange and gold border, her low-backed choli fastened with satin tassels. They are wearing two mangalsutras each—one long, one short—and jhumkis on their ears. I take many pictures of them and discover how gracefully and naturally they pose for the camera.

My mood is good and I'm feeling chatty enough to request Sujata to hold the dusting and tell me why she bunked for two days without informing me.

'My daughter's wedding got fixed. Her future in-laws were visiting,' she beams.

I am instantly silenced. The same daughter who's appearing for her final BSc exam? Yes, the same. And the prospective groom?

'He paid us ₹5 lakh for her hand,' Sujata says flatly.

What? He paid? Isn't it supposed to be the other way round?

She explains in plain lingo, 'The boy is an orphan raised by his uncles … he doesn't earn much, and there is no house in his name. The five lakhs are to be deposited in my daughter's name as her security, in case anything goes wrong.'

Good on you! Practical and no-nonsense when it comes to basics. But why marry off the girl? Does she like the fellow at all?

Sujata's horse sense kicks in again. 'She wants to study for two more years—the boy has agreed. He will treat her well,' she says.

Was any formal ceremony performed to mark the betrothal?

'Yes, we exchanged suparis ...'

That was it? A solemn pledge sealed with a supari? Perhaps, that's where the more sinister usage among gangsters of 'supari' originates? An assassination sealed with a supari.

It made me think of all the complex negotiations parents from my background are forced to get into when a family marriage looms. I think of a recent request from a senior journalist friend who wanted me to 'recommend' a suitable match for her wealthy friend's daughter, reasoning, 'You know a lot of rich people in Mumbai ... the rishta has to be of a certain level.'

Obviously, the level being financial, not emotional, educational, recreational or physical. I replied, 'I have two children who are single ... besides, I don't believe in forging "rishtas".'

And here was Sujata's formula! How simple and direct this down-to-earth, illiterate lady made it sound. I asked her if her daughter was pleased with the decision—sold for Rs 5 lakh to a stranger whose job prospects were far less attractive than hers. Sujata's reply, 'She is already twenty-one,' said it all.

To me, this clinical approach to a child's future may appear cold-blooded and unilateral. To Sujata, it is the right and only way. Who decides what's fair?

'The boy has agreed to wait for two more years ... How much longer could we expect him to wait?'

I weakly stutter, 'There are other boys ...'

Sujata looked away. 'Any guarantee about those boys?'

Sorry, Sujata. You are right. No guarantees. Nobody gave any of us guarantees either. What works, works. What doesn't ...

We are often reminded in harsh tones: you aren't illiterate women
... you knew exactly what you were getting into when you were
getting married.

Did we, really?

—❦—

It's late evening and my cell phone alerts are going nuts! What gives?
Don't tell me Lalit and Sushmita have divorced before getting married?

Oh oh—we have a scandal! Niceeee!

Ranveer has bared his butt and much else while I was busy finishing
my beer. It is all over the news, and I am wondering what the fuss is
about. Had he done the full monty, I might have understood the hysteria
generated by a superstar's exposed genitals. But come on—look! It's just
a well-oiled, well-toned derriere. Get over it! Filing FIRs for a bum shot?
Yashraj Mukhote's instant video 'We can see his bum' is going viral. Those
exposed buns are making waves in India and abroad. Ridic, right? Too
tame and too lame, man! Grow up, have another beer ...

—❦—

It is the first Shravani Somwar today—traditionally observed by young,
unmarried girls, who keep a strict fast on the four or five Mondays that
fall during Shravan, the fifth month of the Hindu calendar. It is a month
dedicated to Lord Shiva, and a vrat is kept to seek his blessings. For several
years, I observed this semi-strict fast on Mondays in this most auspicious
month in the Hindu calendar. Why? I don't know. Did my mother fast
during Shravan? Frankly, I have no recollection. Did we eat hardcore
satvik food for a month? No garlic, no onions, no meats? I draw a blank.

I do however remember Aie making sabudana khichdi, grated sweet
potato cooked in ghee with a simple tadka of jeera, unspiced potato gravy,
varya chha bhaat (broken rice), peanut curry tempered with shahi jeera
and green chillies, thick pumpkin-stuffed puris and a velvety shrikhand

liberally decorated with strands of Kashmiri saffron, pre-soaked in milk. Yes, the daily morning and evening pujas at her tiny kitchen shrine were a little more elaborate on Shravan Mondays, and dinner was served early, as All India Radio Bombay played appropriate aartis and devotional songs on Baba's World War II–era radio.

My determination to fast on Mondays, shun non-vegetarian preparations and abstain from wine for a month may or may not have been a strictly religious decision. I believe it was more an exercise in self-discipline, with a few vanity issues involved. The calories were restricted, and extra kilos got shed without too much pain! By 6 p.m. I would be in a ravenously hungry state, ready to devour just about anything—but, of course, one is expected to wait for the sun to set before putting food in the mouth.

Years later, Aru85 decided to join me and observe Shravan rituals herself. This was great, as we had each other to offer sympathies to. We bonded over bondas and listened to each other's growling tum tums. Believe me, it isn't easy, even though we weren't really 'fasting'-fasting. Speaking for myself, I did feel virtuous and pious for a while. But my body rebelled at one point, my immunity levels tanked, I kept picking up bugs that left me feeling weakened, listless and crochety. It simply wasn't worth it! All I could think of during Shravan was food and wine! I'd start counting the days when I could raise a glass and enjoy myself. Since Aditya's birthday falls in September, often the tail end of Shravan would overlap with the janamdin celebration. And I'd feel seriously deprived, left out of the feasting and drinking.

I recall one particular birthday at a newly opened restaurant in our neighbour's gorgeous hotel, the Art Deco–inspired Intercontinental on Marine Drive. It was just us and a few of Aditya's friends. Everyone was having the best time but me. I heard sounds of animated conversation, much laughter and the tempting clinking of glasses from a private, sectioned-off area in the huge restaurant. Uffff! Another party! Merde! Just then a familiar voice yelled out, 'Shobhaaaa … hey … come and

join us.' It was Tina Ambani celebrating Supriya Sule's something—
anniversary? So much merriment and mirth, and here I was feeling
martyred and khadoos!

Perhaps, that was the night I decided this wasn't working. I wasn't
feeling what I was supposed to feel. My emotions were stuck in the
craving-for-food groove. My thoughts about food and wine had turned
compulsive. This was counterproductive. I had nothing to prove to
anyone. I had tried for a few years and failed to convert this deprivation
into higher thought and a meditative mindset. I enthusiastically accepted
a glass of champagne from Tina—and there my tryst with fasting on
Shravani Somwar abruptly ended.

But this year, I am in Pune. Guilt is weighing heavily on me. Vaishali,
the bai with the strong, white teeth, has walked in dressed in bright, festive
colours to mark the first Monday of the holy month. I look at my own
self, inappropriately dressed in a strappy Anokhi maxi and wonder what
Vaishali must think of her newest 'Aunty'. She is in a rush, but briskly
makes aloo parathas for nashta, karela sabzi and sprouted matki daal for
lunch. I have not dared to ask her to cook chicken so far, or fish for that
matter. Raju, the famous neighbourhood fishwala, provides the best river
fish, the neighbours say. But I'll wait till after Shravan to visit him at his
stall behind the municipal office, close to the Ganpati statue.

My improvised lunch is disgraceful! Smoked salmon with lots of
Tabasco, honey-glazed ham slices with Camembert cheese, to be eaten on
buttered multigrain bread, heavy with assorted seeds on the crust. Narayan
has arranged the lunch tray very neatly and attractively, with wedges of
imported lemon (not local limbu) placed next to finely diced white onion
for the salmon. Ah ... who is Narayan, you ask?

Narayan is an all-weather, all-purpose handyman, valet and much
more. There's nothing Narayan will admit he can't do. In his ambitions
and imagination, he is bigger and richer than Ratan Tata. He dreams
in millions and is desperate to own a fancy apartment. His tastes are so
refined and extravagant, I feel embarrassed to let him judge my far more
modest standards of living. Narayan instinctively goes for the best of

the best—only top of the line products will do. While with me in Pune, he sniffs at poha and upma for breakfast and has located a source for edamame beans close by. When he puts together a breakfast tray, it is better than a seven-star hotel's effort. Only, I am unable to keep up. I dare not complain about the fresh cucumber-green-apple-bitter-gourd-ginger morning juice in a tall, frosted glass, placed on a tiny, enamelled tray I did not know I possessed.

'Baba ko aisa sab pasand hai,' he says about my son, Aditya, Narayan's current employer.

Aditya is a shehzada ... Who am I? I think. A hard-working, middle-class Maharashtrian senior citizen—that's who. Call me 'ghati', it's fine! Proud to be a ghati—I don't look at it as a put-down. My ancestors were from Kolhapur and Goa, not the Ghats, but that's a minor detail. All Maharashtrians are called 'ghatis' in Mumbai. Some mean it as a slur. I take it as a compliment.

I am getting used to the Narayan treatment. For example, this morning, Narayan gave me a long list of what he felt was missing in our Pune lives and from the refrigerator. I am sharing it here, with his unique spellings intact:

Rockit salad pata
Mashrum
Celary
Ice Burg
Roman pata
Cherry tamatar
Bezel patta
Brocali
Englis kukumber
Pinto beans
Tuskan Kale salad
Zukini
Parseley

Kosher salt
Kinoa
Maple syrup
Pomugrant
Blue berry
Mulberry
Rasberry
Strawberry
Extra vargin olive oil
Balsimac bhinegar

Phew!

I was relieved Narayan had skipped foie gras and caviar. I told him I wasn't opening a restaurant in Pune and all I needed was a basic salad at lunch. Narayan looked crestfallen. 'Par Baba ke ghar yeh sab rakte hai …'

Well, I am not my son. Did Narayan just downgrade me?

Narayan is a slight-framed, delicate Nepali, with artistic hands and shining eyes. He's a long way from his home in the mountains, but clearly does not miss his folks. He now works for Aditya in his Malabar Hill flat, but at one point he used to work at our home in Cuffe Parade, till he was asked to leave for a variety of reasons. Who cares? That's history. Only the present matters. And Narayan is my ally and saviour in Pune. He is just there, happy to take on any task with a huge grin on his face. Having Narayan around is like tucking oneself under a soft duvet on a harsh, cold night in an unfamiliar land. This is my emotional state at present. I am in feelings ka wilderness. Narayan makes me feel less alone as he briskly goes about making changes around my apartment, moving things around, fixing stuff that needs fixing. He has repaired a leaking tap in the kitchen sink and shown me how to use a rice cooker. He has successfully handled the highly inconvenient, ongoing internet problem and knows how to pay for groceries over Paytm. Narayan carries four cell phones. That should worry me, but it doesn't. The lad likes his gadgets, I rationalize.

Narayan is a little like the character played by Matt Damon in the 1999 psychological thriller, *The Talented Mr Ripley*. Cunning, mentally agile, charming, observant and wily. But, my God, is he efficient! There is nothing Narayan won't throw himself into with gusto. An extension of my Pune stay has been made possible thanks to Narayan's presence Narayan has given me a gift even he isn't aware of—the priceless chance to just be, since he decides what I eat and when it should be served.

Today, however, the infallible Narayan has erred.

Busy as I've been, dealing with the ever-exasperated Mr Bhimani, my chartered accountant (who speaks to me like one speaks to an inattentive, dull-in-the-head child), going on about suspense accounts and advance tax payments, I have left it to Narayan to fix lunch. When I look up from my writing pad, I see the tray with rolls of smoked salmon, ham, cheese and much else. I promptly take a picture and send it to the children on our Brood chat group. Aditya is the first one to scold, 'Mom! What is this? So much processed food!' He sends me a picture of his lunch—green vegetable juice and lightly sautéed veggies with a few nuts and seeds. I instantly shrivel up with shame. The girls follow with their comments on unhealthy eating habits and how Pune is ruining my discipline. They are right. Instead of eating both the buttered toasts with cheese, salmon, ham, I sacrifice one. And feel instantly better. I pass on the dark chocolate with fruits and nuts which Narayan has solicitously offered. My halo is gleaming! Come on … I'm in Pune. No minders around to control my every waking minute. I am free to eat, sleep, drink, pray, read, dance, sing and vegetate at will.

But the remote control (and my heart) still remains in Mumbai with the Brood. How we kid ourselves, na?

—m—

'Everything slows down with age, except the time it takes cake and ice cream to reach your hips.'

—**John Wagner**

Today, the local cops came a-calling and the big challenge facing me was what I should serve them over high tea, considering it was the second Monday of Shravan.

One of my visitors is Sandeep Karnik, the joint commissioner of police, who was earlier posted in Mumbai. It showed in the informality of our WhatsApp exchanges, where we did not adhere to officialize, preferring short forms, even slang, while setting up a convenient time for the meeting. He said he'd be bringing his DCP with him, and I said I'd invite my Pune-based sister, Mandakini Tata, who, in turn, said she'd bring along her financial advisor. Mandakini relocated to Pune a decade ago, after spending thirty years in New York. Pune is taking its time to grow on my attractive, adventurous octogenarian sister—a former banker and current world traveller. Well ... New York, it isn't ... But does NYC have a Shaniwar Wada? Or vada pav?

It is turning into quite a party and Narayan is getting a bit too enthu, suggesting a fancy Mumbai-style menu. I have to calm him down and remind him it's Shravani Somwar, the cops are Maharashtrian, and grilled ham sandwiches, asparagus rolls, avocado on toast or strawberry tarts, even mango cheesecake, should be strictly avoided. He looks crestfallen, probably wondering what sort of lowly 'ghaas-phoos' to serve. I am about to suggest dahi misal and vada pav but quickly bite my tongue, hastily recalling the trouble I had got into with the Shiv Sena (SS), whose netas accused me of 'making fun' of vada pav. Two-and-half years of living under police protection after irate Shiv Sainiks arrived at my door to present me with vada pav, I don't want the local SS Shakha in Pune to track me down and offer me a 'gift' of dahi misal. By this time, Choudhary has also decided to get involved in structuring the menu for the visiting cops, till I remind him he'd be better off attending to the remote-controlled car key which is on the blink.

I pack off both the men—Narayan and Choudhary—and tell them to go on a focused satvik Shravan faraal hunt in the locality. They luck out soon enough! The triumphant grins on their faces as they walk in bearing parcels of sabudana vada, dhokla, chivda, chakli, mithai and, at my request, eggless walnut brownies from Theobroma, tell me the cops won't leave hungry from my home.

Then, two rather unexpected things happen. I had presumed the DCP and the financial advisor were men and I'm wrong about both. For a few seconds, I'm totally thrown by my blinkered conclusions. Bewakoof aurat, I scold myself, before regaining my composure and greeting the guests. This is stereotyping of the Neanderthal kind, and I'm no better than all those people who automatically address every woman in authority as 'sir', or for better emphasis, 'madam sirji', especially in Delhi.

The evening goes off splendidly. I discover that Namrata Patil, the 'Lady DCP', as she is politely called by her senior, is a mother of three daughters—the eldest followed by twins. She is beaming when I ask if her girls are proud of her—do they feel she is special, particularly when she dons her smart uniform? She replies candidly, 'Not really! They see me in this vardi every day and to them I am just their mother going to work.' She has had to reach for her gun just once, when she was with the prestigious National Investigation Agency (NIA), based in Mumbai, chasing terrorists in a dark forest. It was Mission Accomplished—the men were nabbed and jailed—but not before making her think this was going to be her end. 'At that moment, I was sure I would die during the operation … that fear kept me more alert … I wanted to stay alive for the girls.'

I want to instantly hug her but think better of it. We are Maharashtrians. We are not supposed to act too 'forward' and hug cops. We are too uptight to even hug family members! Besides, she is sipping a cup of piping hot kadak chai and her senior is taking constant calls from some VVIP given the number of times he says 'Sir' and leaves his Chitale chakli half-eaten. The DCP, happily dunking biscuits into her tea, looks up and says, 'Don't mind, na? Purani habit hai.'

I assure her there is no point in serving biscuits with tea if one can't dunk them and then time the retrieval. Too soggy? Just right? Or did the bikkie sink to the bottom of the teacup? I'm really enjoying the biscuit banter with a lady who has cracked the toughest terrorists through her hard questioning. Here we are discussing the merits of cream-filled wafer biscuits versus Irani butter khaari. She narrates an amusing story of a prospective bride from her family who rejected the callow prospective groom based on his tea-drinking etiquette. 'The mulgi did not like it when the mulga dipped biscuits in his tea and later sipped the same tea from a saucer.' We are about to launch into an animated discourse on Kolhapuri chivda when the boss man indicates it's time to bounce. We pose for pics (Insta strikes again!) with Choudhary art directing Narayan's shoot, making sure the frame is good and includes all of us. I'm glad about this visit. My sister is eighty-six and lives all alone in Pune, and I'm on a solo stay myself. It's difficult to mess with women who live on their own if word gets out that their BFFs are top cops who come to tea in uniform, with red and blue lights blazing on their police cars. No wonder the surly security guard downstairs thokos a smart salaam when I leave for dinner later.

The political situation in Maharashtra is at a fascinating stage, with back-stabbing accusations and rebels launching their own rival party. The state's newest chief minister is driving to Pune the next day to inspect Ganpati pandals and to generally make his presence felt as a neta who means business. I can hear sirens as Pune cops—generally invisible—are whizzing all over the city to make sure the new guy in the hot seat stays safe and secure while in the city. I'm dying to chat informally with my visitors and ask if they identify with cop representation in commercial cinema. After all, the handsome and very fit joint commissioner who is busy admiring Tanjores on my wall is dashing enough to play 'Simmba' or take over Salman Khan's role as Chulbul Pandey in *Dabangg* (2010). Thinking it'll seem a bit too flirty, I stop myself. Besides, I don't want my

Mumbai-based friend Sharlene Batlivala, who runs a powerful PR firm dealing with showbiz luminaries, to feel 'what was she thinking?' After all … it was she who had set up the meeting.

Their arrival has generated enough excitement in the complex, with neighbours wondering why senior cops are at my home. Since I hardly interact with anyone and rarely leave my apartment, the unexpected presence of vardiwaley mehmaan must have tickled other residents. Ana-Banana, in faraway Vienna, sees the picture I shared on the Brood chat, and panics. 'Why have the cops arrived? What have you done now? Are you being arrested for something stupid you tweeted? Really, Mama, you are the limit!'

Wow! I love the reputation I enjoy with my children!

My Twitter history is muddled and idiotic. I have a paradoxical, one-sided relationship with this particular social media platform. When I started tweeting back in 2009, I was having fun, recklessly expressing opinions and laughing at the hyperventilation that followed. Since I did not engage with trolls or establish any Twitter relationships, I felt detached enough to compose tweets that were witty and acerbic, at least according to me … But clearly there were powerful people out there who weren't amused. Trolls? Aah—them! I didn't read comments, and that hasn't changed. I tweet … and move on. But that's not how this game is played, right?

Today, I tweet far more infrequently than I did five years ago. It's no longer fun. The thrill's missing. I prefer Instagram—it's less corrosive and more enjoyable. As of now, there are over 136K interested (I like to think!) followers, and the numbers have grown organically from the time I began posting in 2014. At the time of writing this, my posts number 7,500. I follow less than forty people or sites, and the people who comment on my posts on a regular basis sound alarmingly young. This explains my attraction to Insta! Only idiots pontificate on Insta, while everybody else lives in a hallucinatory bubble where all things bright and beautiful exist in perfect harmony. People say Insta causes anxiety. I don't get it! I mean I neither get anxiety because of Insta nor do I understand why it generates anxiety in others. Post away, folks. Nothing is too insignificant on Insta—not even your new pimple. The imaginary and vividly imagined lives of strangers keep Insta 'hot'. I like the heat in this kitchen.

My Twitter account is only as active as I want it to be. It has never been pro-active—and that decision stays. There are over 2.5 million followers—I neither check who they are, nor care. Facebook? Dull and static. Not for me, even though I am on it in a very listless fashion and the account is private. Which is a joke—*nothing* is private in the universe any longer, if it ever was. Every single post, or even call, can be tracked. Privacy does not exist. It's easier to accept this idea and come to terms with it, minus illusions. There is no place left to hide on this planet. Be nanga. Be naked. Big brother has seen everything in any case. I have 150 friends on FB—mainly writers, publishers, painters, photographers, artists. They are not randoms I've connected with on the FB platform—most are old friends. It feels like a cosy community of like-minded people but it sure does get boring to be in an echo chamber minus any fireworks and personal attacks. Just standard polite noises that mean nothing and the anxiety about how many likes a post receives and from whom.

I have never googled myself. Nor have I checked what's on Wikipedia. Not bothering about wiki content is not smart; it's seriously dumb, I know. But then again I am a one-woman battalion, doing everything on my own, without an assistant or a social media team to 'position me' and filter content. Despite this lapse, one of these days, I shall do something about one painful wiki entry that bugs the hell out of me. Let me put it out there: I am not the Jackie Collins of India. Please! Just because over twenty years ago an American foreign correspondent working with *Time* magazine called me that in a lazily written profile he got handsomely paid for does not mean I subscribe to his off-hand description! For better perspective, how about this: I am not the Jackie Collins of India, I am Anuradha from Satara.

Social media is a devil. Can't live with it, can't live without it. FB and Insta wants users to post reels. Stories are out! Reels are in. Keep shooting those videos, darrrrrlings … shake your booty … you are Nora Fatehi …

I often half-joke that if you are not on Instagram, you don't exist. It's worth quoting Walter Bagehot, the brilliant British journalist, businessman, essayist who wrote, 'To be invisible is to be forgotten. To be a symbol and an effective symbol, you must be vividly and often seen.'

India's prime minister must be a big fan of Bagehot.

—ɷ—

'Age is something that doesn't matter, unless you are a cheese.'
—Luis Bunuel

'Is the Discovery Channel still on?' asks Nicku, an old friend from my college days, now settled in Pune with her affable, laid-back husband Sayajirao Gaekwad. There's blue blood on both sides in this love marriage.

I laugh and say lightly, 'Absolutely! A fresh discovery every minute.'

It is our private joke, after Arundhati described my Pune stay to Rana as 'Mom's on Discovery Channel'. Initially, Rana thought I was shooting an adventure series in Pune for the popular international channel till he caught on to what Arundhati was trying to tell him obliquely—I was taking some much-needed time out for myself and in the process making a few startling discoveries, mainly about myself.

Rana calls from Koh Samui to ask how I'm doing and is full of encouragement as he jokes about my newfound freedom. 'About time, Mom!' he signs off after I assure him I'm okay and rather enjoying the new normal, doing mundane things I'm not required to handle in Mumbai. Aru85 had only half-joked when she narrated my day in Pune, saying, 'Mom is cleaning and scrubbing, doing the dishes and washing clothes.' Well, yes and no. The unaccustomed, unfamiliar domestic chores are definitely nightmare-inducing but equally therapeutic in a paradoxical way. My meals are mainly vegetarian, and I have much more agency over my time, food, sleep, activities, even thoughts. Nice. Each new day is like filming a fresh episode for my personal Discovery Channel and I'm having great fun. This is my very own reality show. Savouring a 'new, improved' lifestyle, one bite at a time.

So, it's true. Pune is fast becoming not a second home, a weekend home nor a staycation home. It's becoming my 'home'-home. I like it here. I like the space and all that's in it. These are 'my things'. Only mine. If they are admired and appreciated, my heart soars! Pune has always worked for me. Perhaps it is a karmic connection. Or maybe there's a simpler explanation—I connect to my Maharashtrian roots in Pune, even though, ironically, I don't know any Maharashtrians here. And I am not even all that confident about my own 'Marathi manoos' identity. All I know is that Pune feels good. Pune feels right. Pune feels me.

I see myself gravitating towards a new life in Peshwa City. The sheer pleasure of stopping strangers to make enquiries and breaking into Marathi gives me a kick. Even when I'm spurned. A stern young woman at a local bank I went to yesterday was not amused when I asked her a question in Marathi. She stared at me coldly and snapped, 'Madam, English or Hindi only. No Marathi.' I thanked her for being so polite and helpful, but my sarcasm was wasted. She glared and went back to her laptop. I looked around the shabby branch of the bank near my home and smiled. A Ferrari roared down the road, narrowly missing five buffaloes waddling into a swamp just off the highway. Two young men sporting bright purple and magenta hair looked up disinterestedly when I asked for directions to the nearest supermarket—I had run out of milk, tissue boxes, kitchen towels, toor dal ...

These are tiny but significant aspects of my Pune stay that are telling me so many things about myself, my priorities, my choices. It is the far more relaxed air in Pune that I appreciate. It is not a 'slow life'—it is a richer, less hectic life. I sleep better, breathe better and, clearly, I eat better, especially with Narayan around! Even the fact that I barely have any friends here is most attractive. I am on my own in more ways than one. This is new to me ... the rhythm of my life is changing—has changed. I am discovering that 'slower is superior' indeed—a radical concept, alien to me! My balcony garden is expanding with new potted plants and flowering creepers. I gaze at fluffy clouds and patches of blue sky while I read, swaying gently in an antique, rosewood jhoola, the mid-morning quiet broken by noisy jets from the Air Force base at Lohegaon close by from where the No. 20 Squadron (Lightnings) flies sorties in Sukhoi Su-30MKI fighter jets.

In the early evening, I hear kids squealing with delight in the large sandpit where my grandkids play when they visit Nani. The last time

Adhiraj was here, he told his father, 'We must not leave Nani alone. If she's staying back, we should also stay with her.' I hugged him, making sure to hide my aansoo. Children instinctively sense suppressed emotions that adults frequently miss. Adhiraj had figured out what even I hadn't registered at that point—Nani was feeling sad right now, but Nani was also happy because Nani was finally where she wanted to be!

—⁓—

'Time may be a great healer, but it's a lousy beautician.'

—Anonymous

Star Bazaar, inside Season's Mall next door, has become my regular haunt. It's almost an addiction. I get withdrawal symptoms if I stay away for more than two days, so I find excuses to go there in search of nailclippers, face scrubs, green tea. Local friends tease me mercilessly. Most of them wouldn't deign to step inside such a bazaar when they've been regulars at the far more exclusive and upmarket Dorabjee's, where the sales staff greet them by their names and know exactly what they are looking for—the best of the best cuts in meats, imported artichokes and Brussel sprouts.

'That place! Shobhaa, you can't be serious! You shop *there*?' they exclaim in utter disbelief.

Errrr ... yes, indeed I do, Ma'am, because deep down I am a thrifty Maharashtrian housewife and die when I have to pay a bomb for the best macaroons in Pune at the très chic French Window Patisserie in Koregaon Park. I would rather get my tea cake at the supermarket and stick to ears of local corn, which I steam, slather with Amul butter, and sprinkle salt and pepper on. You can keep your rich, gooey Belgian chocolate cake with kafir lime slivers, thank you.

I kick myself for not discovering Star Bazaar on previous visits to Pune. I'd bring cartons of food from Mumbai, behaving like I was travelling to a desert outpost instead of the bustling, busy, modern, exciting city with every conceivable amenity one could ask for, which is exactly what today's Pune is. On my virgin visit to Star Bazaar, I behaved like a kid who'd been let loose in Legoland. I couldn't get over the vast array of goods, neatly labelled and well displayed in aisle after aisle. The prices were unbelievable as well, so naturally I went nuts buying things I had zero use for. On that visit, my cart was overloaded at the end of two hours of hectic shopping for useless items. Since it's a Tata enterprise, the product range is comprehensive and so is the quality of goods. I called the Brood triumphantly to crow about my latest domestic victory and they were

vastly amused. 'Mom gets thrifty. What next? Ration shops?' No problem.
I had also made three new friends during my time at the supermarket.

Check out this scenario: I was looking utterly lost and bewildered,
walking around peering at shelves, randomly picking up fresh vegetables
… gobi, lauki, gajar … when I noticed people staring and giving me
strange looks. Two attractive young women came up and asked, 'Are you
by any chance …?'

I nodded sheepishly as if to say, 'Please don't judge me, I'm new here.'

Then they squealed with delight as the lady with short hair demanded
an instant hug. 'We love you!' she said, introducing her friend. 'We are
both single moms and shop here regularly. Here … please … allow us to
help you. These are the paper bags … fill your veggies into them, go to
the weighing counter, have the bags tagged, and then line up at any cash
counter to pay.'

Seeing the dumb expression on my face, they did all of this for me,
saying, 'It's okay, we have time and you are not used to this system.' I
was so touched. I mean—who does this? That's not where the story ends.
As I waited for the weighing process, they pointed to another counter,
'Pick up the famous Pune chivda here … and these savouries are great at
teatime … look … north Indian matahadis! You can make quick sev puri
with them. There's dahi in that cold storage, and the tamarind paste is in
aisle number 20. Just add chopped onions and dhaniya on top—it's yum.
Oh don't forget to pick up a packet of whole-wheat pizza bases—very
convenient when you don't feel like cooking.' I didn't say it, but wanted
to: Honey, I never feel like cooking.

We exchanged numbers and they've invited me home! Meanwhile,
I am exulting in how much money I have 'saved' shopping at my new
Mecca! Biodegradable green garbage bags—jumbo pack! Yayy.

As I was exiting the mall and looking for Choudhary, one of the
security ladies walked up to ask, 'Madamji, aapke muh par kya hai?'

My hand flew to my face.

She smiled, put her face mask down and said, 'Aap muh par kya lagati
hai … kaunsa cream?'

Phew! She pointed to her face, pitted with acne, and asked for skincare tips. I reached into my cane handbag from Bangkok and pulled out a jar of Pond's cold cream (I never leave home without a jar or two within easy reach).

She stared at it, and asked, 'Achcha hai?'

I formed 'O' with my thumb and index finger indicating that it was 'bahut achcha'. She turned the jar around in her hand, the other hand still holding the metal detector.

'Aap rakh lo … try karo … Next time, batana achcha hai ki nahi,' I said.

She slipped it quickly into her trouser pocket before the supervisor caught her. Then she touched my cheek lightly and whispered, 'Thhunk you, Didi.'

I now had one more legit reason to revisit the mall after a few days—I had to check on her skin!

I got back and requested Narayan to haul the loot home and place it on the blindingly white counters of the huge island kitchen. Had I lost it totally? What was I planning to do with eight toilet rolls, four jumbo Harpic toilet cleaners, six kitchen mops, twelve airtight storage containers, eight tufted bath mats, two large, bright red plastic bins, three different types of atta, five pulses, four dals, three economy packs of lemony, grass-green, sticky bath gels, and—wait for it—all the Mysore Sandal Soaps I found on the counter.

Why so many soaps? Because Mysore Sandal Soap is not just another soap! It is the luxury soap of my childhood. The one Baba would buy for us during Diwali to be used sparingly for the pre-dawn 'snaan'. The one that effectively washed away the fragrant oil Aie had massaged us with, and the one that stayed firm in the plastic soap dish while inferior soaps got pulpy and yucky. The sight of Mysore Sandal Soap in Star Bazaar, lying hidden behind today's 'it' soaps, made me want to protect it. 'Hold your head high, Soap!' I crooned, cradling it against my cheek and taking deep breaths of the packaging! This was the fragrance of my childhood, the fragrance of innocence and joy. It reminded me of the sandalwood paste my mother ground on a small stone platform to anoint the foreheads of all the framed deities in our modest shrine. At that moment, in the crowded aisle of Star Bazaar, I heard God talking, as my mother looked on and smiled at her child—me!

Of course, it was understood I would be heading back to Mumbai soon. Rather, everyone had taken it for granted I would. But I was in two minds. I was not ready to go back just yet. Nor was I experiencing any withdrawal symptoms. In fact, I was revelling in my newly minted life of being on my own. The brood would have none of it. 'That's enough, Mom … make sure you get back in time for Aru85's birthday …' Well, put like that, I was left with zero options. I didn't want to be a 'bad puppy' with the fam.

By that weekend, I knew it was time. I reluctantly packed my small bag, closed down the flat, switched off the mains, gave all the unused food items to Vaishali, kissed my beloved balcony plants goodbye, kept the laundry bag ready for the dhobi to collect from Vaishali, and informed Narayan and Choudhary we were heading to Mumbai. Just in time for Ganpati Bappa's dramatic arrival …

—⚬—

'None are so old as those who have outlived enthusiasm.'
—**Henry David Thoreau**

'You can tell Bappa anything. Our Ganeshji is known to listen to everyone. He also sees everything. Right now, he is looking at you and hearing this conversation. Ask him for something you are praying hard for ... Your wish will be heard and granted. This is the power of our Ganpati ...'

And then, this exceptionally helpful, highly educated and enormously successful 'volunteer', Gurudatta, at the Goud Sarawat Brahmin (GSB) seva mandal at King's Circle, lowers his voice and tells me, 'Uddhavji had come here before he became chief minister (CM) ... Our Guruji predicted it ... Ganpati Bappa heard his prayer and Uddhavji became Maharashtra's CM soon after.' After this nugget is shared, he casually mentions, 'You just missed Aaditya Thackeray by five minutes. He just left after a good darshan ... and Devendra Fadnavisji is coming at 10 p.m. In case you want to meet him.' There is no reference to Eknath Shinde, the current chief minister. Shri Shinde is Maratha, not GSB. Will he still be CM next year?

Wow! The majestic Ganpati at the sixty-eight-year-old mandal is going to have a pretty busy night ahead of him. God knows what sort of unreasonable demands have been made this evening. I didn't want to overburden Ganeshji with my maamuli requests. Since I am not contesting elections or hoping to become CM of Maharashtra, why waste the God's time on mundanities? Best we join in the aarti, which is about to begin ...

This is the sixty-eighth year of the GSB seva mandal's sarvajanik festival and I am looking around with my chest puffing up with pride and eyes gleaming at the grandeur of it all. These are 'my' people (I am a GSB) and just look at them and what they are doing! All the inspiring socially relevant projects undertaken by them are in the public domain. But the media stories this year are only about wealth—this being the wealthiest pandal in Mumbai. It is the only one with a staggering, record-breaking

217

₹316-crore insurance cover. The idol is richly adorned, with 66 kilos of gold and 295 kilos of silver.[4] I feel rich! My community is prosperous, successful, charitable—and good-looking! But more than that, I am seriously impressed by the impeccable organization and high level of security, all of it achieved through the sevaks who come from around the world to participate in the festival. They are happy to take on any assigned job—from looking after shoes and chappals of devotees, to making sure the oil lamps stay lit throughout the night. I meet doctors, engineers, corporate heads, civil servants, industrialists, teachers, government administrators who are busy making sure everything is running smoothly, no hitches, especially today, the last day before the immersion. There is an unimaginable surge of devotees, waiting in orderly queues for a darshan.

My relationship with Ganpati is far more personal and intimate. It is a bond I forged as a schoolgirl. It was Ganpati I prayed to before leaving for school. It was Ganpati I thanked when I won a cup on the sports field. It was Ganpati I beseeched when I was sick or troubled. He is a buddy. We chat. We share a laugh or two. My secret sorrows are known to him and him alone. I don't take chances—I am surrounded by Ganpatis at home. One has my back—literally! He is behind my chair at the dining table where I write. The other is in front of me, when I look up from the laptop. I carry Ganpati with me when I travel and he stays in a particular place inside my cavernous handbag. I feel secure and protected knowing I have Ganpati on speed dial during a crisis. He is my security blanket and confidant. My go-to advisor on matters big and small.

The GSB Ganpati experience has overwhelmed me. I figure a GSB darshan deserves an appropriate feast! Thanks to Anushree Sardesai, a family friend, we are invited to join her family for a satvik Karhade Brahmin lunch. They host Ganeshji for three days at their home, and

4 'Mumbai's wealthy Ganesh Mandal takes insurance cover of ₹316 crore', NDTV, 29 August 2022. https://www.ndtv.com/india-news/mumbais-wealthy-ganesh-mandal-takes-insurance-cover-of-rs-316-4-cr-3295591#:~:text=The%20GSB%20Seva%20Mandal%20is,festival%2C%20a%20mandal%20representative%20said.

are kind enough to invite me, Avantikka and Anandita to enjoy the most authentic, vegetarian specialities, home-cooked by Anushree's mother Priya. Anushree's jovial father Nandan gives me a crash course in Karhade Brahmin food traditions and how those differ from the GSB's. Ours does not use freshly grated coconut as garnish on virtually every dish. And we aren't as milk and dairy dependent in our cuisine. Karhade Brahmins prefer a far simpler vegetarian fare while GSBs love their fish. Orthodox Karhade Brahmin families avoid garlic and onions. We can't do without both. Of course, Nandan smoothly slips it in, that within the Brahmin hierarchy, the Karhades rank higher than the GSBs! They call themselves 'Rigvedi Brahmins'. They, along with the Deshastha and Konkanastha Brahmins, are referred to as the 'Maharashtrian Brahmins'. Which makes me wonder who or what I am. Instant inferiority complex.

Padmini, Nandan's gorgeous-looking, light-eyed, eighty-five-year-old mother (who models and acts in TV serials) nods her head in agreement as lunch is served. I am there to devour rushichi bhaji, a seasonal, leafy vegetable that's cooked with other vegetables to make a stew-like preparation, which goes best with rice-flour bhakris. We greedily sample everything that's emerging from the kitchen, including basundi puri, puran poli, aloo puri, varan-bhaat, which is a deceptively simple toor daal preparation eaten with steamed rice—all these accompanied by generous portions of the grainy, homemade sajuk tup. I am missing my Aie—she used to make the best rushichi bhaji. Well ... I talk to Aie every night before I close my eyes. That night I assure her Priya's bhaji was terrific, no doubt, but not a patch on hers!

Earlier, I'm sheepishly admitting, I had ordered ukkadi chhe modak online! Sacrilege! That too from Brijwasi and not a Maharashtrian delivery kitchen. Ufff ... it's come to this! I was grateful Anandita had found them while surfing for these modaks at my request. What is Ganesh Chaturthi without modaks? Not just the easier-to-make deep-fried modaks, but these—the steamed (ukkadi) ones? Well, ours came from Brijwasi, delivered by Swiggy, to my utter surprise. Modaks on-the-go. Like ordering burgers or pizza on food-delivery apps. Even though Brijwasi is an established mithai brand in Mumbai (since 1946), and was patronized by Raj Kapoor and other Bollywood gourmets, I was sceptical. Ukkadi modaks are so specifically Maharashtrian! And Brijwasi sounds more Mathura! I bit into one and couldn't stop till I'd enjoyed two more.

My grandmother used to make superb ukkadi chhe modaks, with Aie as her understudy. It is an art, given how tedious the process is. Essentially, this is a rice-flour dumpling, filled with fresh, grated coconut, jaggery and a little elaichi. The rice flour can, optionally, be mixed with maida. One can use readymade moulds or shape the modaks manually. They can be steamed in banana leaves, or in a steamer. At our home, they'd be served piping hot from the copper steamer and enjoyed with either ghee or fresh coconut milk. The skill lies in getting the consistency of the rice flour just right (not too sticky, not too thick, not too lumpy). My spry, formidable grandmother had mastered modak-making, along with other Maharashtrian specialties. All the efforts made by these two women slaving in a hot, dark kitchen were taken for granted. Our family was stingy about many things—and praise definitely topped the list.

Long live, Brijwasi!

Coming back to GSB, I am still wondering why it has taken me this long to come to King's Circle, despite so many years of dedicated pandal-hopping in and around Mumbai, where every other gully has its own 'Raja' or 'Yuvraj'. The GSB one represents my roots. Even so, our trip to the GSB seva mandal this year marked a first. It happened thanks to divine intervention, as such things often do. Our friend, Anami Roy, former top cop (DGP of Maharashtra), recommended the darshan, and set it up with his friendly contacts at the mandal. Am I glad we went by his strong endorsement! It far exceeded what I had imagined when we were escorted inside and had our first jhalak. Sanjay Leela Bhansali could learn a thing or two from the decor, with thousands of diyas illuminating the vast space. Such are the stringent security measures, with the latest CCTV cameras and QRC for each and every visitor, Gurudatta is justifiably proud when he claims, 'Even if a lady's chain falls to the ground in this crowd, our cameras will locate it.' Mine is intact—I quickly check!

But like I do every year, I manage to make it to the best-known Ganpati in Mumbai—the towering and stately Lalbaugh Chha Raja. It is an experience like no other. I have been to the Maha Kumbh Mela and several other religious melas, but nothing compares to the religious frenzy and fervour at Lalbaugh. This year, I am uncertain. Would I be able to handle the bheed-bhaad, the pushing and shoving? I hear aggressive policewomen yelling, 'Idhar selfie mat lena … Chalo! Chalo!', while giving one hard dhakka in the ribs.

Thanks to the good offices of our well-connected friend, Kim Sharma, and Anandita's steely determination to have her annual darshan of the Raja, once we make it inside and are in his magnetic presence, I find myself placing my head on his extended right foot covered with gulal. I am shaking with emotion as I fervently seek his blessings and pray for my family. The tears always flow at this point of the darshan … My cheeks are wet, my tikka smeared, but as I emerge from the pandal, I am beaming …

I can feel it. I know it. The magnificent, benevolent Raja knew we were at his feet and has blessed all of us.

—⁓—

'The secret of staying young is to live honestly, eat slowly and lie about your age.'

—Lucille Ball

It is the second week of September and I am returning from the Ooty Lit Fest. When I get home, I notice Ana Banana's swollen eyes and the dark rings under them.

'What happened?' I ask. Mothers often ask stupid questions.

'What do you mean?' Anandita snaps. 'You know what has happened … I have been crying for two days … No sleep, nothing.'

Since there's no love interest on the scene—at least none that I know of—I dismiss the accusation and ask for tea. I have been travelling for twelve hours, risking life and limb on this treacherous Coonoor Ghat with its forty-seven hairpin bends, with a manic driver named Madhan behind the wheel of a rickety car. I should be the one with those dark circles.

'Mama, please! How can you be this insensitive … she's dead! I have never felt this sad about anyone else dying …'

Oh. 'So sorry, Ana! I forgot! Mama is tired, okay?'

Of course, it isn't okay. Yes, the Queen of England is no more. Queen Elizabeth II has been Anandita's biggest heroine forever. There are just two people in this world Anandita worships—Ratan Tata and Queen Elizabeth II. She has met Mr Tata and now there is no chance left of her ever meeting the Queen.

Anandita is the lone royalist in the family. Her adoration of Britain's royals puzzles me. But I say nothing. Does she ask why I adore Elvis Presley? I try my best to console Ana. She is sobbing and shaking with sorrow. By the next afternoon, she is prepping for the funeral. By then, we are all teasing her and suggesting she wear a black hat with a veil for a few days. Ana is not amused. She pleads with me to watch the majestic procession with her on TV … I go along, even though I'm in the middle of writing a column. Her emotions are genuine, she needs me to share this sentimental moment and she really did love the old girl. In fact, she tells me without the slightest self-consciousness, 'Mama … Don't feel bad, but I loved the Queen more than I loved your mother. I didn't cry half as much when Aaji died …' Truthful daughter. I like her candour.

As we watch the funeral, I spot King Charles leading the mourners and I find myself recalling the first time I met him (he was Prince Charles then and dating Camilla Parker Bowles). This is sounding like we became chuddi-buddies and we met several times. Not so! It was at a charity sit-down dinner for around fifty people at his London residence many moons ago, and I was one of the invitees. While the briskly served dinner itself was entirely forgettable, my brief interaction with Charles remains the only memorable aspect of an otherwise blah evening. For starters, his then lady love, Camilla Parker Bowles, decided at the last minute to crash the party, throwing protocol out of the window. Lovely! I almost cheered. And then, when the formal introductions got underway, Prince Charles surprised one and all by asking pertinent, polite questions to each guest. When it was my turn, he asked, 'What sort of books do you write?'

'Bodice rippers, Your Highness,' I replied.

He wiggled his ears with excitement, his eyes lit up, as he looked for Camilla and asked her to join us. 'This charming lady from India writes bodice rippers, darling!' he announced, much to her delight.

Emboldened and encouraged, I went on to discuss the *Kama Sutra* and how it was India's way of getting back at the West. 'You could damage your knees and break your spine attempting some of those positions,' I cheekily added.

They exchanged meaningful looks, as only couples who are into each other do.

Before I could expound on this theory any further, the aides sidled up and whisked them away. But not before he turned around and gave me a conspiratorial smile, as did Camilla.

The next time we made significant eye contact was at Nita and Mukesh Ambani's grand reception for Charles and the Duchess in Mumbai (November 2013). When we were introduced, there was a vaguer than vague gleam of dim recognition in both their eyes and then they were gone. I noticed a lot of society ladies attempting a curtsy and wondered if they were okay in the head! But that's us! Always willing to make asses of ourselves, over-eager to please and impress the goras—even the ones who ruled and looted us.

During the same nine-day visit to India, we were invited by the Poonawallas to hang with the royals during their maiden trip to Pune. It was a hellishly packed day for the couple and I admired their stamina as they rushed from one event to the next. Prince Charles visited the Serum Institute of India, laid wreaths at the war cemetery in Khadki, met business leaders at the Turf Club, while the Duchess met a few ladies over high tea at the Poonawalla mansion. I had picked a pastel French chiffon saree with frisky sequinned butterflies for the occasion. I was hoping Camilla would wear a tiara to tea (of course, it's never done!), but she was in India with the natives and I'd wondered if the Duchess might throw one on just as a nod to her mum-in-law.

No chance. Camilla was dressed in a discreet, printed afternoon outfit, no big rocks flashing, and sensible shoes—the kind stocky English ladies wear when they tramp all over the heather. Our hostess, the glam and gorgeous Natasha Poonawalla, outshone the Duchess on every front—looks, couture, age and baubles. The catered high tea was laid out in the garden and the Poonawalla home resembled an Ivory–Merchant movie set. Banks of imported flowers, white-glove service, gleaming silver, delicate porcelain, tinkling crystal—altogether, terribly grand and befitting the royal visit. It's not every day that England's future Queen Consort comes to tea. Arrey baba … we also have to show 'hum kisi se kum nahi', and the Poonawallas certainly put on a fabulous show.

I wanted to ask the Duchess about the state of her knees—any further wear and tear since we last met? But we were interrupted by well-heeled, perfectly coiffed Punekars who had perfected the dip. Must have rehearsed for weeks, I bitchily concluded, as we bit into paper-thin cucumber and smoked salmon sandwiches, gingerly tackled freshly baked scones served with clotted cream and jam, nibbled on custard tarts, and helped ourselves to tiny macaroons and pastries that the tea caddies placed on long tables, which were immaculately draped in white damask.

Meanwhile, Mr Dé was twinning with Prince Charles in a beige linen suit. He has a terrific photograph of the two of them laughing into the camera. Not sure if Mr Dé mentioned any erotic text from India's glorious and sensual past, but the men seemed pleased.

Well, nine years later, the same couple is under intense scrutiny. Will King Charles manage to hang on to the monarchy and stay on the throne? Will Queen Consort Camilla ('My darling wife') taunt us, here in India, by wearing the Imperial Crown with 'our' Kohinoor embedded in the centre at the coronation? Or will the royal advisors shoot it down? Who will get the royal invite from India? My guess is it will be 'Pacho' (Padmanabh Singh), the twenty-four-year-old polo-playing maharaja of Jaipur. After all, King Charles III happens to be Pacho's godfather. But, most importantly, when will the Ambanis and Poonawallas host the royals again? Will they make it to the coronation guest list? Unless, of course, it's Gautam Adani's turn now …

OCTOBER

'My face carries all my memories. Why would I erase them?'
—**Diane Von Furstenberg**

I AM FREQUENTLY ACCOSTED, INTERCEPTED, AMBUSHED, WAYLAID, nearly attacked by strangers and other unlikeable creatures (generally after a conference where I have delivered a pretty good address on women's health and related issues), who ask aggressively, 'Madam, your writing *vaghera* is nice … it's okay … but tell us about your diet, daily routine. Give us beauty tips. No Botox or what?' Sometimes, I smile wearily and say, '… or what.' Waste of time. Joke misfires, every time!

I came across a quote on a random reel, which had me chuckling: 'Nobody gives an eff if you are clever or sad if you have high cheekbones.' And added, 'There's no sympathy for pretty people …' Too true!

The festive season is upon us. God help me! I adore all our festivals, but one thing about this time of the year that scares the hell out of me is food! As soon as Navratri ends and Diwali begins, so does the hog fest. I get tempted. I succumb. I gain weight. There—got that out of the way.

Now to tackle the questions I'm frequently asked on both these subjects—food and weight. It is no secret I love all things yummy—food included. Let me start with a few basics. I do not possess a secret formula. No magic potion. If I overeat, the kilos pile on. Same as for everyone else. Neither do I have an esoteric skincare routine that I fiercely guard. My mantra is to moisturize, moisturize, moisturize with whatever is handy at the time—a layer of pre-shower fresh cream (malai) with a few drops of limbu, a pinch of haldi, works for me. So does cold cream throughout the day. And the neck! Always moisturize the neck. That's where the lines and crepe-like skin start. That's why you never saw Dev Anand in his later years without a scarf around his neck that touched his chin! How does a person Botox the neck? Any expert answers?

I have no exercise regimen; I have neither been a member of a gym, nor do I employ personal trainers. No yoga (hot or cold). No Pilates. No jogging. Two years ago, after I tore a cartilage in my left knee, trying to impress my footballer granddaughter, Anasuya Devi, I stopped stretching or doing stomach crunches because my knee would puff up within hours because of the strain. Now I am stuck. I feel like a ball of lead. A chair-potato. I walk around the house before dinner these days but that's a joke. I do it to placate myself that I am not a fossil sitting at the dining table for hours—either eating or writing. So how come I haven't blimped out so far? It's a combination of genes, my personal DNA—besides controlled and informed eating! The last bit is key. It's possible. It's easy.

Food speaks to me. I understand the language of food. Make friends with the foods that suit you. Pay attention to your body when it talks to you.

Metabolism is not a constant. With age, it slows down almost ridiculously. As a teenager I could comfortably eat two portions of biryani in one go; I could also finish a bottle of champagne effortlessly over an evening. This is no longer possible. Getting to the stage when I can enjoy food and drink in a way my body approves, has taken me years. Most people assume you are a glutton if you say you love food. Other curious guests watch me eat at parties and exclaim, 'Arrey … so little on your plate! You keep talking about food—what is this? No wonder you don't put on weight like us.' It annoys me. Am I going on about what's on your plate, you oaf? This is exactly how much and what I want to savour, so bugger off, and stuff your face if you want to!

It's a good thing I don't have a sweet tooth and have bade all things sugary goodbye a few years ago. When a pesky stranger asks, 'No desserts? Try the tiramisu or the ras malai with hot jalebis?' I point to the glass of wine in my hand and say, 'I prefer my sugar fix in liquid form.' If calories must be counted, let the glass decide!

My food censorship includes all things deep fried. Plus, most things white (maida is my biggest dushman). And that sums up my diet plan. Besides, I do everything ulta-pulta—the opposition of what world experts on nutrition and fitness prescribe. My breakfast is minimal—one boiled egg and a multigrain toast. My lunch is lean—soup and salad. By teatime, I'm ravenous and out of control (homemade kebabs and dahi puri are my current favourites). But it's dinner that I look forward to the most—it makes me go nuts with anticipation. I know why. It's a basic insecurity many women harbour, but rarely admit to—going to be bed on an empty stomach. The dread of waking up in the middle of the night with your stomach growling! I need to feel full before I sleep. Ask your women friends about their attitude to hunger. You'll be surprised to know it has to do with childhood and deprivation. Adulthood and abuse.

I have known hunger.

It was during my early thirties, which in retrospect, was the toughest period of my life, emotionally and physically. I was isolated and adrift. 'You have brought this upon yourself,' said hostile family members, who refused to open their doors to me. But, as it often happens, when a few old doors are slammed in your face, a few new ones open. Harinakshiben Shah, a kind and generous lady, who stayed on the second floor of my parents' building, opened not just her door but her heart and home to me. She did so wordlessly, unobtrusively, sensitively ... No questions asked. There was hot Gujju food on the table at whatever hour I walked in, and unlimited affection to comfort me. It's a debt I can never repay.

About those who felt I had 'gone too far' and had 'only myself to blame', they were right. I had indeed 'brought it upon myself'. But I was hungry! I had no money. And too much pride to ask anyone for anything. It was during those months that I fell in love with boiled eggs. They became my best friends; they kept me alive. The staple meal for me at the time was two boiled eggs a day and a bottle of chilled Aarey flavoured milk from the Mafco booth down the road, purchased from a kind, bearded man, who I could instinctively sense understood my hunger and aloneness.

Each time I felt weakened, drained and close to defeat, I would recall the words of a farmer lady in Telangana, who'd said, at a micro-financing conference for women, 'The longest journey a woman needs to understand is the journey of her hand to her mouth. If she can earn enough to feed herself, she has nothing to fear in this world.' I needed to make more money! I needed to feed myself.

A successful and beautiful PR lady, also in her thirties and going through a personal trauma at around the same time, drove the point home still further when she plaintively asked me over the phone, 'Khaana kidhar se khaoongi? I am broke ...' Looking back, I suspect she eventually tied the knot with a man to stave off hunger and have two full meals a day. So many women do that but never admit to it. Imagine the enormity of such insecurity! Women sign up for a lifetime of misery with a man they may loathe, because they fear starvation! I am talking modern, urban, educated women with jobs. Not daily-wage labourers on construction sites. It's not paranoia. It's reality. Ask me!

It's an entirely different script today but who can forget what it was like forty years ago? I certainly can't and don't want to. Each time the boiled-eggs story comes up, and gets thrown at me as a put-down, I smile to myself. It made me stronger back then—I survived on andaas and self-belief! I can do it again, if challenged. There's a lot to be said for andaas, what say?

When I hit an occasional low these days, I hang on to Avantikka's words when she told me gently, 'Ma, hang on to your happy stuff ... places and people who make you happy ... girlfriends who make you happy … something small that makes you happy … just grab your happiness. Tend to plants, dance, sing, travel, read, write, eat.' She went on to describe her happy stuff, apart from the biggest joy in her life— spending time with her three kids and her husband. Morning yoga, Om chants on Alexa, dogs, Netflix binges, fashion websites, charcoal-free dhoop at dusk, evening walks in the garden looking for peacocks, Pilates classes, daily massages, holidays in Phuket or Goa, brekkies at Willingdon Club, Gujju diet farsan and evenings with her incredible support group of bright, sensitive gal pals.

Avantikka understands my hunger.

Today, I value and respect food. I know what it's like to not have any.

Then there's the M-word (money). It embarrasses many women. It shouldn't. Several women I know would rather starve than beg. That suits society just fine. Back to the old 'she's brought it upon herself' rationalization that frees everyone else from assuming responsibility.

These days I constantly remind women: Money is important. Respect it. Make it. Spend it. Keep it. Save it. Do not lend money. And never borrow any. No joint bank accounts, no joint credit cards. Protect yourself and pay your own bills. Dignity cannot be compromised for daily meals in fancy homes. Small-minded, calculating, mean family members will always stay that way. A girlfriend once told me: there are three kinds of men whom women should avoid—drunkards, philanderers and misers. Remember, a drunkard can give up drinks and a philanderer can turn faithful, but a miser can never become generous. Misers don't change, they stay misers. Stay away from misers.

Control freaks look for more control. Most domestic conflicts involve money. And nobody responds to the idiotic line 'Show me the money' by loosening purse strings. Financial independence is the only way to retain your self-respect. Make sure you never compromise. But also make sure you don't subsidize, and become a 'bakri', imagining you can save a marriage by handing over your hard-earned money to your partner. He will keep the money and get rid of you!

Take pride in feeding yourself well. Don't listen to well-meaning but misguided female family elders who tell you, 'Have a large glass of milk … You will feel fine … And then say sorry to your husband.' Never underestimate the role food plays in determining a woman's sense of self. It took a hard knock for me to understand the power of food. Which may explain why I am so disciplined about what I eat, when and how much. No waste. No excess. You never know when boiled eggs may have to come to my rescue once again and save another day!

—m—

'Everything slows down with age, except the time it takes cake and ice cream to reach your hips.'

—John Wagner

'Ma, let's revive our family Pujo Party—it used to be epic!'

Yes, our annual pre-Dusshera dinners were indeed 'epic', to borrow a term that's so overused these days. Everything and everyone is 'epic'—*Fabulous Lives of Bollywood Wives* (2020) included. Let me just say that between 1984 and 2006 (the year we ended the tradition, as a mark of respect to my father who'd passed away), we hosted what came to be called 'the Dé's Pujo Party' without skipping a year. When we started hosting an Ashtami/Navami festive dinner at home, it was considered pretty special by our friends and family. Looking back, it seems insane and demanding in the extreme—for twenty-two years without interruption, organizing such a huge party at home.

(P.S.: No party planners, no event managers, no caterers. Just us.)

What started as a smallish celebration for Bombay Bongs in search of 'bhog' (which is nothing fancier than a delicious khichuri, but rich in its symbolism in the lives of Bongs who leave Bengal), kinship and an animated adda, soon ballooned like the Marvel character Hulk into a gorgeous party that kept growing till it became an annual pan-Indian celebration—a much-looked-forward-to pre-Diwali event on the social calendar. But first, it was our job to explain the significance of 'pujo' to non-Bengalis. A note here: Bengalis may be the only community in India who so clearly separates itself from the rest. In their view, the country is carved up into two distinct groups—the Bengalis and the non-Bengalis. Ever heard anyone else say something as absurd as, 'Oh … so you are a non-Gujarati …'? Or a non-Assamese or a non-Punjabi? It distressed Mr Dé initially to have to decode pujo for the benefit of the vast majority of non-initiates, the non-Bengali friends. Most thought they were being invited to a religious ceremony, an elaborate Durga puja, straight out of Satyajit Ray's *Pather Panchali* (1955) with the Goddess in residence, an evening aarti, conch-blowing devotees in dhutis, women resembling

Charulata with smeared sindoor in the parting of their hair, followed by a pure satvik bhojan! I often stopped myself from snapping, 'You are a nonsense ...' as Bongs in Kolkata scoff when provoked. 'A nonsense.' Got it?

So, yes, there was a lot of nonsense to deal with back then, including questions like, 'Do we leave our footwear in the car?' And, when told it's a *party*, not a religious, pious anything, hopes would instantly go up. 'You mean there's booze, a bar?' Absolutely! Nischoi!

Apart from a full and interesting bar, Bong food was always the star and biggest attraction. 'Hope you are serving mustard fish?' Back then, Bengali cuisine was relatively unknown in Mumbai, with people believing every Bong table featured maach and nothing else. The kitchen being Mr Dé's domain, I used to stay out of it and focus on getting my Dhakai saris and goyna (gehna) organized well in time.

Tapanda, my sari-seller from Bangladesh, would show up in August, carrying bundles of exquisite Dhakai saris with real zari from Dhaka. Getting the perfect Dhakai for the party was a far bigger challenge than making sure we had enough maach, mangsho or mishti to feed over a hundred guests who'd show up in waves during the long evening and take over every corner of the home for their addas. Industrialists, cricketers, corporate heads, diplomats, media tycoons, bankers, top cops, movie stars, writers, painters, film-makers, models, politicians and, of course, several of our family friends, would fly in from across India dressed in gorgeous attire, the women showing off their heritage jewellery and stunning wardrobes, the men strutting their attitude as a fashion accessory. I always looked forward to some notorious character showing up. I was rarely disappointed. Romances happened. So did divorces, heartbreaks and a few notable break-ups. Our bachchalog would take over Rana's room, and soon bottles of vodka would start disappearing from the bar to their adda and a thick fog of ciggie smoke would escape the room, polluting all others. The Bong contingent invariably stood out in starched, pleated dhutis and embroidered panjabis which completely overshadowed the designer suits and embellished bandhgalas of—you guessed right—the 'non-Bengalis'. One year, Vijay Mallya stole the show when he walked in dressed like Mysore's maharaja, turban and all. His bodyguard from Cyprus was spared the fancy dress and came dressed in a dark formal suit. He was told to leave his gun outside.

Yes, those were terrific times. But do I want to revive the pujo parties of old? No chance! I don't enjoy revisiting grand, old celebrations. There's also something called the law of diminishing returns. Such mega-parties are better off as vivid memories of another era in our lives. Our 'baadi' at Cuffe Parade is the same. Alas, it is we who have changed. But what's stopping the children from throwing Pujo Party Part 2—sequels are so in! They owe it to the next generation of Bongs and non-Bongs? I would happily attend, that new Dhakai and old jewels in place!

My current nostalgia has a context. It's the first day of Navratri today. Last evening was Mahalaya, and I was driving home from the suburbs after meeting the family over high tea at the Willingdon Club and gazing at huge idols of Durga Ma being ceremonially taken to pandals—her temporary home on earth for the next ten days. The beat of the electronic keyboards tuning up for garba, the sound of excited children welcoming her, dhols and dhaks. And energetic, uninhibited ladies dancing with abandon to this year's big garba hit, 'Dholida', which had featured Alia Bhatt in Sanjay Leela Bhansali's superhit *Gangubai Kathiawadi* (2022).

The kids are thrilled with the Navratri ensembles I have brought back from Ahmedabad. Aaah—nice story there! It's midnight in the land of Mahatma Gandhi and I want to go shopping. No problem, says the gallant Pinakin, a dancer and teacher working for the past twenty-six years at Darpana Academy of Performing Arts in Ahmedabad. Pinakin's just back from America, where he'd gone to conduct dance workshops for Ukrainian orphans. Don't ask! It's total madness at the Navratri stalls on Law College Road. Mahendrabhai, our driver, looks nervous as I jump out of the SUV and wade into heaps of colourful dandiya raas garments spread over the crowded footpath. Buying frenzy is at a peak, before the cops arrive and fine the stall owners. I grab whatever is within easy reach—chaniyas, kediyas, bundis, cholis in vibrant colours, covered with mirrors and heavy Kutch embroidery. Pinakin briskly bargains with the Kutchi families manning the crammed stalls. The owners are busy gossiping about me, wondering who the hell I am. I reply in Gujarati, which I speak fluently. Ha! Revenge!

The female security cops from Uttar Pradesh at Ahmedabad airport are so attracted to my Navratri shopping, they leave their posts and make me remove all the ghaghras from the jute bags. 'Kitney ka? Kahan se kharida?' For the next few minutes, any determined female terrorist could effortlessly sail past these ladies, while we chat about styles, cuts, backless cholis and mermaid lehengas.

For the past two years, I have missed going to our favourite pujo pandal at Tejpal Auditorium in central Mumbai. As pandal-snobbery goes, this one wins hands down. It is Tejpal that attracts the bhadralok. Corporate India's giants congregate here and participate enthusiastically in the trance-inducing dhunuchi dance. Sheepish admission: I attempted it once, after watching Vidya Balan in *Parineeta* (2005). Super flopped at it! From Dr Ashok Sekhar Ganguly (former chairman of Hindustan Lever) to Sushim Mukul Dutta (HUL chairman, TCI board member, revered by Bongs and corporate colleagues), the biggies show up for pushpanjali, their beautiful wives and daughters taking turns with the aarti thaalis and participating in pushpanjali. Shotti! This here is the real deal.

Pujo hasn't been pujo during the pandemic. Virtual pujo? Not the same. I am overjoyed it's physically on! I receive a text announcing the same. It is from Sushmita Mitra, the dedicated and very enthusiastic president of the Bombay Durga Bari Committee at Tejpal. They are celebrating the 93rd Sharodotsav this year—the bhog will be phenomenal. Sushmita urges me to attend, saying, 'Sova, we are back at Tejpal this year ... I can promise you very good singara!' I am right there! And yes, the singaras were superb. As is our darshan. Aishu-Paishu, swaying to the sonorous beat of the aarti, says, 'Ganpati Bappa's mom has come to meet him.' Aryaman is busy eating sheera—ooops, should that be suji? Halwa? And we are off to eat Baba Ling's Bombay duck at the iconic Ling's Pavilion, a Cantonese-style Chinese restaurant in south Mumbai. Baba Ling's father, Yick Sen Ling, came to India in 1938, and established Nanking, which relocated and was renamed Ling's Pavilion by his sons, Baba (Sem Tian Ling) and Nini. They have stuck to the original menu faithfully and pride themselves in their kitchen's authenticity. We have known Baba (he's close to my age) forever. This time, we were once again perplexed as to what Sahil, since he is a shudh shakahari, would enjoy, given that we had pre-booked a crab and bombils. Baba Ling went flat out by going to the kitchen himself and creating a few outstanding dishes for our 'jamai'. I particularly relished an unusual karela omelette! Thanks, Baba!

—w—

'I'm baffled that anyone might not think women get more beautiful as they get older. Confidence comes with age, and looking beautiful comes from the confidence someone has in themselves.'

—Kate Winslet

It's a lazy Sunday today. White heat outside. Boredom inside. I should be drained of all energy this morning, given the late night yesterday, listening to the DJ at Bombay Gymkhana courteously playing oldie-goldie numbers, after surveying the listless, beer-drinking elderly crowd mindlessly watching some IPL match on the television screen above the bar. Most of us are indeed oldies in this hall. Not too many goldies, but the sweet DJ has a job to do, and he must have noticed the record number of four-pronged walking sticks and a couple of walkers propped up next to tables in the dining area.

Looking around the familiar setting, I realize Mr Dé has been a member of the 137-year-old Bombay Gymkhana for fifty-two years! Most of the people I spot on the premises weren't born at the time he was ordering martinis at the teakwood bar. And here I was getting bugged by a stranger who was Mr Dé's age. Had this man become my reality check? Was he sent by God to convey a message to open my eyes? Or was I just feeling super-defensive?

'Keep it up!' he'd said, with a conspiratorial wink, as I lightly made my way to where my 'young' friends were enjoying mint tea, sev puri and chicken sandwiches with mustard. I looked over my shoulder and grinned wickedly.

You bet I will, Mister—keep it up. Something you certainly can't!

There's a huge challenge confronting female senior citizens tonight. The ladies' room, next to the dining area, is under renovation. The temporary one has been shifted to the other end of the long corridor, beyond the popular shop from where most members prefer to get their veggies and groceries (their swipe the card and pay next month policy being the main reason). A bent old lady at the next table is asking her companions loudly to stop ordering more beers—'I won't be able to hold

240

it in and we don't want an accident here.' The talk turns to adult diapers, hip replacement, physiotherapy and stents. It's getting a bit too depressing, so I order extra portions of 'aamras with puris', along with salt and pepper prawns. The DJ starts playing 'La Bamba' which I used to dance to in the early sixties, possibly when the DJ's grandmother was doing the same. I was the only one tapping my feet and shaking my shoulders. Fortunately, the young members gathered around the bar; the women, some clad in denim shorts, strappy white linen tops and dull gold sandals, were too engrossed to look beyond themselves—most of us seated at the tables were invisible to them. But, to their credit, they parted instantly and offered their arms to help an eighty-five-year-old lady through the crowd as she slowly made her way to the distant loo—she'd managed to 'hold it in'.

I found it difficult to sleep that night. Images of the elderly managing to somehow make an evening out of their Saturday night outing, kept haunting me. I was one of them, wasn't I? So far, I had no problem 'holding it in'. But soon, perhaps, I'd be in the exact same position. Then again, maybe not, I comforted myself. My father passed away at age ninety-eight. He was looking forward to his century. All his life, he'd enjoyed robust health and remained in full control of every body part, the bladder included. Had he not suffered a minor fall, during which he hurt his head, he would have made it to 100. Why would I have to go through the ignominy of incontinence and depend on a walker later in life? Why? I was his daughter. My genes would see me through old age, I comforted myself, as I tossed and turned, and bravely forced myself to think 'positive thoughts'. Along with the aamras puri and prawns, I had defiantly ordered a mutton stew—greed and panic had propelled that decision. I had also run into an old admirer/friend and noticed his fitness levels, while exchanging fake greetings.

'How are you?' I'd enquired, stressing on 'you'.

'Perfect … just purrfect,' he'd drawled smugly.

That made me feel most imperfect and jittery. Who the hell talks like that, I thought. Who's perfect in this world? How can he say it without feeling embarrassed?

Earlier, I'd run into a woman I used to meet socially on a regular basis, fifty or so years ago. She was totally unrecognizable, like she'd shrunk and been put into the deep freezer for years. Her eyes still shone with excitement when I asked after her children (my son had briefly dated her daughter). Her animated face right at that instant reminded me of our first meeting when she was a vivacious new bride who'd joined our small, snooty group and dazzled everyone with her personality and confidence. She'd graduated from one of the Seven Sisters, held a master's degree in French, wore super-chic clothes, flirted and danced with the men in the group, her skin glowing, and jewellery of the very expensive kind, glinting on her elegant fingers, arms and neck. The woman in front of me now looked like a bag lady, shabby and sad. No! I never want to be this person ever, I vowed to myself. But, honestly speaking, who can guarantee that?

Here I am chuckling away as I think of a 'grande dames' dinner I attended recently. The touchy topic of women and ageing seems to obsess every female I meet, regardless of age. The contented ones have made peace with their vintage and own it with pride. It is those who have tried and failed to come to terms with advancing years that have crumbled and look like ancient, neglected ruins. My grande dame hostesses belong to the former category—they have enjoyed their lives to the fullest. It shows! Their faces have lines, of course! But smiles are genuine and reach the eyes. The laughter is spontaneous and the memories always upbeat. There is no negative energy field around these two gracious ladies.

Sadly, grande dames are a dying breed in Mumbai, which once boasted of the grandest. The social pecking order and glamorous parties came much later. That was the time in the seventies and eighties when Mumbai's calendar of events was dominated by one or two strikingly attractive, insanely affluent ladies who knew a thing or two about hosting madly extravagant soirees that got talked about for months. The grandest dame of all was Parmeshwar Godrej. She passed away in 2016, aged seventy-one. There never was or can be anybody who comes anywhere close to la Godrej. Others have strenuously tried and failed to rival her style and hospitality. It is about aura, not extravagance. Many hostesses in India have money, but they have no mystique. No flair. No magic for putting together the most jaw-dropping parties, in which international figures like Oprah Winfrey, Richard Gere, Imran Khan, Goldie Hawn, Elizabeth Hurley, to name a few, would meet the most dazzling personalities from India in a setting that is like no other—the Godrej Villa at Juhu. It is like Kubla Khan's 'vision in a dream' Xanadu, stunningly designed by Parmesh herself. What parties! What guests! And the hostess herself, designer beret firmly in place, out-glittering the biggest stars, clinking glasses and boogeying on a glass dance floor near the subtly lit swimming pool. Her famous table, laden with lobsters, caviar, exotic meats and outstanding barbecues, would see global celebrities awestruck by the star power scattered around so casually. Maharanis and maharajas, mega movie stars and billionaires, chiffons and black ties … I can go on and on. It was all Parmeshwar's eye and instinct for the grand, the spectacular, the gorgeous—that's it. Like releasing hundreds of Thai 'wish lanterns' into the night sky to celebrate her son Pirojsha's wedding to Karla Bookman, … Or lighting countless mashaals along the seafront at the United Services Club for her daughter Tanya's reception after her marriage to Arvind Dubash. Through it all, it was Adi Godrej, Parmeshwar's brilliant and incredibly supportive husband, who would hold his own and bask in his wife's spectacular presence.

No … They don't make them like her anymore. The mould's broken.

—⁂—

Six years after the Parmeshwar era, I was lucky enough to be invited to a small dinner by one such grande dame this month, someone I hadn't met in decades. I jumped at the chance to pay homage (note to self: the 'h' is silent, cherie) and be a humble courtier at her durbar. Should I dress up or pretend I attend this sort of super-exclusive dinner every other evening and therefore opt for a no-fuss look?

Since Avantikka is also invited, I check with her and she says, 'It's an informal mother–daughter evening with just the six of us ... so ... I mean ... you know best.' Actually, I don't. She could have been more helpful! I opt for safe. But wear a couple of extra rings so I don't appear too poor.

Just two days earlier, I had run into a creepy man in a food court on the Mumbai–Pune Expressway who had introduced himself like this: 'Hello! Shobhaa Rajadhyaksha, right? I am a Saraswat like you. I used to see you and your sister when you were in college. You'd be rushing home before "lights out". You were a top athlete ... you looked too good in shorts ... but ... but ... you look so very different now. Can I get a selfie?'

Bloody cheek! My hand rushed to fix my hair. My reading glasses were halfway down my nose, I was dressed in a shapeless, black tee which read 'Ready in a Prosecco' (a gift from Anandita, queen of message tees) worn over baggy pants. But still!

Yes. I was still smarting! I wanted to look divine for the grande dame. Divine ... not just good. I may not have made the cut because when I collected Avantikka, she looked me over critically and said, 'Ma, blot your lips ... Why are you in an old black, shapeless tunic? Those two will be dressed up, and how. I know they've pulled out all the stops.'

I managed a weak laugh, 'Who's competing?'

The imposing residence at one of the best addresses in the city was just the start of what turned out to be a superlative and supremely elegant evening, with every little detail in place. Tiny mother-of-pearl spoons to scoop-up caviar; tofu skewers in teriyaki sauce; a crab salad served in individual porcelain bowls; blanched, lightly grilled salmon off a hallmark platter; fresh asparagus spears; a cheddar soufflé that had obediently risen to the occasion; paper-thin slices of mandarin orange with slivers of dates doused in orange blossom water; rich toffee pudding made from scratch ... Every single dish made in the famous kitchen presided over by two cooks, six butlers, four maids, in a home filled with priceless art, old silver and the fragrance of another, highly refined era where this very space we were enjoying tonight saw men in black ties, women in silken gowns, dancing cheek-to-cheek to Cole Porter!

I held the soft, delicate hand of our very lovely hostess as we were leaving. She is a sprightly ninety-three, and fabulous and together in every sense. I admired her Art Deco diamond brooch, the teal silk blouson worn over slim pants, the ballet slippers, the coiffed silver hair, pampered skin like satin, devoid of any make-up. Then I turned to look at her much more flamboyant best friend of seventy years—the contrast was astounding! I adored the other grand dame's showy, blingy exuberance and complimented her as she surreptitiously pulled down the neckline of her leopard print tunic to better display her deep cleavage. We laughed over her crazy stories of yore—the flirtations, seductions and heartbreaks. She told us about shocking her potential son-in-law when he admired her spectacular emerald pendant by saucily replying, 'Forget the pendant, darrrrrling ... see the landing place!'

I asked her about 'cheek-to-cheek' dancing and she coyly replied, 'Yes, of course darrrrrling ... but only with my husband.' We laughed and raised yet another flute of chilled Dom.

'To us!' we said, meaning every word.

Here are two incredibly vibrant women in their ninth decade, full of joie de vivre and living the good life. I thought of that foolish oaf at the food court and his crude remark about how much I had changed as he stared at me while I was minding my own business and tucking into delicious masaley bhat from the Udipi outlet I patronize on each trip to Pune and back. What did the ass expect after sixty years? I am not a museum piece nor a laboratory specimen preserved in formaldehyde. I am me. I am seventy-five.

Age is simply a number. It depends on how you view it, feel it, live it. One of the grande dames was recovering from a nasty fall. The other one, from the sad death of her beautiful daughter. Which one of us doesn't have major and minor tragedies to deal with? Who is free of anxiety and disappointments? But that glorious evening, as the six of us spent a few short hours together in a beautiful home, laughing at ourselves and sharing notes on a few bizarre life experiences, it was possible to believe in the power of essential goodness, kindness and grace in the face of challenges that can break most folk.

Did these two ladies have a secret formula that has kept them afloat and happy? When asked, they looked at one another and exchanged a conspiratorial smile. They weren't tellin' nuthin'.

—m—

'My advice: Don't waste so much time worrying about your skin or your weight. Develop what you put your hands on in the world.'

—**Meryl Streep**

Monday mornings are … well, Monday mornings. The whole world hates them and a collective groan can actually be heard if you listen hard enough. I used to be one of those annoying eager beavers who'd wait impatiently for a new week to start, fresh adventures to begin, amazing discoveries and activities to look forward to. Anticipation is such a lovely word.

Off late, my enthusiasm has waned a bit, and I have not 100 per cent disconnected from the pandemic hangover that disoriented most of us—what did it matter which day of the week it was? Every day was the same. Trapped in our homes and entirely demotivated from actively planning anything more taxing than the next meal, one dull, uneventful day slipped into the next. For many, even the boundaries between night and day had been blurred. We existed. We'd forgotten how to live.

I decided to become my own therapist, adopting the best therapy I knew—writing! Apart from daily journalling (a discipline I have followed since the age of twelve), I manically wrote two books (*Lockdown Liaisons* and *Srilaaji*), frequently penning 2,000 words a day. The twenty-six stories in *Lockdown Liaisons* were written as first-person monologues, a cathartic device that helped me deal with my pandemic issues. *Srilaaji* got sexier and sexier as I kept going, and offered vicarious thrills in an arid doom-dominated landscape.

I'd kept myself going with steely determination, shooting daily videos which I'd upload on Insta immediately. But even those two-minute videos required a great deal of effort. I'd plan an appropriate outfit, match accessories, wear make-up, do my hair, pen a rough script, find a spot at home with good lighting and get my daughter Ana Banana to shoot it, generally right after lunch. Both of us would be grumpy and irritable. At times, she'd flare up and express her resentment and, very often, I'd snap at her for being indifferent and short with me. It wasn't helping the whole mother–daughter bonding plan. If things got really bad between us, I would cajole Tara, our sweet and kind Nepali house help, to shoot instead.

For fifty days non-stop, we shot these eccentric videos in which I shared my dread and despair, as the crisis worsened, and fatalities kept rising. To lighten the gloom, I would end each clip with an upbeat Bollywood song which—get this—I would croak out myself! Frequently, I mixed up the lyrics and, almost always, I sang off-key. So what? I wasn't auditioning for a gig with A.R. Rahman. I had nothing to lose by putting my shameful lack of singing talent out there for people to laugh at. Zero ego. For all of us believed at the time that we could be dead the next morning, felled by a deadly virus against which there was no defence. Why not sing? I'd remind myself of an old motto: 'Don't let the music stop', as I tiredly filled in the gaps in my eyebrows, outlined my lips with a coral pink pencil, thrown a bright-coloured dupatta over a nightie, and faced the camera, providing a capsule analysis of how the world was coping. Without shame, I'm admitting I did beat a thaali, light candles, shower petals—but I am proud to state I did not shout 'Go, Corona, go!' from the balcony.

Last week, a lady approached me with a big smile to thank me for those fifty videos, saying, 'You have no idea what they meant to so many of us. We would watch you change your outfits and jewellery, wear make-up, and share your thoughts—the best part was your besura singing! I used to feel motivated after seeing your video. I'd wait impatiently for you to upload it and I'd tell myself, if this woman can take the trouble to dress up every day, I have no excuse to stay in my pajamas, with uncombed hair and an unwashed face.'

I spontaneously hugged her and we both laughed. Take that, I mentally said, thinking of a close friend who'd advised me to not make an ass of myself by singing. Especially since my repertoire of Hindi songs is so limited. I'd lightly told her to go ahead and sing in her own videos since she was so much better than I could ever be. I was just having fun, not competing with Alka Yagnik. Strangely, the response to my videos was very encouraging! My Insta followers started to recommend songs for forthcoming videos. Young, unknown boutique owners offered to courier their latest outfits for me to wear on camera. And 'The Boys'—top couturiers and old friends Abu Jani and Sandeep Khosla—were appreciative enough to send gorgeous flowers congratulating me for those fifty back-to-back videos which had cheered them up during the darkest days. Others wrote in their disappointment that I'd stopped at fifty and sweetly asked me to resume at the earliest. I didn't. I'm like Captain Cool, M.S. Dhoni—one must know when to walk back to the pavilion. Overkill is so unsexy!

I think I'll get Anandita to shoot one final video in the series for me today. Nostalgia demands a bow. I have a song in mind. It's from the Dev Anand–Waheeda Rehman movie *Guide* (1965), based on R.K. Narayan's marvellous book published in 1958, titled *The Guide*. The evocative song was picturized on a gloriously youthful, impish Waheeda Rehman. The lyricist was Shailendra Singh and the music was composed by S.D. Burman. It captures all that I'm feeling at this exact moment. Come on, sing with me:

Aaj phir jeeney ki tamanna hai,
Aaj phir marney ka iraada hai …

(Today I have the desire to live again,
Today I have the intention to die again …)

Nothing could provide a more apt closure to the pandemic. Thank you, Shailendra Singh.

'We don't see things as they are, we see them as we are ...'

—Anais Nin

Unlike Bebo (Kareena Kapoor Khan to you!), I am not part of a 'Girl Gang'. But there may be a more apt, age-appropriate parallel, in Bollywood itself, for me. Much to the astonishment of sceptics who are convinced female actors in Bollywood are a Bitch Brigade, there exists strong friendships that have endured through the decades, like the close bond between Waheeda Rehman, Asha Parekh and Helen. These gorgeous 'gal pals' of a certain vintage travel together frequently and are one another's support systems, through thick and thin. My girlfriends, too, are very precious to me. While some friendships have been recently forged, most go back four decades or more and bring back warm, fuzzy memories.

Like the time Babyeeee (the ever-ebullient author and food expert Rashmi Uday Singh) organized a special fiftieth birthday bash for me—a party that also marked the launch of my book *Selective Memory* (it remains my personal favourite). Invitees were given smart white t-shirts with the cover of the book printed on them, and requested to wear them to the party in the most creative/inventive way. To my absolute delight, most guests obliged. Babyeeee also travelled across many miles and seas, hand-carrying an incredible birthday cake to Phuket where a small group was celebrating my seventieth. I, of course, had my cake and ate it too! But I can never forget the arduous journey taken by both—Babyeeee and the cake!

Art historian, curator and director of the Dr Bhau Daji Lal Museum, Tasneem Mehta, as beauteous as she is cerebral, followed up the celebrations in Phuket with a smashing dinner party she hosted in her art-filled home. She has promised an encore for my seventy-fifth! That's something to look forward to, even though at least five guests from that night five years ago, have left us. We shall raise a glass and toast them— toast us, toast our friendship.

Late last night, I received a jaunty text from Babyeeee; she was wondering how I was doing. As always, she had just checked into a grandiose heritage hotel in an exotic destination, posted a zillion reels on Instagram, showing her eating all kinds of food that resembled décor. Our time zones rarely overlap, but I'm always delighted to hear from her at bizarre hours, as she flies in and out of destinations whose names I can barely pronounce. Last seen, she was in Thessaloniki dancing to 'Zorba the Greek' with the most celebrated chef in the region. Next, she was doing the cancan with a maître d' in Istanbul. I love her free spirit. Bless my Babyeeee, who sure has come a long, long way … I am so pleased to count her among my handful of close friends.

The first time we met was in a crowded flea market in Paris. She had chopsticks holding up her top knot. Hmmm. Thinking back on that image today, I'm saying, 'How apt!' At the time she was an income tax officer (with the Indian Revenue Services). But her passion for food, travel and adventure was boldly announced by those chopsticks in her hair. That unusual hair accessory had heralded the birth and blooming of India's best-known food writer, who has authored more than forty food books and been awarded all sorts of amazing culinary honours. Besides, she is the only bona fide globetrotter I know.

Babyeeee has been a loving and steadfast friend. I am aware I am but one of her countless 'close and intimate friends and admirers', going by her effusive Instagram posts, but I try not to be too jealous! Babyeeee loves everybody! She finds wonderful traits in the most hateful individuals. I feel ashamed after bitching about someone we both know, for Babyeeee only has good things to say about that nauseous person. God bless her kind and uncritical heart. My dislikes cannot be camouflaged, unfortunately. The expression in my eyes says it all and gives me away every single time.

What I marvel about Babyeeee is how she manages to juggle so many intimate relationships across continents and age gaps. She was a great buddy of my father, the venerable G.H. Rajadhyaksha, till he passed away when he was ninety-eight. Later, when she quit a girl gang (mostly journos) I was part of, who'd meet regularly to celebrate birthdays, I was hurt and surprised. Babyeeee explained she didn't enjoy the hardcore gossip that was exchanged after a few glasses of wine. In retrospect, I am saying 'salaam' with genuine respect. How right she was! Soon, the gang disbanded, but at the time I felt she was being sanctimonious and goody-goody. That's also when she told me that the only movie she watches over and over again is *Cinderella* (1950). She avoids any movie that features violence because negativity affects her health.

Her messages say she is zipping off somewhere again. Perhaps in search of an amazing chef on the North Pole—the one who creates gastronomic wonders out of walrus livers and the blubber of seals. And it reminds me of another impromptu adventure a few years ago when we risked our lives sailing across a stormy, rough sea to savour reindeer meat in Helsinki.

It was my brilliant idea, so I plead guilty. The channel crossing from Tallinn in Estonia to the port of Helsinki was no more than four hours. I was in a buoyant and reckless mood. Gita Pandit, our wonderful friend, was feeling adventurous as well. 'Let's go!' I said, sounding like a Boy Scout setting off on a hazardous trip. The sky looked ominous as we got on the gigantic catamaran. It was wet and chilly on the deck, and it was suddenly not looking like the best plan for a Sunday. But I was with two international foodies and had boasted about enjoying reindeer-meat sandwiches on my previous trip! They looked sceptical. It had started to rain. Gita, who always has the most incredible travel solutions, announced there was no need to worry. If the weather worsened, we could always charter a chopper and get back to Tallinn in half an hour. Gita was right— there was no turning back—we had to taste reindeer meat.

These are ladies after my own heart—sporting and daring, like those actors one sees on reality shows grappling with snakes and eating spiders, diving from great heights and clambering over slippery rocks. Yes, we were in Roadies mode that miserably wet and soggy morning. For me, it was a major *izzat ka sawal*—what if we couldn't find reindeer meat after so much trouble? How stupid would I look? Gita tried to google the best restaurants in Helsinki with reindeer meat on the menu. No luck. Babyeeee was taking a long snooze in the carpeted lounge close to the casino, while the damn catamaran pitched and swayed over a dark, scary sea.

Gita decided to shoot the storm that was heading in our direction—she's a superb photographer. I adore Gita—she is one of the most genuine people I know. Selfless, giving and loyal to a fault. Gita is also a healer, painter, poet and singer. Recently, when I was in pain (emotionally more than physically), Gita called from Kolkata for our regular chat.

'How are you?' she asked gently, perhaps sensing I was not feeling great.

'Gita, come to Mumbai soonest. I need your crystal therapy ... like yesterday,' I replied.

She chuckled, 'What crystal therapy can I offer you? Don't you know you are the crystal?'

I felt instantly cured!

But during that nutty expedition in search of reindeer meat with that catamaran listing dangerously and all of us pretty certain we were going the *Titanic* way, methods had to be found to retain our sanity and contain our panic. For me, there was just one thing to do to steady my nerves—shop! I went to the arcade looking for socks with reindeer motifs. No socks. Not even a scarf with reindeer prancing all over it. Ominous sign, indeed. Maybe all the reindeer in Finland had died? I went in search of a coffee. There were dozens of Chinese shoppers lining up for chilled beer at the cafeteria. Later I was told they made the weekly crossing from Finland to Estonia and back to stock up on booze, groceries and other essentials, which were far cheaper (taxes!) across the channel. They were on their return journey laden like oxen. Those bulging plastic bags were filled with toilet paper rolls. Gosh. Bad tummy, anyone?

As soon as we disembarked, we set off in search of reindeer meat. Babyeeee wanted to go to the finest, most exclusive restaurant in Helsinki. We reached there hungrily just in time for lunch but were told they only served haute cuisine—and, sorry, but reindeer meat did not make the cut! Miffed and snubbed, we were now determined to accomplish our mission. We had lost not just precious time at this fancy-shancy place,

I'd left my fancy-shancy sunglasses behind in the fancy-shancy cloakroom where I had felt almost too shabby to pee in those grand porcelain pots! I should have worn my pearls and diamond earrings to eat reindeer meat, I thought to myself a little crossly. Then that snooty blonde bitch in a sharp suit ushering aristocratic-looking guests resembling Björn Borg (okay okay ... he's Swedish, but still) to their tables next to the large windows overlooking the main square would not have been as frosty. I would show her next time! I would go back looking like a TBZ showroom, wearing such pricey baubles even three generations of her snotty family could never afford! There! I was feeling better already as we trudged to a cafe that featured reindeer meat on the limited menu—hip hip hurrah!

Honestly, I have to say here how much I treasure my girlfriends. They ate those dry, stringy, awful sandwiches without grumbling, and even smiled for the photographs. Not a word of complaint escaped their mouths as we made the long trip back to Tallinn. I had persuaded Babyeeee to splurge and get herself a silver fox trimmed shawl from a boutique nearby. Babyeeee generously gifted me a gorgeous metallic gold bomber jacket, which makes me feel like Michael Jackson each time I don it and I inevitably sing, ' Beat It', even though my poor pelvis can't keep up with MJ's trademark thrusts. Girls need a little something by way of compensation after ridiculous expeditions. And no, thank you very much, the services of a chartered chopper were not needed—the storm had passed!

Looking back, one thing's obvious—good and lasting friendships are based on weathering storms at sea and earnestly hunting for inedible rubbish like reindeer-meat sandwiches in alien lands.

—⁓—

'Why not just embrace it, go along with it and welcome it?'
—Helen Mirren

I am listening to 'Jalebi Baby' and dancing in my chair. Why? Simbbly. Frantic planning is on for Diwali, and the mood is 'phessstiv' as we Maharashtrians say. I survey the tokri of hand-painted diyas sent by the Cancer Patients' Aid Association (CPAA). I love their 'Saloni' diyas and torans. I greatly admire Y.K. Saprusaab and his wife Rekhaji, who started CPAA over fifty years ago, along with Siloo Jasdanwala, to help underprivileged cancer patients. I have a close bond with the whole CPAA family, and it makes me so happy each Diwali, to know that their diyas are so coveted. Each diya sold, helps someone suffering from Cancer. Each diya counts.

It occurs to me, while I move my bottom on the chair and shake my head to 'Jalebi Baby', that our family Diwali—like most aspects of our lives—is hybrid. Diwali delirium sets in right after Dusshera, once we've recovered from enjoying the Ashtami bhog and pushpanjali. This year will be a heightened experience; after two years of COVID-19 darkness, let there be light!

I am trying hard to recall what I did last year to mark Diwali. Did I bother to make that tedious trip to Girgaum to buy traditional Diwali faraal (traditional sweetmeats and savouries)? Yes, I vaguely remember it was a muggy, sultry October afternoon when Arundhati, Avantikka and I set off in search of faraal and paper lanterns (aakash kandeels)—both small-scale businesses used to be family enterprises in the old days. The industrious ladies of the house would meticulously prepare Diwali sweets (flaky chirotey, coconut karanjis, shakkarpali, besan laddoo, rawa laddoo, anarsey, to name a few) and Diwali savouries (spicy 'nylon' chivda, thikkat shev, crunchy chakli), while schoolgoing kids managed the sale of colourful kandeels strung up between lampposts on the footpaths. These would sell as fast as they could make them out of neem sticks, rice glue and colourful paper.

Today, there are hardly any Maharashtrian faraal shops. Most are run by Marwaris, who sell packaged faraal by the kilo, along with khakra, thepla, fafda, dhokla and imported chocolates, dates, cookies from Dubai, besides baked bakarwaddis (masala-stuffed deep-fried rolls) and other 'healthy' snacks. There's nothing healthy about anything on sale. And I deeply miss my old vendors, people who had become annual 'Diwali' friends, the conversations we had, the gossip we traded. Even the ladies selling flowers on the footpath these days come from Saurashtra. I miss the Sakhubais wearing nine-yard kashta saris and gold Kolhapuri bead necklaces. There is no first-pressed jasmine oil (sugandhi tel) for the ritual Diwali bath, nor is fragrant utney (roughly ground mixed herbs to remove the extra oil during the snaan) the same. What I buy in branded packets now resembles scented sawdust. No point cribbing. Like I said, our lives and loves are hybrid. We eat hybrid. Drink hybrid. Cook hybrid. Talk hybrid. Think hybrid. Dress hybrid. Authentic? What's that?

Jalebi Baby …

I remain undaunted. I will do as I have always done over the years. Our hybrid home will be given a huge, old-fashioned scrub from top to bottom with soapy water and a hard-bristled brush, while I look around at familiar but strange objects, and even stranger furniture that is strewn in an eccentric way which somehow works for us. Yes, even the decor is hybrid! So many Buddha heads in different materials, from different periods; two solemn Catholic saints in wood from an antique dealer in Goa; a bronze Radhika statue sitting on an old Portuguese stand; ancient carved jharokas from a Rajasthan haveli; two English Chesterfields; old silver attardaans from Lucknow; a Waterford elephant from Ireland; carpets from Turkey and Kashmir; an inlay-work screen in intricately carved rosewood acquired at an auction; an upright piano none of the children now play; a beautiful bronze bust of Lalla Rouk, a fictitious princess from Persia, atop a marble pedestal from Italy; framed pictures of family on a tiled, marble-top Irani table; a huge, hand-painted porcelain vase from Japan … and, of course, the many paintings on the walls which tell their own story.

Jalebi Baby … sings Canadian rapper Tesher in Punjabi–English:

Baby lookin' like khaana khazana on a plate
… like mithai … like kulfi …
like ras malai … Jalebi Baby …
Baby, let me see it … I just wanna eat it …

He totally gets it! We are in sync …

—⁂—

My Diwali sari is still to be bought. I have enthusiastically planned a family dinner. The card states: expect fireworks! And the dress code reads: desi chamak-dhamak. Mr Dé's thoughts are on Britain's distressing economy and Liz Truss. I don't stand a chance, with or without a sari. I have designed the clothes for the children and grandchildren—fingers crossed, they will be approved and worn! We will celebrate Bhau Beej for sure. It is an annual ritual at our home, but after my beloved brother passed away five years ago, I have told the girls to take turns and host it at their respective homes. There is no 'bhau' for me to do aarti to … I miss Ashok desperately. Especially during Diwali, when he'd give me a Chimanlal's handmade paper envelope with cash, after the aarti and say, 'Baby sister … Go buy yourself something.' I have all the unopened envelopes in my special drawer. I see his neat handwriting, the carefully dated message on the cover and my heart aches with love for a good, kind man who mixed the bloodiest Bloody Marys ever and charmed the ladies with his deep dimples and sparkling wit. Without a brother to honour during Bhau Beej, what's the point?

But the other traditions and rituals carry on, as they must.

Mr Dé announces triumphantly, 'I have kept a special towel for you … I love the colour!' For a moment, I am stumped. Then seeing his enthusiasm for the fluffy, sage-coloured towel, I feign delight. And instantly make the connection. It's a hint and a reminder. On the fifth day of Diwali, Maharashtrians celebrate their New Year (Padwa, not to be confused with Gudi Padwa) and Mr Dé gets an oil bath treat. He refers to it as 'Husband's Day' and boasts to all his Bong friends about the focused attention he receives from his Maharashtrian wife. He taunts them, 'Does your wife worship you with an aarti? Does she touch your feet and seek blessings? Do you receive an oil massage with fragrant tel before bathing?' They shrivel up and die of shame, I imagine, while turning green with envy at this level of absurd pampering. When Bongs get acutely jealous, Mount Etna gets a complex. I grew up watching Aie and Baba following these practices during Padwa, and decided to take a cue and follow the ancient custom. I continue to find these old-fashioned rituals very moving.

My children watch with amazement and amusement, as I perform the aarti and touch Mr Dé's feet, bowing deep, my eyes shut and my mouth moving in prayer. I do it for myself, mainly. It makes me feel good. I do it with sincerity. Mr Dé blesses me with equal sincerity. The children wait patiently till we are done … The bar only opens after I gently replace the aarti thali in front of the silver Lakshmi. Soon, the champagne is being impatiently popped by the girls, and ice is on the way, along with soda and tonic water for the very thirsty adults. Mr Dé readjusts his brand new dhuti–panjabi and demands to see all the videos and phone camera pictures of the ceremony. Proof! His face lights up with delight seeing me bow down. He smugly forwards the ones in which he is looking good, and the rear-view shot of me bowing which focuses on my bottom … My big bottom … Like a wide angle shot which is not a wide angle shot. No face in view. It can be an impersonator! Another woman with a generous derriere holding an aarti thaali and bowing to him. Right?

Where's the evidence, Mr Dé?

—ɷ—

NOVEMBER

'Inside every older person is a younger person wondering what happened.'

—Jennifer Yane

'WOULD YOU LIKE TO SIT DOWN? CAN I GET YOU A COFFEE? TEA? Something else?' An elderly man has leapt to his feet while I'm staring at the breads on display, wondering which one to get—with pumpkin seeds, gluten-free, sourdough, wholewheat, focaccia. The counters are laden with goodies at the newly opened deli in our favourite club. Uff, too many to choose from.

I look at the man's smiling face, but don't recognize him. Or the lady seated next to him. Maybe I am afflicted by prosopagnosia, a condition I was unaware of till the bubbly vivacious Shenaz Treasurywala, actor and travel blogger, went public with the info. It's a cognitive disorder in which the brain is unable to put faces together. Let's call it 'face blindness'. And it happens to me all the time.

Am I supposed to know this couple? I smile broadly just to assure them I'm friendly, not snobby, just blank, as I wave vaguely in the direction of the table where I am seated with Anandita and her friends—two stylish gay men and a gorgeous girlfriend. The unfamiliar man hastily fixes his thinning grey hair and mentions having met me thirty-five years ago. Okayyyyyy. I hear that a lot and pretend to instantly recall that encounter, to establish I'm not being stand-offish. Encouraged, he starts rattling off names of people he knows whom I must also know (same vintage). My smile is still in place, but I really want to join the youngsters, who are much more fun. I can see this is not going to end quickly.

'Weren't you friendly with Gulu? Do you know he is very, very sick these days …'

Which Gulu? I should never have asked. Five more minutes wasted. A few more names are thrown around.

With a sad change in tone and expression, the man says, 'Most of them are dead …'

His wife has either not heard him or she didn't like the dead people because she's beaming. Now I'm in a quandary—should I beam back? But that will mean I'm an insensitive woman who neither remembers nor cares about those dead people. The man is looking at me in a puzzled sort of way. I wave to my daughter again to indicate I'll be joining all of them in a jiff.

He looks at the group and says, 'Young people …'

'Yes! My bachchas,' I reply brightly.

He looks again, 'All?'

I hastily clarify, 'No, no … not all. Just the girl in black.'

He stares pointedly at them, 'And the rest?'

'Friends,' I answer.

He is still looking puzzled, 'Yours or hers?'

This is getting a bit much. I shrug, 'Hers … and mine.'

He stares at me and says, 'Achcha? You look young … for your age. Very good, very good … I am also your age. We used to meet during your modelling days when I worked in an ad agency.' His wife continues to beam.

Sir … You want bitchy? I can do bitchy.

'Are you still writing?' he asks, in an effort to keep this weird conversation going.

'Are you still reading?' I reply.

His wife stops beaming. 'We have stopped reading newspapers,' she snaps.

It's my turn to beam.

Anandita and her friends are giggling away. I turn to join them, but the man isn't done yet.

'Your brain also works really well—very sharp. Good, good, good … and do remember my name the next time we meet.'

My smile reaches my ears as I skip away. 'I can never ever forget your name Mr … what did you say it was?' I know. Childish. Silly. Petty. But hey, I didn't ask to chat with him or his wife. He intruded into my private space and time with his opening remark, while I was minding my own business, scanning a selection of breads. Silly chap! If half the people he referred to are dead, why bring them up? To gloat he's still alive and not ready to join them?

Wait. Was that the real cause of my irritation? The dead people? Maybe I didn't want to deal with the fact that so many friends and acquaintances I grew up with are no more. A dear friend from school just passed away, after ailing for months. As our friend and former sheriff, the late Nana Chudasama of 'I Love Mumbai' (an organization he founded to clean and beautify Mumbai) fame, would frequently say about his contemporaries, 'They are sitting in the departure lounge, waiting for take-off.' We would laugh. Feeling reassured our flight wasn't scheduled. But this smarmy man's conversation at the deli has upset me and made me acutely aware of my age and vulnerability. My rushing to join the 'young people', as he described them—what was that? For one, they were far more entertaining than this bore. I could laugh and gossip with them like I couldn't possibly do with two dour-faced strangers all set to narrate some more stories about how many contemporaries were no more, how they'd died and where—complete with gory medical records of suffering, neglect and sorrow. Failed kidneys. Malignancies. Prostate problems. Lung collapse. I didn't need tragic tales. I needed laughter. And hope.

I was flattered by how interested the 'young people' were in my anecdotes from the distant past, when they weren't even born. They were urging me to stay and join them for dinner. They didn't want me to leave. 'You're gorgeous!' they gushed. I was preening and showing off, in a very classy, nonchalant way, of course! Besides, I genuinely enjoyed their company. I don't want to hear morbid stories about rectal cancer, Parkinson's, Alzheimer's and worse ... Death and disease. Doctor's prescriptions and alternative therapies. Bowel movements and blood tests. Sometimes, one can overhear scraps of conversation—acquaintances speaking in hushed tones about those of us who are still alive and in circulation. Almost as if we have no right to be living, even less, enjoying ourselves. Excuse me! I want to talk about the Next Best Thing.

I prefer the world that my children's vibrantly alive generation belongs to. My children's buddies are welcome to call me 'Aunty'—not 'Auntyji—there's a difference. I expect them to respect my boundaries. Just as I respect theirs. I am not their jigri dost—I am their friend's mother. It's a pity boundaries have to be emphasized and re-emphasized constantly with people who ought to know better than to cross them nonchalantly and sometimes even brutally. That oafish man in the deli could do with a crash course in age appropriate lingo before waylaying a startled stranger innocuously buying flat breads.

—⁓—

'Anyone who keeps the ability to see beauty never grows old.'
—**Franz Kafka**

Understanding, sensitive friends never embarrass you when you are making an idiot of yourself and talking rubbish—sometimes after an extra glass of vino and sometimes simbbly because you are in 'that' mood. My children don't like me to be in 'that' mood—it upsets and embarrasses them, even though I am never in 'that' mood in public. Alas, these days my mood has been disappointingly straightlaced and boring. I am a bit too well-behaved for my own amusement. Only because someone or the other around me is constantly talking about death and dying. Just this morning I woke up to the sad news of two close and wonderful friends passing away—just like that—poof! They're gone.

I am having dinner tonight with friends I have not met for two years. We have booked a table well in advance at the sexiest restaurant in Mumbai—the Shilpa Shetty-owned-and-promoted Bastian. It is the kind of super-glam place where top Bollywood stars like Ranveer Singh frequently put on impromptu performances like they are on stage during IIFA Awards, dancing energetically to a medley of their own hit songs. Ranveer Singh is that kind of a guy—spontaneous, unselfconscious and always himself. But I am feeling morose and low after digesting the terrible news of my friends' passing. Neither the scrumptious menu (imagine a dish called Animal Prawns, featuring tiger prawns doused in chilli-mayo) nor the exotic, yummy, fruity cocktails created by Big John, the Brit mixologist, are likely to get me out of the funk. I am craving 'that' mood despite the pall of gloom.

Nearly every other week, I have been losing someone or the other I have grown up with. With mounting dread, I open the newspapers to check the obituaries. Today's wretchedly shabby obit featured one of my dearest and oldest friends, the beauteous M. Nobody has come anywhere close to this divine woman, who was Lady Gaga before Lady Gaga. She died a lonely death, after enduring Parkinson's for years. Her evil brother's hypocrisy is evident in the obit, in which he has 'forgotten' to name her only child—possibly the only person she truly loved during her colourful but tragic life. I guess it's about grabbing her fancy apartment and other assets. Typical story. M truly deserves a book, not this sketchy tribute, such was her natural force and energy when she was alive.

A younger friend tells me bluntly, 'What do you expect? Age is cruel. People are cruel. Most of your contemporaries are dead or seriously ill. Deal with it, Shobhaa.'

I don't want to 'deal with it'. I get defensive and say a bit too sharply, 'I *am* dealing with it but in my own way, which is not to deal with it. You have a problem with that?' Excuse me, am I really dealing with anything sad or morbid or both, these days? Is that why I secretly want to run away to Bastian tonight, half-hoping Ranveer Singh will show up and dance for me?

All of us occasionally harbour contradictory feelings that end up generating guilt. Today, I don't want to think about the loss of two beloved friends. Double whammy. I don't want to connect the twin tragedies to myself, my own age or the thought: it was them yesterday; it could be me tomorrow. No! I want to dress up to the hilt and step out. I have a sleek, black, one-shoulder caftan with pretty mirror work on the sides meticulously steam ironed by the lovely Lakshmi. I have carefully picked out a silver cuff (a beautiful, arty cuff gifted by Raisa Husain years ago—I bet she won't remember giving it to me). I shall wear the two new rings created by my daughter Arundhati's talented jeweller-friend in Jaipur—so chic! Ebony and gold with tourmalines. This is my official reason for not cancelling dinner and dressing up: I need a mood lifter, okay? Please don't ruin it all by exclaiming 'how shallow'!

'That mood' will not be as easy to manifest tonight, no matter what Big John adds to the cocktail and even if the impossibly svelte Shilpa Shetty personally serves it to me! It's got to be something else … something I am not able to process because it is too painful.

Given that our friend circle is rapidly shrinking—if they aren't dead, they have dementia and don't recognize us any longer—the few we run into are tactless and crude. Age is the excuse for insulting others. I met such a bunch sitting around at the club looking as sour as the limbu-paani they were sipping. One of them said in an offhand manner, 'Let's see your face in strong daylight … Arrey, arrey … wait, I need to get my glasses on … oh … you don't have too many wrinkles … plastic surgery? These days it has become so common. Everybody gets a nose job, bum job, tit job. Nothing wrong in self-improvement.' The rest cackled. The oldest of the lot bragged, 'Look at me! I have my own teeth … no bridges or dentures. My own knees too!' The one in blue with lipstick on her teeth (dentures, were they?) chipped in, 'I toh am a full original—no cataracts, no stents, no major surgeries, no hair transplants …' Her friend interrupted, 'Didn't you have a hernia problem? Or was it piles?'

Some people are born seventy-five.

I'm determined to impress Shilpa Shetty and other glamzines doing tequila shots at the long bar in Bastian. There has to be a way to make age and death less intimidating. I glance at the usual mess on my dining table before we leave for dinner and find a bouquet of fresh flowers waiting for me with a charming note. Those particular flowers (pale green hydrangeas) remind me of my beautiful girlfriend who passed away. She and I were seated at the same messy table a few months before her death. Like me, she lived to eat and travelled on her stomach, looking for specific gourmet treats. We could talk food ad nauseaum.

Both of us were in 'that' mood one evening. We'd ordered Chinese food from Royal China—all our favourites—wanton soup, flaming fish, salt and pepper prawns, egg fried rice, pork puffs, chilly beef, hakka noodles with extra bean sprouts. Our conversation was going all over the place. We were discussing our respective kids (sweetly!), husbands (less sweetly), weight (uffff, avoid!) and travels (if only our knees were better behaved). The help at home asked when we'd like our dinner served. M looked at me and said, 'Never!' But served it was. The hour was late and our well-chilled Sauvignon Blanc was down to the last few sips. I indicated with a slow motion of my head and hand to go ahead and feed us. I was actually slurring by now. Anandita, trying to sleep in her room close by, had stuck her head out of the bedroom door from time to time and rolled her eyes (daughters are born with this particular talent). The food appeared ... I stared at it long and hard. My friend was staring at me.

'All good!' I declared unconvincingly and a bit too loudly.

She smiled and said, 'Yes, Shobhaa, all good!'

Then, we did the unthinkable. We discarded chopsticks, pushed away forks and knives, asked for ghar ka everyday thaalis and ate the Chinese feast with our fingers, desi style! I swear to you, Chinese never tasted better! 'That' mood happened! Our fingers deftly picked up mouthfuls of noodles, we used chilly oil like aachhar, fried rice was enjoyed like pulao, flaming fish became maach bhaaja ... The incomparable sensual delight of tasting our own fingers, licking soya sauce off a thumb soaked in it—unbeatable!

With my friend's passing, this unforgettable experience has also been buried. But in her honour, I would love to do a repeat. Though, this time around, I plan to eat a grand banquet in a posh Chinese restaurant, using my fingers, with my legs folded up on the chair, palati-style. But I am also worried. What if I weep into the wonton soup we both loved and drank like rasam that night?

A few days later, I was taking the elevator up to the business centre, where R had organized an intimate memorial service to honour the memory of her mother—M—and one of my oldest, most cherished friends. The sunflowers in the lobby of the Taj Mahal Palace Hotel this morning looked a bit too upbeat and cheerful. I hadn't met her only child for over forty years, but we had remained in touch. R lives in America. She was back in Mumbai, where she grew up, to immerse her mother's ashes and finish incomplete business. The usual tale of property matters, hefty files and complicated legal work.

R being her stylish mother's daughter, the medium-sized conference room in the impersonal but efficient business centre had been converted into a soothing, pleasing space, with beautiful arrangements of fragrant white flowers and her mother's framed portrait at the entrance. The moment I embraced R, I took a sharp breath—I thought I was embracing M herself—the resemblance was uncanny. R had become her mother. Ever so gently and with enormous poise R started the intimate, short ceremony by reading out her mother's favourite Khalil Gibran verse from 'On Death':

If you would indeed behold the spirit of death, open your heart wide
unto the body of life.
For life and death are one, even as the river and the sea are one.
In the depth of your hopes and desires lies your silent knowledge of
the beyond;
And like seeds dreaming beneath the snow your heart dreams of
spring.

R's voice was breaking. A few hours before her mother died, R had spoken to her from America, as M lay motionless on her bed in Mumbai. R told me she'd shared with her late mother all that had remained unsaid over more than fifty years. R had finally forgiven her mother and set her free. How did R sense so many thousands of miles away that this would be their final call?

A child always knows.

I was asked to speak about my friend by R and I couldn't. The words stuck in my constricted throat. No words emerged. In a flash, all the joyous memories of our days together, when we travelled across India as models, shared rooms, shared our lives and food, played back in past-forward. The other people at the service were staring at me, as puzzled relatives from across the world, joining us over Zoom, waited for me to regain my composure. I cry very easily these days … and a lot. Maybe I am making up for all the times I needed to cry but didn't. My tears and emotions no longer embarrass me as much. For too long I had convincingly played Tough Titty—a role not chosen but assigned to me. 'Shobhaa, the

Invincible!' I am anything but, I would often want to cry out and protest. Now is my time to turn into a marshmallow without feeling sheepish. I took my time before speaking about M; nobody was catching a flight. After I spoke, R recited one more poem, Robert Hayden's 'Those Winter Sundays' that affected me deeply. The last two lines were:

What did I know ... what did I know ... of love's austere and lonely offices...

As I hugged R before leaving, I half-jokingly said, 'My beloved friend is blessed to have received such a thoughtful and sensitive send-off from her loving daughter. I hope my children organize something similar when I go.'

Stupid remark, I know. But at that moment, I envied M. No matter how troubled and complex her relationship had been with her only child, here was R generously acknowledging her mother. I wanted to share this quote by the poet Atticus with her: 'I have never met a strong person with an easy past.' M was one of the toughest persons I knew.

Live and let go! How many of us can? In the show *Fleabag* (2016), the heroine says: 'Women are born with pain built in.'

The thought of death followed me home. M was eighty-one when she died. Not that much older than I am today—what is six years? My emotions weren't morbid; but maybe they were overly and uncharacteristically sentimental. I stopped by the sunflowers display in the lobby and nodded to them, like they were my friends and would empathize with my sombre mood. Offer solace. Well, they did! By the time I reached 'Smart and Hollywood' (my lifelong darzee), I was feeling more emotionally settled.

I greeted Masterji and pulled out the lime green Chanderi fabric from my voluminous recycled tote. 'Sleeveless and low neck,' I said, staring brazenly at him.

He nodded and asked, 'How low?'

As low as the law permits, I wanted to say but didn't.

Masterji's young assistant, a recent recruit from Lucknow, suppressed a smile. He'd definitely noticed the grey framing my face (Oh ho! Late for my touch-up, again!). Since I am not Helen Mirren (I wish I was!) and haven't joined the #greyhairdontcare tribe, I grinned back and thought of M—the lady who over forty, even fifty, years ago, had dared to wear micro miniskirts, topped with lame bikini tops around Mumbai without giving a damn. She would have approved of my instructions to Masterji. Yes! I was doing this for her!

Rest in peace, my darling friend, I hope you are sporting your avant garde Mary Quant wig and false eyelashes wherever you are …

—m—

DECEMBER

'Aging is an extraordinary process where you become the person you always should have been.'

—David Bowie

THERE'S A NIP IN THE AIR THIS MORNING. WOW! WINTER IS COMING! But in a pleasant, not *Game of Thrones*, way. For Mumbaikars, it's officially winter when the mercury drops to 24 degrees in the first week of December. We whip out our best pashminas to attend concerts at the NCPA, while starlets climb into thigh-high boots to get photographed at the airport. Our winter lasts for five whole days and we shiver through it. Don't laugh.

Goodness! It's already the last month of the year, and I'm wondering, like most idiots do, where the hell the other eleven months went. A neat disappearing act, that's what it was. They canned on me, the little swines. But wait. Where's last year's fake X-mas tree? And all those shiny baubles, the cherubs and angels? That's my December plan. Get the X-mas vibe going, gurrrl. You'll feel instantly better.

I enlist the help of the ever-enthusiastic Pushpa and one other Nepali TikTok star, this one with gleaming, glitter nails and a shy smile. 'Memsaab … apna tree sabse best hai …' they say as we prop the damn thing up on its unstable stand which shamelessly states 'Made in China'. I strategically place a bright red reindeer (also made in China) to cover the embarrassment. Why do we put up an X-mas tree, I ask myself while handing over personalized decorative tags bearing the names of Gong Li and Bijou to Pushpa. Silly question.

We all love our synthetic X-mas trees, don't we? White ones made from cleaning brushes and the standard emerald-green ones on which we place strips of cotton wool and pretend it's snow? In our family, we compete outrageously to out-bling one another.

'Mom, don't tell me you are going back to Lohar Chawl for more things for the tree. You have cartons and cartons of stars and things?' Avantikka groans.

'Darling, somehow the tree is looking a little naked this year. Naked is cool. Our tree is doing a Gigi Hadid,' I reply calmly. 'Maybe one of those TikTok girls helped herself to the props for her videos …'

Arundhati objects to the false accusation. 'That's just so meannn, Mom!'

Agreed, it is mean. I could borrow a few spangles from the TikTok girl myself. Besides, it's December, a time to be jolly, say 'ho ho ho', and get ready for the family X-mas fun evening at home, with grandkids pouncing on gifts under the tree, while the adults pose for selfies wearing Santa caps and goofy smiles. The turkey has been ordered—slices, not the whole bird. And smoked ham too.

We have standardized a drill for X-mas parties over the years. Agreed, standardized is boring, but it simplifies my life. Since not everybody enjoys turkey, and ham doesn't have many takers, but both must be ordered 'because it's X-mas', I begin the challenging task of ordering all sorts of idiotic 'side dishes' that have nothing to do with X-mas. The kiddies have to be fed and packed off after fighting energetically over their gifts ('I wanted the car not this dumb board game'), we have to drink some more, open our gifts, hug and kiss by the tree for the mandatory annual X-mas group shot, continue drinking, and finally come to the dining table to attack all that's on it. This year I forget to serve the steamed X-mas pudding, even though I have taken the trouble to get brandy sauce and kept a ladle handy to flambé more brandy over the pud. All is forgiven when cake and choccies are wheeled out on the trolley, while we head back to the bar for more drinks.

As always, Sahil, our vegetarian son-in-law, has been forced to suffer and half-starve. Verrry bad! Honest admission: I have zero imagination when it comes to amazing vegetarian options and it's awful to keep serving artichokes and asparagus mousse to him year after year, while we stuff our faces with delectable smoked oysters and pork puffs. I plan to take a crash course in gourmet vegetarian in 2023 … just for Sahil.

Aah … the bar! Gin is big this year. All sorts of artisanal gins from Goa are being avidly debated. Since it's X-mas, we are all clad in Western clothes and feeling very chic. The babies are wearing identical reindeer sweaters I had ordered months ago on a dodgy website. This is for the all-important group shot, where the family has to be perfectly colour-coordinated and look super-fabulous. The younger babies are wailing, fidgeting and clearly want to do instant nini. No chance! Not before the photos are done! I am feeling 'appreciated' for once. The girls have admired my table with all the bright red, scented candles melting over gleaming crystal stands, and a sweet nativity scene, too! Even Aditya has complimented me with a laconic, 'Not bad, Mom … not too shabby at all,' after seeing the spread.

My eyes are glistening and a bit too bright (champers, anyone?). I can see stockings, candles, flowers, a crystal angel dancing on top of the X-mas tree and I'm dizzy for sure. With joy? Let's just say it's joy. I love December. Soon it'll be New Year's and won't that be something?

I'll be in Kolkata and I can't wait to wander around Park Street, Flury's. Tolly. Last X-mas, I had run into Leander Paes and Kim Sharma near the glazed ham counter at the Tolly X-mas lunch, clicking selfies. I liked their coyness—nayya nayya pyaar, I'm wondering who we'll run into this year; hoping it will be Mohua Mitra wearing one of her designer bags. We can discuss Paresh Rawal and fish.

Every new year is something. Something extraordinary. A reminder. A bugle call. I love the first day of the year, irrespective of how the past twelve months have treated me. I become Scarlett O'Hara when the sun rises on the first of January and repeat her line at the end of *Gone with the Wind* to myself: 'After all, tomorrow is another day.' I spell the last word differently, of course. But it rhymes nicely … You get the gist…

Like Scarlett, Anuradha is not a quitter.

'I am a woman, dear. I can be as contrary as I choose.'
—Dowager Countess, *Downtown Abbey*

I am thinking back to this exact time last year when we had hosted a hysterical OTT celebration at home after watching *House of Gucci* (2021) and going gaga over Lady Gaga playing Patrizia Reggiani, who 'finds the heart of a killer'. It was a stellar performance. I'd loved the movie. I wanted all things Gaga, especially her tiny waist. But I didn't want all things Gucci, since I am not Ranveer Singh. However, I was restless enough and bored enough to giddily and gaudily host a 'Gucci party' for like-minded nutjobs who'd get the theme and the irony.

The children were excited but pretending to be scornful. I heard them discussing their Gucci lewks and smiled to myself. It was only Anandita who was genuinely enthu and working the phone to get inflatable alphabet for the front door. I died looking at the entrance of our home which had been converted into House of Gucci, thanks to those balloons. Thank God, Mr Dé was safely out of town and in the dark about this outrage. I was game for anything, now that we were neck-deep in this absurd plan. I dug up old, musty, mildewed Gucci merchandise from forgotten boxes and placed it on tables, just in case the point was lost on the invitees. Since I possess precisely three Gucci items—decades old sunglasses I never wore because my hair used to get caught in the two inter-linked 'Gs' on the arms, a tiny tote that now qualifies as an authentic vintage handbag and a bright yellow scarf with the initials (aaaaargh!) gifted by Avantikka. I brought out ropes and ropes of fake pearls and synthetic mink collars with jewelled brooches, collected from boutiques across the world. I was set! I rehearsed a few dialogues from the film and channelled my inner Gaga, hoping Maurizio Gucci would walk in and kiss me.

Surprise, surprise. All the attendees did a Gucci!

In they trooped, parading Guccis by the yard—bags, stoles, jackets, loafers, head gear. Vintage, contemporary, limited edition, the works. Honey Bunny walked in wearing black lace gloves and diamonds—so

Gaga. We spoke in a fake Italian accent throughout the evening, which was as bad as Lady Gaga's in the movie. Nothing terribly shocking happened—much to my disappointment. I did not serve Chianti or pasta, but the mood was pagal all the way. Exactly what it should be when the theme is loco and it's December. Kuch bhi!

—ꝏ—

'You cannot find peace by avoiding life.'

—**Virginia Woolf**

The local farmers are selling gigantic jackfruits in improvised stalls lining the pavement outside the complex where I live in Pune. It's not too far from the futuristic tech hub at Magarpatta. Jackfruit, corn, yam, beetroot, green peas, green cucumber, white cucumber, cauliflower, cabbage, palak and methi. I can see the sun's rays bouncing off the gleaming glass casing of buildings in the tech park close by. Cybercity and pumpkin fields nearby. I have to show off!

'Let's drive through Magarpatta before you head back to Mumbai,' I tell my friend Meenakshi, who has spent a couple of days with me and is driving home to Mumbai later. We are halfway to 108 Café in Koregaon Park for our farewell brunch. I love this place as much for its location next to a lush nursery as for its great salads and something wildly decadent called 'eggs in hell' (heavily spiced baked eggs with onions, tomatoes and fresh herbs, served on sourdough toast). I am going to miss Meenakshi's invigorating company! But first, she has to see Cybercity and gasp!

'Why not? Sure,' Meenakshi replies. She's the kind of relaxed, sporting girlfriend who is always game to experience something new.

I tell Choudhary to turn the car around and head to Cybercity. We cruise around at a comfortable speed and Meenakshi comments, 'I could be in Washington …' as we drive through the complex and I point out different avenues with specific indigenous trees lining each one.

The area is indeed spectacular and scrupulously clean, with young techies walking around the woods, chatting and flirting with colleagues. Paradoxically, Pune is a great place for young *and* old people. Rarely does any city offer these advantages to both age groups. I can see myself growing old—rather, older—in Pune. I feel myself here, without knowing exactly who this mysterious, relatively new 'me' is! I trust my gut instincts; I always have.

As I lean on the railing of my balcony, looking at the glittering lights of the city in the distance, I can hear my voice telling me to keep listening to the messages of the universe and follow my heart. Once again, I am

280

standing at a major crossroads wondering where to go next. Over the years, it has only been this deep-down feeling that has helped me make crucial decisions that have not only felt right, but have eventually turned out to be right. Some of these decisions definitely involved a great deal of pain. A pain that never quite disappeared. But I went ahead and took it regardless. The price I paid was often a bit too steep—the wounds still hurt. But these are *my* scars. Self-inflicted and raw even to this day.

Pune is gently telling me to savour every moment and move to the next and final phase without hesitation or regret. To go easy on myself and others. To not judge or let someone else judge any part of me that has nothing to do with the happiness of others. I am there for all my loved ones—that's a given. But I'm also there for myself on this final stretch. The relay will end when it does and I'll run this race at my pace, not someone else's. The family is welcome to join me in Pune, as and when I'm here. Of course, I'm over the moon if they actively seek me out. But there's no pressure on any of them to come 'and keep Motherji company'.

A woman must have her options. As the ladies in Iran are reminding us by raising a simple slogan, 'Women. Life. Freedom.'

I am not relocating to Pune. Just commuting.

These days I'm free-floating. I ask myself, 'You answer to many names—Mataji, Mummy, Ma, Mom, Mad Mom, Mothership, Mama Dé, Supermom, Mashima, Mauvshi, Suvadi, Boudi, Shobhaa-ben, Aunty Shobhaa, Shobes, Sho, Shobhaa Rani, Shobha Pishi, Nani, Dadi, Shobhaa Mem, Ma'am, Bhabhiji, Mrs Dé, Madame Dé ... Who are you in this clutter? And why is Anuradha missing?'

Being a real sucker for cheesy motivational memes that pop up on my Instagram feed, I come across this one today by C.S. Lewis: 'You can't go back and change the beginning, but you can start where you are and change the ending.'

I'm listening to the wind chimes strung up on my balcony. I have never been 'lucky' with wind chimes, invariably picking the wrong ones from different cities across the world—too large, too heavy, too loud, too tinny, too hideous. But these chimes are perfect. A gentle, sweet, tinkle that heralds the arrival of tiny wood nymphs, fairies and elves. I found them in Pune, of course. There! It's a sign! A symbol! A signal! A nudge! An invitation! An instruction! I must listen to the divine music of my chimes.

I am actively missing Darnesh Bharucha, who brings bits of Paris to Pune. He has spent more than forty years living in the French capital, and now shuttles between his home in Pune (where he leads a rich life, surrounded by cousins, music, art, students, friends). We go back fifty years and I cherish our mutually enriching friendship deeply. Darnesh—the Parisian-Parsee—j'adore.

One North was meant to happen—this apartment is my birthday gift to myself. I have come full circle. And to think I bought it on a whim—from a person I had never met, introduced by a broker I didn't know, in an area I was unfamiliar with, at a price I could barely afford … and best of all, putting down hard-earned money to acquire a place I had not seen! Call it blind faith. Or destiny. Three years later, as another birthday rolls up, my party plans are in place. And so is the theme—Elvis Presley. Why Elvis? Because, for an Elvis devotee like myself, Elvis never left the building! (On a slightly more serious note, there are three things every woman should work towards and achieve during her lifetime: a home to call her own, a bank account in her name and a credit card that is not shared.)

I would not have reached this critical point in my search for Anuradha had I not left Mumbai when I did and given myself this do-or-die chance to embark on a daring journey of many delights and discoveries. A deep dive into the unknown. My very own 'Discovery Channel'! Perhaps I rediscovered myself after years of role-playing. I have found my andaz. A beautiful balancing act. Pune was calling. Is calling! I can smell the Mysore Sandal Soap. 'Ek ladies' is waiting to greet me. It's time to celebrate my amrit utsav with full-on josh. I'm going to make sure my seventy-fifth birthday party rocks!

Anuradha is finally where she wants to be …

—⚬—

ACKNOWLEDGEMENTS

BIRTHING A BOOK IS A LOT LIKE BIRTHING A BABY. ASK ME. I AM A veteran of both activities!

A big thank you to the few I shared the idea of the book with—and who 'approved'. Writers crave 'approval', no matter what they claim.

Kanishka Gupta—a literary agent who smells out books and authors like those pigs that forage the much-coveted white truffles, extracting the fruit bodies of the fungi from as deep as three feet underground. He makes me feel like a precious fungus.

Trisha Bora, my editor, whose eyes shone with delight as they met mine across the dining table during our first meeting. She has been an invaluable ally in this madcap adventure, encouraging me to satisfy all my hungers, but only if I stick to the deadline!

Poulomi Chatterjee, whose bewitching beauty distracts me way too much. She makes me feel valued as her author at HarperCollins India.

My hungry family and friends, food fanatics each one, with a perpetually voracious appetite for life's infinite bounties. May we continue to share many more meals and feast on love in the years ahead.

30 Years of

▰ HarperCollins *Publishers* India

At HarperCollins, we believe in telling the best stories and finding the widest possible readership for our books in every format possible. We started publishing 30 years ago; a great deal has changed since then, but what has remained constant is the passion with which our authors write their books, the love with which readers receive them, and the sheer joy and excitement that we as publishers feel in being a part of the publishing process.

Over the years, we've had the pleasure of publishing some of the finest writing from the subcontinent and around the world, and some of the biggest bestsellers in India's publishing history. Our books and authors have won a phenomenal range of awards, and we ourselves have been named Publisher of the Year the greatest number of times. But nothing has meant more to us than the fact that millions of people have read the books we published, and somewhere, a book of ours might have made a difference.

As we step into our fourth decade, we go back to that one word – a word which has been a driving force for us all these years.

Read.